ECONOMICS: AFTER THE NEW RIGHT

Studies in Human Issues

An International Series in the Social Sciences

Previously published books in the series:

Barnett, Larry D.; *Population Policy and the U.S. Constitution*
McKenzie, Richard G.; *The Limits of Economic Science*
Tullock, Gordon; *Economics of Income Redistribution*

This series is devoted to books by qualified scholars that deal with national or international themes from a variety of social science disciplines. It is intended to serve as a bridge of information between the academic community and those serving as policymakers. Furthermore, the series is intended to stimulate debate as well as to point out areas where further social science research is needed.

ECONOMICS: AFTER THE NEW RIGHT

Nick Bosanquet

Springer Science+Business Media, B.V. 1983

To Anne

ISBN 978-94-017-5588-7 ISBN 978-94-017-5586-3 (eBook)
DOI 10.1007/978-94-017-5586-3

Library of Congress Cataloging in Publication Data
Bosanquet, Nicholas.
Economics — after the New Right.
(Kluwer-Nijhoff studies in human issues)
Bibliography: p.
Includes index.
1. Economics. 2. Chicago school of economics.
3. Economic policy. 4. Great Britain — Economic policy —
1945- . 5. United States — Economic policy —
1981- . I. Title. II. Series.
HB71.B645 1983 330.1 83-69
ISBN 978-94-017-5588-7

Originally published by Heinemann Educational Books in 1983
Softcover reprint of the hardcover 1st edition 1983

Contents

Foreword by Samuel Brittan

There has been a revival of interest in the market as a decentralised method for co-ordination of human activities. This has been accompanied by a renewed scepticism about some of the more ambitious claims made for state action. As a great deal of government activity will obviously remain, thinkers of this school have been preoccupied with the difficult task of devising ways in which state activity can be regulated by general rules rather than the discretionary judgment of those temporarily in office.

The New Right is an entirely fair term for expressing the way in which these doctrines have entered the political arena. But the treatment of free market ideas as playthings of partisan debate has had the inevitable side effect of vulgarising the discussion. Both the valuable insights and the true weaknesses of thinkers such as Hayek and Friedman — and a host of others less well known — have been lost to sight in the public slanging matches about 'Monetarism,' 'Wets and Dries,' 'Thatcherism' and other similar slogans.

Thinkers of the free market school have suffered not only from the knee jerk reaction of hostile critics, but even more from their supposed admirers, who applaud before they have read and who are blind to the nuances and subtleties which alone can carry the argument forward. Speaking as a critical and qualified supporter of the new free market school, I welcome this sensitive study by an understanding critic. It will do more for public understanding than any number of partisan declarations. (I wish I had thought of Bosanquet's remark about Friedman insisting that, while there can be no free lunches, his own can be very cheap.)

Indeed Nick Bosanquet has managed to draw the strands of 'New Right' thinking together in a way that has eluded its protagonists — at least in their popular presentations. His concept of a thesis — the beneficial effects of free market progress — and the antithesis — the retarding and corruptive efforts of politicisation — is as far as I know a novel way of bringing together a vast number of statements which otherwise seem to veer between Panglossian optimism and apocalyptic doom warnings.

Bosanquet is sensitive to the many conflicting strands within the 'New Right,' which is not the reactionary monolith which it appears to hostile outsiders. He is clearly much more sympathetic to Hayek than to Friedman. But that only redresses the balance among the economics profession, which tends to ignore as 'not economics' work written outside the approved econometric framework —

rather like seventeenth century theologians who disapproved of studies which were not written in Latin.

There is nothing incompatible in wanting to extend the use of competitive markets and at the same time to support a generous measure of redistribution and provision of 'public goods.' This is an ideal known as the social market economy, which has at least as much to offer social democrats (spelt in lower case) as to the political right.

Indeed it is a weakness of 'New Right' literature in Britain that it has been so preoccupied with frontier raids on state provision of social services that it has not paid sufficient attention to the growing threat to market principles in their former heartlands in industry and commerce. A Government led by Mrs Thatcher has been every bit as anxious as Wilsonian and Heathite Administrations to set European steel production quotas or to limit imports from the Third World to whose welfare such lip service is paid.

The excessive influence of producer groups in extracting subsidies and (more sinister because more indirect) support of other kinds, as Bosanquet points out, reduces the state's ability to make 'an effective response to the problems of poverty.' It is possible to be in favour of redistribution without either being an egalitarian or believing that there is such a thing as a 'just reward' for particular occupations which a body of wise men can ascertain.

The biggest obstacle to an effective social market economy is the epidemic of recessions, slow growth and rising unemployment from which the world has suffered since 1973. This gives the protectionists and special interest groups their chance. The problems of the industrial world have not been brought about by unions; but the existence of union and other institutional obstacles to the market pricing of labour has made adjustments to a more difficult world environment a thousand times more difficult.

A social market economist should make common cause with the New Right in an onslaught on state monopoly, union monopoly, and practices and institutions which price people out of work. But unlike the New Right, he should be concerned with the distribution of capital ownership and with transfers through the tax and social security system. He has nothing to learn from the Old Left with its romantic view of unions and the state, or from the Old Right, which behind all its talk about moderation and pragmatism, at heart still believes

The rich man in his castle,
The poor man at his gate.
God made them, high or lowly,
And order'd their estate,

and would like to buy off trouble by tossing out a few more crumbs to the man at the gate.

Preface

Sam Brittan, Julian Le Grand and Colin Crouch made helpful and detailed comments on the whole of an earlier draft. I am most grateful to them. Alan Maynard, David Piachaud and Brian Abel-Smith made useful comments on particular chapters. Lord Robbins discussed Hayek's work in the 1930s with me: John Barnes and Tessa Blackstone were helpful in discussing voucher experiments. Rupert Sheldrake told me what to leave out. I have benefited from the unwitting help of Sir Keith Joseph whose reading list issued to his civil servants increased my curiosity about the New Right's system.

Betty Lucas spent many hours on the draft. There may be disagreement, but as a result of her efforts people will be much clearer on what they are disagreeing with.

Graham Cannon and Frank Topping of the King's Fund Centre lent me an office to hide away in at a critical moment and the staff of The City University Library were courteous and patient. Unlike the manuscript, Mary Keane's typing was beyond reproach, as was Patrick D'Arifat's research assistance.

My greatest debt is to Anne.

NB

London, April 1982

Introduction

The economic philosophy associated with Milton Friedman and the Chicago School has become increasingly dominant in Britain and in the United States. There is a presumption that government activity is the result of manipulation or conspiracy and that the only legitimate form of organisation is through the market. The views clearly set out by Friedman in *Capitalism and Freedom* have found a large following among politicians. Liberals are on the defensive: uneasy about big government but willing to be persuaded into specific extensions of government activity under tugs from compassion or from interest groups.

The election of Margaret Thatcher as Britain's Prime Minister in 1979 and of Ronald Reagan as President in 1980 demonstrated the new political power of the New Right. The political stereotype has evolved over a long period of time since Adam Smith. I began to look at how the stereotype fitted to the underlying ideas. In the summer of 1979 an unusual opportunity presented itself. Sir Keith Joseph, a leading member of the new Thatcher government in Britain, produced a kind of intellectual testament — a list of books that he regarded as background reading for his civil servants. It included two books by Adam Smith and others by De Tocqueville, Frank Knight, Robbins, Niskanen and Schumpeter, as well as seven books and pamphlets by Sir Keith Joseph himself and an attack on J.K. Galbraith by a former Chairman of Shell Transport and Trading. It compared favourably in weight and depth with President Reagan's rumoured preference for the works of Laffer, Gilder, and the *Reader's Digest.*

The books on Sir Keith's list and other like them are not just an academic orthodoxy created by the economic decline. They are one manifestation of the political market for extreme solutions. The taxpayers' revolt is not the most distinctive feature of this decline, although rising shares of public spending in GDP have produced greater hostility to taxation (some of the strongest reactions were in Scandinavia long before Proposition 13 in California). Adherence to sound money and distrust of inflationary finance are also not the peculiar property of the New Right. The really distinctive features of the New Right both in Britain and in America have been its criticism of government and its view that the overriding condition for greater freedom is a reduction in the role of government. The taxpayers' revolt is everywhere, but the social doctrines of the New Right are not.

The causes for this Anglo-American blessing should be sought mainly in the special nature of the economic problems that the two countries share. They have both experienced not only recession but relative decline and a growing sense of fatalism. For Britain, the decline has been most complete and can be charted in high rates of inflation, low rates of growth, worsening unemployment, and trade competitiveness. For the United States, chronically high inflation and low growth came first; higher unemployment and deteriorating trade competitiveness followed. Over the past fifteen years, economic performance has been worse in Britain and the United States than in other industrial countries of Europe and Asia. There was a market for something other than the incremental programs that form the main stock of political parties in more successful countries. Economics decline has shown uneven social effects. Most of the costs of the decline have been borne by the poorer groups in the population, and the process of decline has involved more day-to-day political argument about how incomes are to be distributed. The declining political influence of trade unions is also common to both countries.

The effect of economic decline was reinforced by changes among economists and among voters. Among economists there has been a marked swing towards monetarism and a general preference for market solutions. Among voters, changing patterns and attitudes have favoured the Right.

All these changes helped to bring about what is usually seen as a shift to the Right, in contrast to the situation in the 1930s in the United States when there was a turning away from market solutions in the face of economic decline. Differing patterns of interest among voters probably have a great deal to do with this. In the 1930s a majority of voters saw themselves as outsiders: now, even in a severe recession, many do not.

The shift to the Right is not simple. In macroeconomics it involves the rejection of Keynesianism and the turn first to monetarism and then to "Reaganomics." It includes a preference for market solutions in many detailed areas of policy. Finally, it involves a hardening of attitude towards poverty, extending at times almost to a glorification of inequality.

The aim of this book is to provide a reasoned challenge to the New Right's views on the role of government and on poverty. I hope this book will encourage debate on what freedom and social justice really mean under current conditions. I also look at the relationship between general ideas and particular policies for the welfare state and income distribution. The main conclusions are that the New Right's views on the role of government are not soundly based in principle, and that its central propositions about the distribution of income and government failure in the welfare state cannot be supported by evidence. The conditions for freedom are not just the reduction of government. The social and economic policies of the New Right have immediate costs with little real hope of gains in the longer term. In the face of social attrition, the New Right has little to offer except complacency and facile optimism. I finish by suggesting an alternative that can meet the real questions about government role and potential.

I hope this book will help to broaden discussion among my fellow economists. Many are uneasy about the trend of opinion, but except for a few courageous spirits, they have kept their heads well down. There has been more debate about income distribution, but still a reluctance to come to clear conclusions. I conclude that the case in principle for government action can be made in terms different from those of welfare economics. I also suggest that the evidence on income distribution will bear the rather strong conclusion that, in the absence of countervailing action by government, the distribution of income will become much more unequal.

The first part of the book deals with the New Right on its own terms. What have Friedman, Hayek and the Virginia School actually said? It is particularly important to fit together the thoughts of Friedman at different times and in different fields. How does the Friedman of myth, fable and television fit with the Friedman of detailed work over forty years? How has Hayek's thought developed since the *Road to Serfdom.*

Beyond the important differences between individual thinkers, the New Right has a core — certain propositions which are shared by many thinkers. This core goes far deeper than assertions about the merit of the market. It has doctrines about the role of government and about the changing distribution of income under a market system. The core propositions can be summed up as follows:

1. The growth of government is the product of malign political forces. The one overriding condition for freedom is that the growth of government should be reduced.
2. The actual course of economic change has been towards raising the living standards of the poor. Left to itself the process of growth would eliminate poverty.
3. There is no legitimate reason for changing the distribution of income in society beyond the change required to provide a subsistence income for all.
4. The welfare state has been a failure. Britain and the United States have programs for social security and health care.

> These have been wasteful and unrelated to consumers' real interests, and in the case of social security, have redistributed money perversely from the poor to the rich.

The second part of the book takes issue with these views. Our society is made up or organisations and of households. The organisations include large firms, professional associations such as the American Medical Association, large trade unions and nonprofit organisations. Households may be small, poorly informed, and vulnerable, but they have civil and political rights. The usual state of such a society will be one of constant struggle between households using the weapons of civil rights and organisations with their potential for unpublicised and far-reaching action. The New Right has ignored the possibility of private coercion, and its plans would shift the balance between households and organisations in favour of the latter. The natural state of society is not one in which freedom flourishes simply because of the absence of government. It is one in which private interests will organise to win gains for themselves through political and commercial means. Private coercion could be exercised by economic interest, by people with strong opinions or religious beliefs, or by class-based or ethnic groups. An appeal to a third party or government is one of the few recourses open to the weak against various forms of coercive power.

The New Right has, of course, pointed out fairly enough that government agencies may themselves act coercively; but it has ignored both the potential for coercion in nongovernmental agencies and the reasons why, in spite of the faults of government, households will be driven to appeal to it.

The Smith/Friedman doctrine on government raises questions of principle and logic. The other core propositions about income distribution and the welfare state are more specific and can be tested against evidence. The historical record does not support the New Right's rather definite statements that growth and the market will raise the incomes of the poor, nor does recent evidence for Britain and the United States suggest growing equality. In fact, the recent movement in both countries has rather clearly been towards growth in poverty and inequality. The New Right's evidence on health services ignores many problems about health insurance and third party payment in the United States and does violence to the facts about the National Health Service in Britain. Friedman's discussion in *Free to Choose* is especially misleading.

This evidence is taken from the United States as well as from Britain, but some American readers may be uneasy with the amount of attention paid to Britain, especially in chapter 9 on income distribution and chapter 11 on health services. I would strongly support the relevance of such comparisons, since the detailed policy issues on health and social security have become more alike. Constraint on health spending forces unpleasant choices, and there are serious problems about financing social security programs. This similarity in the detailed issues represents a more general convergence in the kind of economic and social problems that are faced by the United States and Britain. The United States now faces economic problems of a type that have long been familiar to Britons. Problems of industrial decline, low rates of productivity growth, and competition from imported manufactures have long been high on the British agenda and now figure on the American one. Britain, on the other hand, shows signs of the increasing social inequality that has long concerned many Americans. Differences in unemployment rates between more favoured primary and disadvantaged workers in the British economy have grown. The British labour market, like the American, now has very high levels of unemployment among young people, among ethnic minorities, and in big cities. Job prospects in the suburbs and for more qualified workers remain fairly good. These changes in labour market create stronger interest groups in favour of employer-based schemes for financing social security and health services. The good risks would be pooled and would be able to buy a higher standard of service, while the disadvantaged would have to rely on a residual publicly run service. These changes in the labour market exert similar pressure on the financing and organisation of health care and of social security. In the case of health care, international comparisons have both new relevance and a long history. Britain is the country whose experience Americans have used as evidence of the effects of socialised medicine.

The New Right's system is sometimes seen as a monolith, but in fact, it has many different sides to it. It is new, however, only in comparison with the Old Right of traditional Conservative thought. The Old Right now finds few followers. It was based on political philosophy and on ideas about tradition and hierarchy. The social order has a certain pattern of inferior and superior that has the sanction of tradition. The New Right, on the other hand, is mainly based on economics and on ideas about individualism and markets. The Old Right can be timed in millenia: the New Right in decades.

In chapter 1 we look at the New Right's system as a whole. Society is a battle between light and dark, between forces for creation and for destruction. Left to themselves, forces for growth and change will work themselves through. Society has a natural tendency to order, and the economy has an inherent tendency to growth. Adam Smith's invisible hand can produce growth as well as coordination through the market. The main inpulse to growth comes from entrepreneurship. A dynamic minority sets the pace, takes the risks, and pulls the economy forward. Left to themselves, market forces will lead to constantly rising incomes for the poor. All this might suggest that Utopia is around the corner, but there are destructive tendencies inherent in political democracy. Political democracy sets up intense stresses. Pressure from special interest groups brings about a growth in public spending and in centralisation. In the recent past, the forces of destruction have grown in power and now the forces of creation are under threat.

In chapters 2 through 5, we look at some main modern contributions to the New Right. Hayek's contribution is perhaps the most profound, and it is certainly not to the credit of economists that political scientists have paid most attention to it. Hayek has suffered a great deal from misrepresentation. To some he has become a demon figure. In fact he offers work of deep interest in its own right. He has made, perhaps, the first and fullest case for decentralisation. This began as a case for the market in his well-known paper in the *American Economic Review* in 1945 on the use of knowledge in society: but he has since made a much more broadly based case against centralisation, showing how it must inherently be inefficient. His emphasis on the subjective quality of knowledge and the danger of what he calls scientism — the misapplication of methods drawn from the natural sciences to the social sciences — is still of great interest, and there are few more devastating critiques of Conservatism than his short piece on "Why I am not a Conservative." Finally, his account of the social causes of inflation has close kinship with the approaches of those on the Left,who see inflation as rooted in social conflict.

Hayek has been a totem of the New Right, which has paid little attention to the actual details of his work. Friedman, on the other hand, has a large readership for his work on a range of different subjects. His unifying theme seemed to be "positive economics" — the doctrine that most differences of view on economic issues involve facts rather than values and could be settled by an appeal to facts. However, he has never applied this consistently across the whole span of social, labour and macroeconomics. Some of his most important assumptions, such as that contracts made between individuals and organisations in a modern economy are free and voluntary in the same way as contracts made in a simple exchange economy, are, in fact, based on a priori reasoning rather than on an appeal to facts. There is a contrast between his dogmatic views on social issues and the empirical cast of his work on monetary issues. His emphasis on scarcity fits uneasily with his optimism about growth. "There ain't no such thing as a free lunch," but left to itself, the market economy can certainly get you a cheap one. Hayek's thought is consistent both in method and assumptions, Friedman's lacks this rigorous consistency, and even with the work on monetary topics, it is hard to reconcile his work on monetary history with his writings on monetary policy.

The economics of politics (EP) was not, to begin with, wholly possessed by the New Right but has tended to become part of its territory. This is unfortunate because there is much real interest in its analysis of collective choice and bureaucracy. More questionable is the faith of EP practitioners in constitutional rules and their neglect of private coercion.

The main conclusion from the first part of the book is negative. Economics is not equipped to deal with the wider issues over which it has shown increasing domination. Helped by the prestige of positive economics, economists have asserted squatters' rights in territory where positive economics are of little use. The social teachings of modern economics show an alarming dogmatism.

Chapters 6 and 7 deal with the role of government in principle. The conditions for freedom go much further than the mere absence of government. Freedom is to be valued because it produces results in terms of choice, progress, and higher living standards. It will not produce these results without a shared sense of commitment to the social order. The conditions for a sense of responsibility go beyond the absence of government. This sense of responsibility requires protection from man's own impulsiveness and from the greater force of motives, rather than of potential consequences behind action. In the age of Adam Smith, the possibilities for damage were limited to the cannonball; now, the possibilities for destruction are much greater. The sense of responsibility also requires some minimum of opportunity and of social rights. All this creates a role in principle for a third party, or government.

The core propositions about the changing distribution of incomes are dealt with in chapters 8 and 9. They argue that the New Right is not only wrong in principle in setting such a restricted agenda but wrong in fact about the present course of income distribution. The evidence suggests that mature economies such as those of Britain and the United States are now entering a period in which the pressures from economic change are towards growing inequality. The shift away from manufacturing and towards services has been of benefit to the more qualified. This change in the pattern of demand has increased the effect of recession by adding to the number of people who are at the end of the labour queue. The actual course of income distribution is not benign, and the labour market is now showing a powerful trend towards greater inequality.

In chapters 10 through 12 we turn from the case for government in principle to government in practice. The New Right has argued that the practical record of government is very bad in social security, health services, and education, and that the record in practice outweighs any arguments in principle. The New Right often argues as if some ideal model was available. These chapters assess the most likely alternatives. Thus, the social security system has to be assessed against a private and usually employer-based scheme. The New Right's judgments on social security have been one-sided; for example, they make a great deal of its favours to the higher paid but ignore its redistributive effects from men to women arising from the greater longevity of women. Women survive to draw their pensions. The New Right has also ignored much evidence about the problems of employer-based pension schemes with vesting and financing. In health services, the New Right has vastly underestimated the problems raised by the power and discretion of doctors. Friedman and others have also distorted many facts about the National Health Service in Britain. Friedman's discussion of efficiency is based on strange measures of output, and he exaggerates the number of doctors emigrating from Britain. On education, Friedman has again made the running with his advocacy of voucher schemes. Voucher schemes would only produce a greater equality of expenditures if poorer parents were willing to pay a larger proportion of their lower incomes for education. The implausibility of this is one reason why voucher schemes have made so little progress. The New Right's assessment of the record in practice in the social services has been misleading and one sided.

Many reforms for government and public spending have been suggested, and one possible program for change is set out in the final chapter. I believe that economics has an important role to play, but the orthodoxy of the New Right has had the effect of reducing this role. I hope this book will add to discussion of what freedom and social justice really mean under current conditions.

1 The New Right

The New Right is best known for its macroeconomic prescriptions which are summed up as 'monetarism'. But monetarism is only one of a set of deductions from a broader economic philosophy. The policy prescriptions of monetarism cannot be understood in isolation from this philosophy.

The philosophy of the New Right is set out in a large range of works, in which the main contributions are those of Adam Smith, de Tocqueville, Schumpeter, Hayek and Friedman. To these texts have to be added the many contributions of Sir Keith Joseph which have sharpened the political edge. There are also more topical or empirical studies: on bureaucracy; on employment subsidies and industrial intervention; on the conflicts between entrepreneurship and union power and on the Galbraith thesis. This is a big field in terms of time, space and subjects covered – but it can be described in a basic series of propositions or a 'model'.

This includes a *thesis* and an *antithesis*. By the *thesis* society has a natural tendency to order and the economy an inherent tendency to growth. Government and conscious design are not the main source of order and institutions in society: in fact they are far more likely to inflict damage than to confer benefit. The main source of order is to be found in unintentionally created social institutions – the result of human action but not human design. As Friedman puts it:

> Adam Smith's 'invisible hand' is generally regarded as referring to purchases or sales of goods and services for money. But economic activity is by no means the only area of human life in which a complex and sophisticated structure arises as an unintended consequence of a large number of individuals co-operating while each pursues his own interest.[1]

Language, culture, scientific knowledge and social conventions all grow through voluntary exchange. The main impulse for economic growth comes from entrepreneurship. The entrepreneur takes risks and in return profit. The rate of profit represents essentially the degree of risk. Risk arises from the unpredictability in tastes and in technology. To take Friedman's view again:

> In every country, a tiny minority sets the pace, determines the course of events. In the countries that have developed most rapidly and successfully a minority of entrepreneurs and risk-taking individuals have forged ahead creating opportunities for imitators to follow, have enabled the majority to increase its productivity.[2]

The economy has its entrepreneurial leaders who take big risks for the chance of large profits: but the labour market rightly ordered gives returns to many for skill and 'human capital'. These everyday choices are a source of growth second only in importance to the 'gale of creative destruction'. Government policies for equality and for progressive taxation will interfere with this natural struggle for self-enrichment. Without planning or pattern it is of great benefit to society.

Left to themselves market forces will in fact lead to constantly rising minimum incomes. They may well not bring about greater equality defined in relative terms: but they will be strong enough to abolish primary poverty. Friedman even finds that 'Another striking fact, contrary to popular conception, is that capitalism leads to less inequality than alternative systems of organization and that the development of capitalism has greatly lessened the extent of inequality.'[3] Changes in the level and pattern of production will of themselves alter distribution so as to serve humanitarian ends. Government cannot remain completely aloof from distribution because of the possible threat to social cohesion arising from great inequalities – but the natural course of economic change will generally take care of these.

This thesis might suggest that society was well on the way to Utopia. But unfortunately these processes of growth and change though powerful are long-term. At any one moment in time they are open to misinterpretation. People may register the element of destruction more strongly than the element of creation. As well as genuine misinterpretation there is scope for wilful exploitation of ignorance. This possibility has been vastly increased by the coming of political democracy. Democracy in its current form will lead to short-term and changing decisions being taken under pressure from organised producer groups, unions and intellectual agitators. Dynamic forces inherent in the operation of bureaucracies will also be important. They will give an additional momentum to the decisions of democracy.

This tendency of democracy to run against nature can partly be checked by stronger local government: but mainly by entrenching rights and procedures so that they cannot be uprooted by crude majoritarian democracy. The New Right supports the limited sovereignty of the people.

These stresses create the *antithesis* which can be summed up as 'politicisation'. The atmosphere of class conflict in society will grow more sullen. The power of producer groups will increase. Politics will be concerned with vote-buying rather than with general rules to help along the process of creative destruction.

Friedman believes that the process of political choice is in itself bound to lead to greater dissension. Politics is about choice between clear-cut alternatives. Politics does not, as does the market, allow proportional representation of minorities. 'The use of political channels, while inevitable, tends to strain the social cohesion essential for a stable society . . . . Every extension of the range of issues for which explicit agreement is sought strains further the delicate threads that hold society together.'[4]

'Politicisation' will have consequences for public expenditure and for taxation. One will be a 'subsidy morass'. Another will be steeply progressive taxation to finance growing public expenditure and as class conflict stimulates a damaging search for equality. Bureaucracy will add to the pressure for increased public spending and for progressive taxation. In time a country could become a 'totalitarian slum'.

The *thesis* – the integrating force in society – is the underlying process of economic growth. The *antithesis* is the impact of 'politicisation' set up by the short-term stresses of 'creative destruction' and the nature of the political process itself. 'Politicisation' gets a hold mainly because of the plasticity of a democratic system with universal suffrage and without a carefully drafted constitution. Politicisation has economic effects through increases in public expenditure and taxation. These then reduce the rate of economic growth. This change in the economy then adds to the difficulties in politics and in public finance. Society is a battleground between the forces of light working in the longer term through the economy and the forces of darkness working through the political process. Choices freely made in the economic sphere will nearly always be in society's interest – even if they turn out to be wrong they are the price of risk. But politics presents extreme dangers: attempts to bring about improvements through conscious design however well intentioned will almost always go wrong.

The views of the New Right cover many thousands of pages. To do some justice to them we have to go beyond the main model to more detailed propositions. Some relate to the *thesis* and some to the *antithesis*. The first kind deal with the natural forces for order in society: the origins of social institutions, the correct view of equality, the process of economic growth, the role of the entrepreneur and the nature of poverty. The second kind have to do with the origins of politicisation: the reasons for more intensive class conflict, the irrelevance of 'social cost', the wrongness of the Galbraith thesis, the folly of rising public expenditure and of industrial subsidies, the shortcomings of the public sector, the failure of the welfare state, and the pressures inherent in the growth of bureaucracy. The two kinds of propositions result from different intellectual methods and different people. The theses are mainly derived from Adam Smith by economists who have been heavily influenced by the Austrian school. These are intuitive conclusions from the sweep of western history since the Industrial Revolution. The antitheses are more topical and empirical: infected by modern attachments to fact and statistics which the Austrians have always regarded with the greatest suspicion. Chicago not Vienna is the intellectual capital of the *antithesis*. The propositions of the thesis are mainly qualitative.

The Thesis

(a) Society has inherent tendencies towards order and justice.

The classic statement of this view is Adam Smith's *Theory of Moral Sentiments*. The spring of human action is to be found in self-interest and in self-love: 'every man therefore is much more deeply interested in whatever immediately concerns himself than in what concerns any other man'.[5] There might then have been a state of open warfare in society – but for the sense of justice and that 'nature has implanted in the human breast that consciousness of ill desert and those terrors of merited punishment which attend upon its violation'.[6] There is an inner sense of fair play which can be seen in terms of the judgement of an impartial spectator. This sense of justice is found naturally in man: 'It is thus that man who can subsist only in society was fitted by nature to the situation for which he was made.' The feeling of benevolence is much less important to society than the sense of justice. 'Justice . . . is the main pillar that upholds the whole edifice. If it is removed the great, the immense fabric of human society . . . the peculiar and darling care of nature must in a moment crumble into atoms.'[7] Nature fitted man with the attitudes needed for life in society, with what Smith called 'an original desire to please and an original aversion to offend his brethren'.

These natural instincts of justice are found in private citizens: but not often in nations and courts. These are affected by the 'furious zealots' of parties and factions. Nations rarely observe the rules of justice and their conscious designs are all too likely to fail. The 'natural course of things cannot be entirely controlled by the impotent endeavours of men'. Government cannot replace the sense of justice. 'What institution of government could tend so much to promote the happiness of mankind as the general prevalence of wisdom and virtue? All government is but an imperfect remedy for these deficiencies.'[8]

The natural course of justice will also shape the distribution of income. People will be rewarded according to their deserts. 'In all the middling and inferior professions real and solid professional abilities joined to prudent, just, firm and temperate conduct will very seldom fail of success.'[9] There are general rules by which prosperity and failure are commonly distributed. 'Notwithstanding the disorder in which all things appear to the world, yet even here every virtue meets with its proper reward.' *The Wealth of Nations* traced out the spontaneous order within the economy. Wealth came from rising labour productivity which by turn relates to the division of labour and the extent of the market. The division of labour is 'not originally the effect of any human wisdom which forsees and intends that general opulence to which it gives occasion. It is the necessary though very slow and gradual consequence of a certain propensity to truck, barter and exchange one thing for another.'[10]

Hayek's work is mainly concerned with the antithesis – the process of politicisation and how to stop it – but his view of the thesis is close to Smith's. Hayek starts from a distinction between spontaneous order and conscious design. The self-generating and spontaneous order exists mainly in the economic sphere where adaptation takes place through decisions by private economic agents. The work of conscious organisation mainly takes place in the political sphere.

The possibilities inherent in spontaneous order become even more significant if we accept that there are bound to be serious limitations to the information guiding conscious design. We are much less likely to be damaged by ignorance if we allow the spontaneous order to take its course. Completely rational action demands complete knowledge of all the relevant facts. In practice we are faced with a 'necessary and irremediable ignorance on everyone's part of most of the particular facts which determine the actions of all the several members of human society.'[11]

From these statements about spontaneous order follow definitions of justice and of the functions of government. Justice is about clear general rules within which the spontaneous order can evolve – it is not about assuring justice to particular people. Justice is about establishing rules for the game – not about weighting the results. As long as the rules are observed any one of a number of results becomes fair. Most of these rules will in any case arise from the spontaneous order through a process of natural selection. Social Darwinism in Hayek's view made the error of stressing the selection of individuals rather than of institutions and customs. Justice is 'not a balancing of particular interests at stake in a concrete case, or even of the interests of determinable classes of persons, nor does it bring about a particular state of affairs which is regarded as just'.[12]

The function of government too is to set the rules of the game – not to weight the results. This rule-making function must be distinguished from the role of the state in administering resources. Efforts at administration and conscious design are likely to end by disturbing the spontaneous order. For Hayek government is a maintenance department in a factory. Its object is not to 'produce any particular services or products to be consumed by the citizens, but rather to see that the mechanism which regulates the production of these goods and services is kept in working order'.[13] Government must provide some services and also prevent coercion – but in ordinary times this does not mean that 'the private citizen need be governed in the sense in which the government directs the personal and material resources entrusted to it for rendering services'.

Friedman's view of government is rooted more in reasoning about the role of markets. He does not have Hayek's width of approach, preferring *The Wealth of Nations* to *The Theory of Moral Sentiments*. Friedman believes that it is not easy to improve on Smith's exposition of the 'obvious and simple system of natural liberty' in which 'the sovereign is completely discharged from a duty, in the attempting to perform which he must always be exposed to innumerable delusions, and for the proper performance of which no human wisdom or knowledge could ever be sufficient; the duty of superintending the industry of private peoples and of directing it towards the employment, most suitable to the interest of society'.[14] Yet Friedman was at one time rather pragmatic about the role of government. Each case for intervention has to be weighed on its merits. There has to be a clear and large balance of advantage if government is to go beyond its major functions of preserving law and order, fostering competitive markets and protecting voluntary contracts, but at times 'government may enable us to accomplish jointly what we would find more difficult or expensive to accomplish severally'.[15] Government can also intervene, Friedman thought in 1962, on grounds of 'paternalism' in order to protect minors. As he said then, it is difficult to set any firm limits to this kind of undertaking. However as the sphere of government has expanded, so the Friedman view of the role of government has lost any tinge of agnosticism. The shadow of the Chicago conservative Henry Simons with his somewhat embarrassing advocacy of public as against private monopoly has become fainter.

(b) Inequality is the inevitable and tolerable result of social freedom and personal initiative.

The argument here has been most carefully put by Lord Robbins.[16] The pursuit of equality is a loose phrase because the term covers 'four quite distinct and in some senses inconsistent alternatives. These are equality before the law: equality of opportunity: equality of reward and equality of property.' Equality before the law presents no difficulty. Equality of opportunity has merit as an aspiration – so long as it is recognised that it cannot be realised in full given differences in home background. The positive side of equality of opportunity is that it 'involves at once removal of obstacles to choice and the widest field for the recruitment of potential excellence'.[17] However total equality could only come about through the abolition of the family. Lord Robbins sees 'no justification for confining the advantages of superior spending power to ostentatious display and personal enjoyment and imposing an upper limit to spending on education and health'.

Equality of reward is a different matter. This is almost wholly objectionable. There is a case for spending to relieve absolute poverty – Professor Hayek goes even further by endorsing a minimum income for all[18] – but beyond this there is no case for any levy on personal income. According to Lord Robbins: 'the inequality of reward which the market system engenders does not seem to me something which persons of good sense should worry about over-much'.[19] The gains in income to the less well off arising from redistribution would be negligible compared with the gains which they would enjoy as a result of increased production under the stimulus of proper incentives. Lord Robbins does not deny that equality of reward would in principle be practicable, but he stresses the heavy costs and the increased coercion that would be involved in maintaining it. The first result of this kind of equality would be 'at least some diminution of production' and later effects would include coercion in the labour market and higher unemployment.

Equality of property ownership would not only be undesirable but impossible. Even if all property were redistributed differences in thrift would soon restore inequality. Equality would only be possible if the community took over all property rights.

Sir Keith Joseph's own work on equality mainly deals with the symptoms of politicisation such as progressive taxation: but in its more positive passages it strikes some of the same notes. 'Since inequality arises from the operation of innumerable individual preferences it cannot be evil unless those preferences are themselves evil.'[20] Inequality in the form of different holdings of property is for Hayek part of the natural and spontaneous order. Property serves the interests of those who do not own property as of those who do 'since the development of the whole order of actions on which modern civilization depends was made possible only by the institution of property'.[21]

Friedman stresses the importance of risk and uncertainty about outcome in giving incentive. There is no conflict between freedom and equality of opportunity, but much between freedom and the search for equality of outcome.

> The system under which people make their own choices – and bear most of the consequences of their decisions – is the system that has prevailed for most of our history. It is the system that gave the Henry Fords, the Thomas Alva Edisons, the George Eastmans, the John D. Rockefellers, the James Cash Penneys the incentive to transform our society over the past two centuries. Of course there were many losers along the way – probably more losers than winners. We don't remember their names. But for the most part they went in with their eyes open. They knew they were taking chances. And win or lose society as a whole benefited from their willingness to take a chance.[22]

People have muddled notions that certain types of inequality, such as those arising from inherited talent, are fair while those arising from inherited money are unfair. But these differences represent the operation of chance which is a vital stimulus. It might seem fair that there should be equal shares for all, but is it equally fair that Muhammad Ali should have to share his prize money with everybody else? In the earlier *Capitalism and Freedom* Friedman has argued in rather more general terms that inequalities in the distribution of income were a vital part of an efficient allocation: now the argument is racier and more international. In fact capitalism has promoted equality as compared with other systems. In the few cases where people have been free to choose – as citizens of Israel have been free to move to *kibbutzim* – they have chosen to stay in an open society with greater inequality.

(c) Capitalism is a system which has ensured growth and improved living standards in the long run.

Friedman has spoken of the 'economic miracle' of the development of the United States in the last 200 years – achieved without government. Generous natural resources certainly helped – but they cannot explain for him the success of nineteenth-century Britain and Japan or twentieth-century Hong Kong. For Friedman 'the combination of economic and political *freedom* produced a golden age in both Great Britain and the United States in the nineteenth century'.[23]

The achievements of capitalism are not purely materialistic. The share of income arising from property declines and that arising from human capital rises. According to Friedman 'The great achievement of capitalism has not been the accumulation of property; it has been the opportunities it has offered to men and women to extend and develop and improve their capacities'.[24]

Schumpeter was among the first to stress just how far the process of growth under capitalism had raised the living standards of the 'masses'. 'The capitalist achievement does not typically consist in providing more silk stockings for queens but in bringing them within the reach of factory girls in return for steadily decreasing amounts of effort.'[25] These improvements are great but they take place through economic change – a process of 'creative destruction'. There are long waves in capitalist evolution, a 'recurrent rejuvenation of the productive apparatus'. Each of these waves results in an avalanche of consumer goods that permanently deepens and widens the stream of real income, although in the first instance they spell disturbance, loss and unemployment. The capitalist process progressively raises standards of life, but 'it does so through a series of vicissitudes the severity of which is proportional to the speed of advance'. There are long-run tendencies for real incomes to grow without any long-run trend for unemployment to rise.

Capitalism can only be assessed properly over the long run. As Schumpeter put it: 'Since we are dealing with a process whose every element takes considerable time in revealing its true features and ultimate effects, there is no point in appraising the performance of that process, ex visu of a given point of time.'[26] Capitalism must inevitably involve violent change. We are dealing with competition from 'the new commodity, the new technology, the new sources of supply, the new type of organization (the largest-scale unit of control for example) – competition which commands a decisive cost or quality advantage and which strikes not at the margins of the profits and the outputs of the existing firms but at their foundations and their very lives.'[27]

Capitalism however creates a culture and patterns of organisation which will destroy it from within. Improvements in standards of life include support for new kinds of social critic. The hostility of the intellectuals affects the labour movement. Although investment opportunities show no tendency to vanish in the long run, the role of the entrepreneur becomes less important. Innovation is reduced to a routine and technological progress. Invention becomes the business of specialists who simply turn out what is required and make it work in predictable ways. The economic basis of the bourgeoisie is undermined. 'Dematerialized, defunctionalized and absentee ownership' does not call forth the same loyalty as property did. Schumpeter anticipated much of the *antithesis* as well as the *thesis*.

(d) The entrepreneur is the key figure in ensuring for all the gains to be had from economic growth.

Schumpeter saw the entrepreneur as driving the chariot of 'creative destruction'. As entrepreneurship declined so then later would capitalism. Other economists such as Frank Knight see the role of the entrepreneur mainly in terms of meeting uncertainty and shouldering risk. Entrepreneurs will earn high profits where there is a low level of initiative in the community.[28] Neoclassical economics was wrong to see the main economic problem as that of efficiently allocating resources in the light of preferences, tastes and techniques that are known to be given. The actual discovery of these preferences, tastes and techniques is just as important – and it is the entrepreneur who makes the discovery.[29]

(e) Economic growth will first reduce and then eliminate poverty in absolute terms.

Adam Smith was perhaps the grandfather of this proposition with his view that 'it is not the greatness of national wealth but its continual increase which occasions a rise in the wages of labour'. de Tocqueville saw society as progressing towards an inevitable equality of conditions.

Schumpeter later argued that the distribution of income would become more equal over time. If capitalism continued to grow at the same pace as in the years before 1928, within fifty years poverty would be abolished, 'pathological cases alone excepted'. Reforms such as higher social benefits could be paid for out of economic growth without any interference with the capitalist process.[30] Friedman has stressed more the achievement of capitalism in freeing 'the masses from back breaking toil'.[31] At the extreme Sir Keith Joseph concluded that in an absolute sense there is little poverty in Britain today. Our continued anxiety about poverty arises from bogus attempts to define poverty in relative terms. There are groups with special needs such as single-parent families, but 'by any absolute standard there is little poverty in Britain today'. As Joseph and Sumption wrote in *Equality*, 'it is not right to turn a discussion of real needs into a discussion of something else by so defining poverty as to introduce into it the very different concept of inequality'.[32]

The Antithesis

(a) The origins of politicisation

'Democratic institutions', wrote de Tocqueville, 'have a very strong tendency to promote the feeling of envy in the human heart'. de Tocqueville distinguished between a 'manly and lawful passion for equality which excites men to wish all to be powerful and honoured', and the 'depraved taste for equality, which impels the weak to attempt to lower the powerful to their level and reduces men to prefer equality in slavery to inequality in freedom'.[33] There is also a serious chance of a developing 'despotism' of the majority. The practice of democracy can release forces which will waste enormous amounts of resources, retard economic growth and poison the atmosphere in society.

Political feelings aroused in a democracy would have certain practical results in terms of rising public expenditure and growing centralisation. The poor have votes and are likely to use them to secure public expenditure for which they do not pay. Citizens of democracies are 'perpetually seeking for something better, because they feel the hardship of their lot'.

In this quest there are likely to be frequent changes of mind. Democracy does not understand the art of being economical. It often gets both heavy spending and poor results 'as it frequently changes its purposes, and still more frequently its agents. Its undertakings are often ill-conducted or left unfinished'.[34]

Democracy also implies strong tendencies towards centralisation. As the rage for equality takes hold people become much more sensitive to small differences and small privileges. de Tocqueville's is perhaps the first statement of the theory of relative deprivation. 'The desire of equality always becomes more insatiable in proportion as equality is more complete.'[35] People insist on uniformity – which can only be brought about by an increase in centralisation. In a democracy people are also much more sensitive to privileges held by private individuals. de Tocqueville summed up the process as follows: 'This never dying, ever kindling hatred which sets a democratic people against the smallest privileges is peculiarly favourable to the gradual concentration of all political rights in the hands of the representative of the state alone; the sovereign, being necessarily and incontestably above all the citizens, does not excite their envy.'[36] The central power in its turn encourages the feeling of equality in its own self interest. 'Every central power, which follows its natural tendencies, courts and encourages the principle of equality; for equality singularly facilitates, extends, and secures the influence of a central power.'[37] The search for uniformity will lead to growing bureaucracy. Democracy certainly shows an ambivalent attitude to those who are actually in control of the central government, but it is constant in its attachment to central power. 'Democratic nations often hate those in whose hands the central power is vested; but they always love that power itself.'

The extreme centralisation of government ultimately 'enervates society' and in time weakens the government itself.[38] Centralisation grows also because of the powerful and plausible illusion that it is a more effective way of doing things. It may even be true that at a particular point in time a centralised social power may be better for certain tasks: but in the long term this leads to loss of economic potential and a loss of freedom. 'Everywhere the state acquires more and more direct control over the humblest members of the community and a more exclusive power of governing each of them in his smallest concerns.'[39]

de Tocqueville saw society as moving towards democracy and an 'equality of conditions'. But his observation of America led him to hope that the worst effects of politicisation might be avoided. His aim was to show 'by the example of America that laws and especially manners may exist which will allow a democratic people to remain free'. Equality of conditions – not to be confused with egalitarian envy – does produce a love of independence. Economic progress produces a large middle class. Between the extremes of rich and poor in a democratic community 'stands an innumerable multitude of men almost alike, who without being exactly rich or poor possess sufficient property to desire the maintenance of order yet not enough to excite envy'.[40] The love of wealth and the possibilities of getting it in small amounts influences the social atmosphere as well as the feeling of envy. Social competition establishes a certain amount of social mobility instead of the old pattern of fixed privileges. In practice social mobility is to a degree an illusion: the barrier has changed its shape rather than its position – but it is an influential illusion. The citizens of democracy are materialistic – subject to 'an inordinate love of material gratification' as well as living a mood of illusion. Democracy leads to centralisation but also to a certain kind of individualism.

The pace of technical progress also acts as a countervailing force against democracy. Everybody in society has to live with the fact that the best laid dispositions and the best made investment are going to be overtaken by technical change. As de Tocqueville described it, 'I accost an American sailor and inquire why the ships of his country are built so as to last for only a short time: he answers without hesitation that the art of navigation is every day making such rapid progress that the finest vessel would become almost useless if it lasted beyond a few years.'[41]

Institutions in the political sphere can also help to retard the process of politicisation. One 'social power' will always predominate over the others, and in a democracy this will be the power of equality but society needs obstacles 'which may retard its course and force it to moderate its vehemence'. In America such checks are to be found in the strength of the local unit in government: the weakness of the central government and the strength of the judiciary: but these checks and balances would certainly be much less important than the 'manners' within society which might or might not influence events.

It is worth quoting de Tocqueville at length because his views have deeply influenced later conservative thinkers. Again and again his successors have stressed the tendencies towards disintegration inherent in democracy and the various results in terms of excessive public spending, bureaucracy and the growth of state intervention. The fullest modern restatement of de Tocqueville's underlying theme is to be found in the three volumes of Hayek's *Law, Legislation and Liberty*. Hayek finds the main impulse to politicisation within the political system rather than outside in the wider society. For de Tocqueville the main impulse came from the feeling of envy: for Hayek it is to be found in the reality of majority rule. It is impossible to reconcile constitutionalism [limited government] 'with a conception of democracy according to which this is a form of government where the will of the majority on any particular matter is unlimited'.[42] Government has ceased to be about maintaining general rules and has come to be about coercion on behalf of particular interest groups – and coercion which is bound to be clumsy and ill-informed. At the outset Hayek states this central part of the new antithesis: 'the predominant model of liberal democratic institutions, in which the same representative body lays down the rules of just conduct and directs government, necessarily leads to a gradual transformation of the spontaneous order of a free society into a totalitarian system conducted in the service of some coalition of organised interests'.[43] We get too much administration and too little government: the conscious designs are bound to come unstuck because of lack of adequate information.

Economic misfortune together with the influence of agitators create intense pressure towards action on behalf of special interests. People may be disturbed by the loss of accustomed positions. They may not realise that the 'frequent recurrence of such undeserved strokes of misfortune is however an inseparable part of the steering mechanism of the market'. They may start to follow the marsh lantern of 'social justice', which in time will lead towards a defence of entrenched interests.

Hayek takes the view that public action will nearly always produce bad results while individual action will nearly always serve the interests of the 'spontaneous order'. As Hayek writes towards the end of his second volume: 'Though the pursuit of the selfish aims of the individual will usually lead him to serve the general interest, the collective actions of organised groups are almost invariably contrary to the general interest.'[44] In the second volume the language has become stronger. Democratic government is 'corrupt', 'weak', 'immensely and oppressively powerful', 'lurching like a steamroller driven by one who is drunk', 'slave to particular interest groups'. We now hear about the inevitable tendency of public spending to grow: the capitulation of government to special interest groups – beginning with the Trade Disputes Act of 1906 – and about the growth of bureaucracy.

In an 'unlimited democracy' the 'holders of discretionary powers are forced to use them to favour particular groups on whose swing vote their powers depend'.[45] This development is closely allied to the growing power of producer-dominated pressure groups. At best this will set up a permanent and damaging clash of interests. 'The interests of organised producers are therefore always contrary to the one permanent interest of all the individual members of society, namely the interest in continuous adaptation to unpredictable changes. At worst in the extreme form of the disease known as socialism there will be an inevitable movement towards a totalitarian state and the destruction of the democratic order.'[46] The only hope lies in a series of drastic economic and political changes ranging from the denationalisation of money to the vesting of sovereignty in an assembly elected for fifteen years and with a membership limited to those over 45. Thus democracy is to be tamed by recourse to a Swiss constitution, the caution of middle age and an immense increase in role for joint stock banks.

For Friedman power in a market economy is widely diffused. Such an economy not only diffuses economic power but separates it from political power. If both are in the same hands it is unlikely that political freedom will survive for very long. Economic freedom is not a sufficient condition for political freedom – Friedman in 1962 had the inter-war experience to the front of his mind – but certainly political freedom has never been found without economic freedom.[47] The contrast is between a pluralist capitalistic society and a monistic socialist society. Politicisation takes place through the natural tendency of political power to concentrate itself.

Economic power can be widely dispersed. There is no law of conservation which forces the growth of new centres of economic strength to be at the expense of existing centres. Political power on the other hand is more difficult to decentralise.[48] There seems to be something like a fixed total of political power to be distributed. Consequently if economic power is joined with political power concentration seems almost inevitable. Friedman would limit the role of government and would also strengthen local government. At least the citizen can escape local government by moving away.

The root of politicisation is to be found in the political sphere and the holiest texts of the antithesis are those that deal with the worms in the bud of democracy, but the full phenomenon of politicisation includes other elements. The original impulse leads to consequences and sympathetic developments in various intellectual, fiscal and administrative spheres. It also has consequences for mood in society. In terms of mood there will be an intensification of class conflict. Within economic thinking there is the so-called 'Galbraith' thesis and the tendency to attribute vast significance to the concept of social cost. Then there are fiscal and administrative ramifications to be mapped out: the 'mushroom' growth of public expenditure, the subsidy 'morass' and, as a subsidiary theme, the malign influence of bureaucracy. Another strand of the analysis lies in the corruption of the trade union movement, half victim and half aggressor.

(b) A more intense class conflict

According to Professor Bauer, Britain has 'class on the brain'. For him the evidence suggests that there is much more mobility than is usually allowed for. Nevertheless there is a deeply rooted and powerful belief that Britain is a class-ridden society. In Bauer's view the 'belief that British society is class-ridden and therefore restrictive has paved the way for the politicisation and bureaucratisation of life'.[49] We tend to have misleading stereotypes of the class system. In fact nowadays 'political muscle' is much more important in raising income than any favoured position within the class system. Bauer believes that British society is in fact becoming *less* open and less flexible than in the past. The establishment of small businesses has become more difficult because of 'nationalisation of many activities, widespread bureaucratisation and heavy taxation'. Increased politicisation will lead to more conflict between groups which will shake the social fabric. This is partly because the political process involves a search for clear decision, and as it attempts to deal with more issues, the stresses will become greater.

(c) The fallacy of social cost

'Politicisation' carries with it its own characteristic set of fallacies in the sphere of economic thought. The New Right has spent a great deal of time in trying to rebut both the classic and newer arguments which are often used to justify state intervention. Since Pigou's day economists have stressed that economic decisions will often have social costs or impacts on third parties which could justify government intervention. There is a large literature on whether this intervention should take the form of taxation or direct regulation, but there is broad agreement about the need for some form of state action. The IEA has published an interesting attack on what Professor Cheung calls the 'myth of social cost'.[50] The classic arguments were supported by various empirical examples about the effects of land tenure and the costs arising when the market does not take account of the pollination activities by bees. Professor Cheung has both tracked down evidence on land tenure in pre-revolutionary China and conversed with beekeepers in the state of Washington.[51] His conclusions are that the traditional examples were mainly wrong; the market did for instance take account of pollination effects. With other thinkers on the New Right he does not see the existence of externalities as providing a 'clear case for some kind of public intervention'.

(d) The shortcomings of the Galbraith thesis

The economics of John Kenneth Galbriath are for the New Right a 'study in fantasy'.[52] Size does not necessarily bring with it market power or the ability to cut out uncertainty. McFadzean argues that even the largest firms have to deal with uncertainties arising from world market conditions. These produce fluctuations in raw materials prices and in product demand and lead to big changes in levels of profit from year to year. Galbraith has also failed to provide a clear way of distinguishing the giant corporation capable of rigging the market from the rest. Where does the great divide lie and why in practice do corporations show such very different corporate development and approaches to management? McFadzean also takes issue with various points in Galbraith's detailed account of the strategies by which giant corporations build up their power in the 'New Industrial State'. There is less vertical integration than he supposes and they do not withdraw from the external capital market – in fact they have large external debts. Nor have the planners the power to foretell the future suggested by Galbraith: in fact in the 1970s they have been just as likely to be wrong as right. 'To take a practical example: The Royal Dutch/Shell Group's actual performance in 1975 was recently compared with the estimate made in 1971 of what it would be four years later. In volume terms the forecast sales of oil outside North America were approximately 7 million barrels a day: actual sales were 4.2 million barrels per day.'[53] The relative pressures of total demand and total supply set the market discipline – not the number of producers.

(e) Rising public expenditure

Politicisation has its most obvious and significant fiscal consequence, in rising public expenditure. While Wagner promulgated his law of rising public expenditure as something both inevitable and in society's interest, the New Right sees this trend as wholly disastrous – and also as self-reinforcing. Faced by falling output and employment as the rising share of public expenditure crowds out private wealth creation, governments are tempted to intensify their expansionary policies. Some of the arguments go back to de Tocqueville and very early fiscal thinkers, notably Adam Smith. Where the payments for expenditures are not wholly made by the people getting the benefits from those expenditures, then there will always be temptation towards increases in public spending. Democracy increases the pressure. The benefits of spending programmes are concentrated often on vocal pressure groups while the payment is diffused. Pressures for vote-buying and special pleading lead to a growth in public expenditure. The inefficiency and rising relative cost of public expenditure together with the deadweight of bureaucracy reinforces the process. Bureaucracy not only has its impact through the creeping growth in the number of administrators but also in Britain by setting procedures for regulating public expenditure which ensure that it will regularly rise ahead of GDP. Thus for many years spending was set in real terms in line with over optimistic forecasts of growth. The demand management process encourages an in-built bias against cutting taxes. As Galloway has put it: 'when output is rising fast a "responsible" Chancellor justifies higher taxes as being necessary to reduce demand: but when output is falling increases in public expenditure are proposed to increase employment'.[54] Friedman in 1960 attacked what he called the 'balance wheel' approach to fiscal policy.

When private expenditures decline for any reason, it is said, government expenditures should rise to keep total expenditures stable; conversely when private expenditures rise, government expenditures should decline . . . The haste with which spending programmes are approved is not matched by an equal haste to review them or to eliminate others when the recession is past and expansion is under way. On the contrary it is then argued that a 'healthy' expansion must not be 'jeopardised' by cuts in governmental expenditure.[55]

Older arguments about fiscal pressure in a representative system have come together here with newer ones about macroeconomic balance and, for Britain, declining growth.

(f) Industrial subsidies

The 'subsidy morass' is another fiscal consequence of politicisation and one which reinforces the process. The New Right here both tries to establish that government will always fail in intervening in industry and also to show why it is always trying to do so in spite of this manifest failure. Weinstock has stated his pontifical belief: 'Government intervention in industry is invariably incompetent, and this applies to government subsidy as to every other form of arbitrary interference with the economy.'[56] But subsidy programmes continue because of the intense political pressures for them. Their benefits, as with public spending generally, are much more concentrated than the costs in taxation. In practice the objectives of the subsidy programmes are muddled. Their main rationale is the creation and preservation of jobs, but they are also justified by the new industrial policy, the balance of payments and the 'national interest'. The arguments for them stress the low net costs because of savings in unemployment benefit – but typically ignore the displacement effects in terms of lost jobs in firms not subsidised and also do not measure properly the duration of subsidisation (long) against the duration of unemployment (short). In practice there will often be a bias towards subsidies of capital intensive firms supported by powerful producer groups. This is what is known as the 'Drax B' phenomenon – where 'staggering amounts' of money were pumped into capital intensive firms to avert a few thousand jobs lost 'at heaven knows what cost' to jobs displaced or crowded-out in labour intensive industries. The subsidy programme also has long-term effects on employers and unions which reinforce the process of politicisation. The employment relationship is based on an implicit contract: if there is always a possible appeal to a third party, government, the other two will have no incentive to build and sustain their own relationship and their own ways of adjusting to economic change. Burton predicts that the long-term effect of the subsidy programme will be to bring government into direct confrontation with industry and unions in subsidised companies over the issue of efficiency productivity and wage demands.[57] The atmosphere of class conflict will grow tighter and the pressures to more public spending increase.

(g) The failure of the welfare state

Friedman in the United States together with the Institute of Economic Affairs in Britain have both contributed especially detailed and intense accounts of the misdeeds of the welfare state. But while the New Right in Britain has recently put less stress on detailed attacks on the welfare state, Friedman has continued to mine this lode energetically. Whether he looks at education, housing, health services or social security, the basic themes of the Friedman attack are the same.

1. Expenditures have grown enormously. For example, the Department of Health Education and Welfare spent $2 billion when it was set up in 1953: by 1978 it was spending $160 billion.
2. An increasing proportion of these expenditures in fact favour the better off; an extreme example is higher education where the poor are taxed to pay for the higher earnings of a few. They fail in their stated objectives of redistributing income.
3. In spite of the manifest failure of government activity to provide satisfaction, there are strong political forces, vested interests, clients and the bureaucrats who run the programmes, which seek to preserve and even to extend them.
4. The poor would generally benefit from a market orientated system, for example from the use of vouchers in education.

There have been some significant shifts of ground over the years. Thus it was held by Friedman (following Lees) and others in the early 1960s that the NHS had unduly limited expenditures compared with the level which consumers would have chosen for themselves.[58] Now the emphasis here and in the public services generally tends to be more on waste and inefficiency, rather than on parsimony, but the main themes have been followed consistently from *Capitalism and Freedom*, published in 1962, to *Free to Choose*, published in 1980.

(h) The pressure from bureaucracy

Bureaucracy also works both independently and under pressure from political democracy to raise public spending. The New Right distrust the 'Woodrow Wilson' view of bureaucracy – that all we need to do is to put good men in public office and then give them the power to follow the public interest. Bureaucracies follow their own patterns of behaviour, in relation to their sponsors and their clients. There is often very little definition of the 'output' which bureaux are supposed to be producing; so decisions typically tend to concentrate on the sizes of the budget and the levels of activity. There is also little opportunity for choice at the margin. Bureaux offer a total level of output in return for a budget. In this hazy situation the rational bureaucrat concerned with survival will try to maximise the size of his budget. A larger budget will make the bureau easier to manage and will increase his own prestige.

The central prediction of the main 'Niskanen' model is that bureaux tend to be too large. 'For given cost and demand conditions they supply a quantity of services larger than would maximise the net benefits of the service.'[59] So far from able to control these inherent drives in bureaucracies, parliaments operate so as to reinforce them. Advocacy of spending programmes tends to be concentrated and opposition diffused. The political benefits of spending programmes accrue to a small group of advocates, while the political costs are diffused among all the legislators.

(i) The fall of the trade unions

Finally there is the fallen Lucifer of the trade union movement. There is no inherent and necessary contradiction between the trade union movement and the capitalist ethic. Sir Keith Joseph is always quoting the example of Germany with approval; but British unions have developed destructive tendencies because of false monetary policies and lack of definition of their own legal position. Over the years a growing conflict has grown up between trade union drives in wage bargaining and the entrepreneurial needs of the system. For Peter Jay these can only be resolved through workers' control[60]: however, the New Right follow him in his diagnosis of the problem – but not of the solution.

Friedman argues, as he has since the early 1950s, that unions have little effect on the real earnings of their members, apart from the power to restrict entry. But this has been done much more effectively by the American Medical Association than it has by trade unions. 'The most reliable and effective protection for most workers is provided by the existence of many employers.' Unions create a world of dramatic incident which lead people to over-estimate their power. In fact they are the thermometer rather than the furnace.[61] However the situation gets more complicated and the effects of unions potentially stronger if they are combined with nationalised monopoly operating in an uncertain budgetary context.

How does the New Right's macroeconomic policy of monetarism relate to this wider social philosophy? Certainly it also has some independent origins in evidence about the relationship between money and economic activity, most of which Friedman has provided, but it also fits in very neatly with the wider philosophy. The ideal policy for monetarists would be to set a steady moderate growth of the money supply and then simply to switch the economy onto the automatic pilot.

The economy would then of its own accord find its natural rate of unemployment, and entrepreneurs would have room to build. With little government intervention, the forces for growth inherent in a free market economy would begin to show themselves. Thus monetarism gives scope for society to find its *thesis*: but it also weakens the *antithesis*. It gives little scope for political logrolling. Without an active fiscal policy questions about the distribution of income are in the background. There is little scope for a lurch towards equality. The labour market will establish a natural distribution of income. Nor will there be so much opportunity for growth in public spending or in subsidies. Through their powers in relation to public debt the monetary authorities will be able to weaken the urges of democratic representatives towards higher public spending. Thus monetarism in effect creates a new permanent authority with substantial power to check elected governments. With bureaux increasingly forced to rely on charging, the momentum of bureaucracy will be slowed down. Finally the new atmosphere will deeply influence the conduct of the trade union movement.

References

Much of this chapter first appeared in *Political Quarterly*, July/September 1981, under the title 'Sir Keith's Reading List'. I am grateful to the editors for permission to use this material.

1. M. Friedman and R. Friedman, *Free to Choose*, London; Secker and Warburg, 1980, p.25.
2. *Free to Choose*, pp.60–61.
3. M. Friedman, *Capitalism and Freedom*, Chicago; University of Chicago Press, 1962, p.169.
4. *Capitalism and Freedom*, pp.23–24.
5. A. Smith, *The Theory of Moral Sentiments*, Oxford; Oxford University Press, p.119.
6. *The Theory of Moral Sentiments*, p.125.
7. *The Theory of Moral Sentiments*, p.125.
8. *The Theory of Moral Sentiments*, p.269.
9. *The Theory of Moral Sentiments*, p.87.
10. *Wealth of Nations*, London; Everyman, 1960, Vol. I p.12.
11. F. Hayek, *Law, Legislation and Liberty: Vol. 1, Rules and Order*, London; Routledge and Kegan Paul, 1973, p.12.
12. F. Hayek, *Law, Legislation and Liberty: Vol 2, The Mirage of Social Justice*, London; Routledge and Kegan Paul, 1976, p.39.
13. *Rules and Order*, London; p.47.
14. *Free to Choose*, pp.28–29, quoting A. Smith, Vol II (Cannan Edition), pp.184–5. *Wealth of Nations*, Vol. II, pp.184–5.
15. *Capitalism and Freedom*, p.3.
16. Lord Robbins, *Liberty and Equality*, IEA Occasional Paper no. 52, 1977.
17. *Liberty and Equality*, p.13.
18. *The Mirage of Social Justice*, p.87.
19. *Liberty and Equality*, p.16.
20. K. Joseph and J. Sumption, *Equality*, London; John Murray, 1979, p.78.

21. *Rules and Order*, p.121.
22. *Free to Choose*, p.138.
23. *Free to Choose*, p.3.
24. *Capitalism and Freedom*, p.169.
25. J.A. Schumpeter, *Capitalism, Socialism and Democracy*, London; Allen and Unwin, 1979, p.67.
26. *Capitalism, Socialism and Democracy*, p.83.
27. *Capitalism, Socialism and Democrary*, p.84.
28. F. Knight, *Risk, Uncertainty and Profit*, New York; Kelly Reprint of Economic Classics, 1967, p.284.
29. S.C. Littlechild, *The Fallacy of the Mixed Economy*, London; IEA, 1978, p.1.
30. *Capitalism, Socialism and Democrary*, p.69.
31. *Capitalism and Freedom*, p.170.
32. *Equality*, p.28.
33. A. de Tocqueville, *Democracy in America*; New York; Phillips Bradley edition Vintage Books, 1945, Vol. 1, p.56.
34. *Democracy in America*, Vol. 1, p.224.
35. *Democracy in America*, Vol. 2, p.147.
36. *Democracy in America*, Vol. 2, p.312.
37. *Democracy in America*, p.312.
38. *Democracy in America*, p.317.
39. *Democracy in America*, p.322.
40. *Democracy in America*, p.266.
41. *Democracy in America*, p.35.
42. *Rules and Order*, p.1.
43. *Rules and Order*, p.2.
44. *The Mirage of Social Justice*, p.138.
45. F. Hayek, *Law, Legislation and Liberty: Vol. 3, The Political Order of a Free People*, London; Routledge and Kegan Paul, 1979, p.139.
46. *The Political Order of a Free People*, p.151.
47. *Capitalism and Freedom*, p.9.
48. *Capitalism and Freedom*, p.16.
49. P. Bauer, *Class on the Brain, The Cost of a British Obsession*, London; Centre for Policy Studies, 1978, p.6.
50. S. Cheung, *The Myth of Social Cost*, London; IEA, 1978.
51. *The Myth of Social Cost*, pp.55–64.
52. F. McFadzean, *The Economics of J.K. Galbraith*, London; Centre for Policy Studies, 1977.
53. *The Economics of J.K. Galbraith*, p.36.
54. J. Galloway, *The Public Prodigals*, London; Temple Smith, 1976, p.184.
55. *Capitalism and Freedom*, p.76.
56. A. Weinstock, Foreword to J. Burton, *The Job Support Machine*, London; Centre for Policy Studies, 1979.
57. *The Job Support Machine*, pp.51–2.
58. *Capitalism and Freedom*, p.95.
59. W. Niskanen, *Bureaucracy, Servant or Master*, London; IEA, 1973, p.31.
60. P. Jay, *Employment, Inflation and Politics*, London; IEA, Occasional Paper, 1976.
61. M. Friedman, 'Some Comments on the Significance of Labor Unions for Economic Policy', in D. McCord Wright (ed.), *The Impact of the Union*, New York; Harcourt Brace, 1951 p.222.

2 Hayek

Hayek has been honoured by his colleagues, not least by the Nobel Prize in 1974, but they have not followed very far into the complexities of his thought and its implications for policy. Friedman is partially correct in saying that Hayek's influence has been tremendous.[1] It is only in the senses of a title a general inspiration and an organisation. *The Road to Serfdom*[2] remained for many years the most uncompromising statement of liberalism and the one which commanded the greatest public attention. The inspiration was contained in the insistence on a few fundamental principles. Others followed him in his principles but without the rigour and clarity of his supporting argument. Hayek's case for the market is a deeply considered one. The organisation was the Mont Pelerin society, which Hayek did so much to found, perhaps influenced by the example of Beatrice Webb whose ability to influence opinion he held in great esteem.[3]

Hayek's system of thought has received far less attention. This is partly because it deals with issues that economists see either as insoluble or as 'not economics'. Hayek aspires to deal with issues about man in society which economists normally see as outside their normal business. He was also unlucky in the timing of his major work *The Constitution of Liberty*, which was published in a period of political apathy.[4] Ten years later it might have had a much wider hearing. Most of the attention to Hayek's system has been from political scientists.[5]

This chapter shows how Hayek's system has developed to allow a comparison with Friedman's system. It has sometimes been argued that the differences between them are not of major importance. It will be argued here that they are of major significance: that the New Right follows two quite different economic approaches which lead to different conclusions about society and to different approaches to policy. There is much in the Hayekian canon which could be accepted by all schools of thought in economics and more widely in the social sciences.

Much of Hayek's work before the Second World War was of a technical kind which is difficult to fit into the later framework: but even then it contained some important anticipations. His first major work in English *Prices and Production* showed a suspicion of aggregate relationships and of crude quantification. He expressed some dismay at Irving Fisher's recent revival in America of the 'mechanistic' version of the quantity theory. This crude theory certainly had an important function of social control: it would be 'one of the worst things which could befall us if the general public should ever again cease to believe in the elementary propositions of the quantity theory.'[6] But the theory stood in the way of real understanding. He was suspicious of attempts to 'establish *direct* causal connections between the *total* quantity of money, the *general level* of all prices and, perhaps, also the *total* amount of production. For none of these magnitudes *as such* ever exerts an influence on the decisions of individuals' (emphasis original).[7] It was important to bring modern subjective theory to bear on these problems. The trade cycle moves with changes in preferences between consumption and investment which affect the pattern of real demand in the economy. Such changes in preferences can cause changes in the monetary side of the economy which are difficult to reconcile with the crude quantity theory. The money supply will adjust to the volume and composition of production through the creation of money substitutes. This 'elastic' quality of the currency will make it very difficult for central banks to control the stock of money.[8] The quantity theory needs to be rethought as a much more sophisticated relationship. Indeed Hayek began his book with a quotation from Cantillon: 'He realised well that the abundance of money makes everything dear, but he did not analyse how that takes place. The great difficulty of this analysis consists in discovering in what path and in what proportion the increase of money raises the price of things.'[9]

His writings on the economics of socialism are even clearer precursors in their distrust of centralisation and their emphasis on the element of discovery in market processes. The main case for the market is that it can live with uncertainty. Here we have the beginnings of the case against planning which was to be much more fully made in the *Road to Serfdom*. His work during the 1930s on the impossibility of central planning and its disastrous results in the USSR was also closer to intense issues of day-to-day politics. For Beatrice Webb, Hayek appears in the 1930s at the London School of Economics mainly as the representative of a certain type of abstract economics. On 1 May 1937 Beatrice Webb wrote in her *Diary* that 'Robbins who with Hayek and Plant thinks, talks and writes abstract economics . . . has always been our antithesis at the school.'[10] However, in one entry Hayek appears in a rather different light (even though his name is still misspelt as 'Hyack'). Beatrice Webb wrote of a visit by a Russian refugee couple, the 'unfortunates Turins'. She wrote that 'Turin has been deprived of the fees which he received from the London School of Economics – he is now merely an adviser to students because Hayek and Robbins objected to the subject of Soviet planning, etc. being raised among the students except by themselves.[11] Whatever the truth of that matter the sections written by Hayek for *Collectivist Economist Planning*, published in 1935, are very much closer in tone and content to his post-war work than most of his other writings in the 1930s.[12]

Although Hayek clearly regards the *Constitution of Liberty* as his major work, the consumers – on best subjectivist principles – are not likely to take him at his word. The *Constitution of Liberty* is certainly a major step, but it has a static, negative quality. Some of the earlier contributions on 'scientism' as well as parts of the later three volumes on *Law, Legislation and Liberty* seem more directly personal and challenging. Hayek's thought can be seen as the development of consistent perceptions on a number of issues starting from a few central propositions about knowledge and behaviour. There would seem to be three main phases in this development.

First, the Hayekian views of knowledge, psychology and social science were formulated. The division of labour was redefined in terms of the distribution of information. But the social implications of these views were drawn out only sketchily in the *Road of Serfdom*.

In the second phase detailed inferences were drawn from the theory of information about economic development and social ordering. A set of moral definitions – of freedom and coercion – were now added to the earlier thesis. In the later sections of the *Constitution of Liberty* he attempted to illustrate the damage already done to 'freedom' by the drift to the welfare state.

In the last phase the *thesis* remains unchanged but the Hayekian view of the *antithesis* changes. It is no longer just ideas and intellectuals which determine policy. Policy is determined by competition for votes in the political market-place. In this last phase too, Hayek in his 'despair' about the crisis of inflation returns to commentary about day-to-day economic affairs for the first time since the 1930s.

Hayek's Subjectivism: The First Phase

In this phase we find certain propositions which remain the foundation pillars of the Hayekian system throughout.

Hayek viewed his lecture on 'Economics and Knowledge', given in 1936, as a landmark in this intellectual development.[13] Hayek, talking to a Japanese audience explained in 1964 how he had moved from technical economics into 'all kinds of questions usually regarded as philosophical. When I look back, it seems to have all begun, nearly thirty years ago, with an essay on economics and knowledge.'[14] In this he takes issue with objective approaches to economic concepts such as equilibrium. Equilibrium simply means that the expectations of a number of individuals are fulfilled. Hayek ends by setting out the problem which he puts at the centre of all his subsequent work. 'How can the combination of fragments of knowledge existing in different minds bring about results which if they were to be brought about deliberately would require a knowledge on the part of the directing mind which no single person can possess?'[15]

The next step is 'The Counter-Revolution of Science', published first as a series of articles in *Economica* between 1942 and 1944.[16] This continued the war against the unreasoning faith in quantification and the 'tyranny' of the natural sciences which he had declared in his inaugural lecture at the LSE. It must surely rank as one of the best written and stimulating of Hayek's works and also the one which has been most completely ignored by economists.

Modern science has come to be about objective facts, 'using special language and quantitative techniques of measurement'. The aim of science is '. . . to produce a new organisation of all our experience of the external world, and in doing so it has not only to remodel our concepts but also to get away from the sense qualities and to replace them by a different classification of events'.[17] But there is another world beyond science, the 'views and concepts people hold'.[18]

Later Hayek half admitted that his view of the natural sciences had been something of a caricature. But he was surely right in his direction of a certain type of science. Most of the book is about the consequences of uncritical imitation of the methods of the natural sciences – 'scientism'. Science aims to move away from experience into a formal mathematical language. Social science, on the other hand, has to deal with the views and concepts people hold – '. . . all they know and believe about themselves, about other people, and about the external world, in short everything which determines their actions, including science itself'.[19] Individuals have their own knowledge and beliefs. They can communicate because of the similarity of these views: but knowledge is always subjective and dispersed. 'But the concrete knowledge which guides the action of any group of people never exists as a consistent and coherent body. It only exists in the dispersed, incomplete and inconsistent form in which it appears in many individual minds, and this dispersion and imperfection of all knowledge is one of the basic facts from which the social sciences have to start.'[20] There is also a subjective character to human beliefs whether they are about the natural world or about social relationships. 'Even such a seemingly purely biological relationship as that between parent and child is in social study not defined in physical terms and cannot be so defined for their purposes.'[21] Our knowledge of external objects is diffused and highly subjective. Yet our perceptions are similar enough to allow recurrent, recognisable and familiar elements of a social structure to develop.

Hayek then proceeds to a catalogue of the cardinal sins of the scientists. They include the attempt to deal with man in society through objective and abstract approaches. 'Objectivism' is concerned with the material and physiological. It busies itself with such interesting problems as the physical roots of psychological processes. It usually includes a major interest in quantitative data and abstractions such as 'society'. It carries over very easily into the second cardinal sin of 'collectivism', a tendency to treat 'wholes' such as 'society' or the 'economy' etc. as objects about which we can discover laws by observing their behaviour as wholes. The last sin is more familiar, that of historicism – or the ex post search for historical laws relating to these wholes, laws which tend to create a false identity and a false determinism for each historical epoch.[22]

These fallacies make people unable to grasp 'how the independent action of many men can produce coherent wholes, persistent structures of relationships which serve important human purposes without having been designed for that end'. This blindness leads directly to political collectivism. Hayek finished this part of *The Counter-Revolution of Science* by contrasting the approaches of the engineer and of the economist. Engineering problems are solved by dealing with objective facts: the engineer is not taking part in a social process in which others may take independent decisions, but lives in a separate world of his own. The merchant, on the other hand, relies upon the '. . . knowledge of particular circumstances of time or place . . .'.[23] This is much more critical to the efficient use of resources than the knowledge of the engineer. The second part of *The Counter-Revolution of Science* traces the origins of the scientific hubris in the Ecole Polytechnique and in the work of Saint Simon. Saint-Simonian influence on the pattern of industrial enterprise in France was enormous, partly through the work of his disciples in banks and railway companies. Napoleon III, or 'Saint Simon on Horseback' as he was called, and Bismarck were others who were indirectly influenced by Saint Simon's ideas.

To economists, Hayek's best known work in this phase is his paper of September 1945 in the *American Economic Review* on the 'Use of Knowledge in Society'.[24] This identifies the price mechanism as the crucial means by which society makes use of differences in the knowledge of individuals. The price mechanism also economises on intellectual effort making it possible for people to adjust almost automatically to change.

Taking this first phase as a whole from 1936 to 1953 we can define Hayek's main ideas as follows:

1. Economic decisions are made subjectively by individuals. This proposition was based on the subjective 'Austrian' school of economics: but in *The Sensory Order* Hayek also made a detour in psychology in order to try to establish it there.[25] Our classification of the world is based on certain sets of perceptions within the mind. 'It is thus the existence of an order of sensory qualities and not a reproduction of qualities existing outside the perceiving mind which is the basic

problem raised by mental events.'[26] We all have maps which are sufficiently similar to allow communication, but which are not simply created by external stimuli. Human knowledge is also limited by the limitation of the apparatus of classification, the brain.

2. No one person can know more than a fraction of the information available in society.

3. Society advances by making use of dispersed knowledge: but it does so through the price system and the market. Collectivist central planning is bound to fail: it will be the 'road to serfdom'.

4. Social action is guided by opinion: opinion is set, in turn by thinkers and intellectuals. Thinkers and intellectuals control politics from the grave. Hayek approved of rather few of Keynes' statements, but one of which he would have approved was that practical men are ruled by long-defunct economic theorists. The emphasis on opinion was most fully put in *The Counter-Revolution of Science*, but it appears later in the Introduction to *Capitalism and the Historians*.[27] Here it is the historians rather than the political theorists who are controlling society by giving the stamp of scholarship to myths.

5. The forces of the market are impersonal and men often cannot understand them. Progress depends on man giving an unthinking deference to the market.

The Road to Serfdom was a political and polemical work which made use of these ideas but in a rhetorical way. It also gained force from its many references to Nazi Germany. Only concern for the wartime alliance prevented Hayek from giving a more extended analysis of the Soviet system. *The Road to Serfdom* had its main success in the United States where like Orwell's *Animal Farm* it was a political event. Perhaps the chapter of greatest interest is that on 'Material Conditions and Ideal Ends'.[28] Here Hayek defends the free market as a concept of moral choice to which he was to return in his later work. 'What our generation is in danger of forgetting', he wrote in a paragraph which Keynes called 'extraordinarily good and fundamental',[29] 'is not only that morals are of necessity a phenomenon of individual conduct, but also that they can exist only in the sphere in which the individual is free to decide for himself and called upon voluntarily to sacrifice personal advantage to the observance of a moral rule.'[30] Later we are told that the workings of an individualist society depend on virtues such as 'independence, self-reliance, and the willingness to bear risks, the readiness to back one's conviction against a majority and the willingness to voluntary cooperations with one's neighbours'.[31] We have here a fuller – even if vague and diffuse – definition of moral conduct than appears in any of Hayek's later works. It is also somewhat conventional in its stress on 'British' virtues. The shock effect of the *Road to Serfdom* has, however, worn off.

The Second Phase: Hayek's Constitution of Liberty

The *Road to Serfdom* had mainly been about the pernicious effects of central planning. It looked backwards to the earlier writings of Hayek about socialism. The defence of freedom was incidental. In the crucial first part of *The Constitution of Liberty*, Hayek sets out his real conception of freedom at length. It is a highly negative conception. Freedom for Hayek is the absence of coercion. By coercion he means such '. . . control of the environment or circumstances of a person by another that, in order to avoid greater evil, he is forced to act not according to a coherent plan of his own but to serve the ends of another. Except in the sense of choosing the lesser evil in a situation forced on him by another, he is unable either to use his own intelligence and knowledge or to follow his own aims and beliefs.'[32] Coercion is evil precisely because it thus eliminates an individual as a thinking and valuing person and makes him a bare tool in the achievement of the ends of another.

This narrow conception of freedom is best understood as the opposite of slavery. Anybody who is not a slave – whose will is subject to the will of another – is free under this definition. Freedom is not about content: it is not about having a wide range of opportunities to choose from. 'In this sense "freedom" refers solely to a relation of men to other men, and the only infringement on it is coercion by other men. This means, in particular, that the range of physical possibilities from which a person can choose at a given moment has no direct relevance to freedom. The rock climber on a difficult pitch who sees only one way out to save his life is unquestionably free, though we would hardly say that he has any choice.'[33] This is claimed as the original meaning of the word freedom, as distinct from slavery. It is to be distinguished from a number of other common meanings of the term, including political freedom. In fact Hayek has suggested various limitations on franchise which he describes as no more arbitrary than the ones which now exist. His freedom is to be distinguished from political freedom – the 'participation of men in the choice of their government, in the process of legislation, and in the control of administration'.[34] Freedom is not about consent to the political order. Nor is it to be mistaken for inner freedom. But the most dangerous confusion of all is between liberty and the ability to do things. Liberty is not power. Such ideas lead to philosophies of redistribution by which liberty is further confused with wealth. A minimum of coercion may be unavoidable in order to preserve liberty, but this coercion should be in the hands of government and limited to general rules.

However, Hayek accepts by implication that this definition of liberty would only survive if it would provide the context for 'progress'. Progress is not explicitly defined in *The Constitution of Liberty* but would seem to be roughly equated with the state of affairs prevailing in England during the nineteenth century. Progress can only occur in a society which has stumbled on the arrangements which have made it possible for man to transcend the boundaries – soon reached – of his own ignorance. The decentralised market economy allows pooling of information through price signals. There is a tilt towards social conservatism in the Hayekian approach here. Man is best served by a semi-conscious adaptation to existing forms not only in the economic sphere but in many others.

> These 'tools' which man has evolved and which constitute such an important part of his adaptation to his environment include much more than material implements. They consist in a large measure of forms of conduct which he habitually follows without knowing why; they consist of what we call 'traditions' and 'institutions' which he uses because they are available to him as a product of cumulative growth without ever having been designed by any one mind.[35]

Hayek is even more explicit in a later passage. 'It is this submission to undesigned rules and conventions whose significance and importance we largely do not understand, this reverence for the traditional, that the rationalistic type of mind finds so uncongenial, though it is indispensable for the working of a free society.'[36] The 'foundation' of the argument for liberty is that through such utilisation of dispersed knowledge, achievements are made possible greater than any single mind can foresee. But this is not an argument against organisation. Organisation is likely to be beneficial and effective so long as it is truly voluntary. The rationalist wants to control all through reason – but in fact progress depends on the unpredictability of human action. The main argument for this is in terms of results. 'The history of civilisation is the account of a progress which, in the short space of less than eight thousand years, has created nearly all that we regard as characteristic of human life.'[37] Progress is basically a process of learning, of formation and modification of the human intellect, of adaptation in which not only the possibilities known to us but also our values and desires constantly change. Progress will usually have as one of its consequences rapidly rising incomes for many. The enjoyment of personal success will be given to large numbers only in a society, which as a whole progresses fairly rapidly. Inequality is vital to progress in that it makes possible the accumulation of personal wealth.

Greater stress is put here on the role of tradition as the carrier of the conventions which lead to progress than in any of the later works.

The conception of freedom is clear enough, but it is not at all clear how such a conception is going to find support in the world as it is today; Hayek himself at times seems despondent. He expresses some doubt about whether man can feel a sense of local responsibility in a mass society. 'The essential condition of responsibility is that it refer to circumstances that the individual can judge, to problems that, without too much strain on the imagination, man can make his own and whose solution he can, with good reason, consider his own concern rather than another's. Such a condition can hardly apply to life in the anonymous crowd of an industrial city.'[38] Even more important is the growth in the number of employees. 'Where this class predominates, the conception of social justice becomes largely adjusted to its needs. This applies not only to legislation but also to institutions and business practices.'[39] Hayek professes to believe that the employees can be persuaded to accept that the existence of their own freedom depends on the self-employed. 'The existence of a multiplicity of opportunities for employment ultimately depends on the existence of independent individuals who can take the initiative in the continuous process of reforming and redirecting organisations.'[40] Similarly the employed masses depend on the wealthy for the advance of culture. 'It is one of the great tragedies of our time that the masses have come to believe that they have reached their high standard of material welfare as a result of having pulled down the wealthy . . .'[41]

Hayek also looks at the moral consequence of his particular idea of freedom. One is that naive ideas about reward being proportional to merit are no longer applicable. Reward will go to those who make the best judgements about the disposition of their own resources and merit in the usual sense will have little to do with it. Justice also has a particular meaning within this scheme of things. It does not have any implications for distribution, but for the deliberate treatment of men by other men. It also requires certain limitations to democracy. The ideal of freedom is incompatible with the absolute sovereignty of the majority. Political decisions only become legitimate if they are guided by freely formed opinions. 'The ideal of democracy rests on the belief that the view which will direct government emerges from an independent and spontaneous process. It requires, therefore, the existence of a large sphere independent of majority control in which the opinions of the individuals are formed.'[42] The final section on 'Freedom in the Welfare State' traces the continuing decline of the ideal of freedom in a number of areas: the growing weight of progressive taxation, the increasing rate of inflation, the increase in the social security system, the pernicious effects of rent control. But all these issues are discussed in empirical and institutional terms. They are not linked to a central thesis about change in society.

Hayek is clear on the historical change at issue – the road to serfdom has suddenly taken a new turning. Socialists have given up completely their traditional faith in control of the means of production and have taken up the other road of achieving their objectives – changes in the welfare state. This will gradually lead to the sapping of individual initiatives in a number of fields and to a 'new despotism'. The power of trade unions is only one symptom of this. However Hayek's trumpet call has a more uncertain sound than Friedman's. Hayek does not have the strength of faith in the market mechanism as a means of solving the problems of urbanised societies. Nor is the welfare state as definite a target as was central planning. 'We shall see that some of the aims of the welfare state can be realised without detriment to individual liberty . . .'[43] Government can also provide security against severe physical privation, the assurance of a given minimum sustenance for all, even though it cannot end and should not assure a '. . . given standard of life, which is determined by comparing the standard enjoyed by a person or a group with that of others'.[44] The welfare state tends to develop an ambition to use the powers of government to ensure a more even or more just distribution of income. The welfare state also tends to lead to the creation of government monopolies, and to other kinds of barrier to entry such as those inherent in the growth of trade unions. These general theses are then worked out in application to particular fields – social security, taxation, housing. Yet, even in some of the detailed discussions of issues, the ambivalence continues. Thus in the excellent chapter on housing Hayek wrote:

> In many respects the close contiguity of city life invalidates the assumptions underlying any simple division of property rights. In such conditions it is true only to a limited extent that whatever an owner does with his property will affect only him and nobody else. What economists call the 'neighbourhood effects' . . . assume major importance. The usefulness of almost any piece of property in a city will in fact depend on what one's immediate neighbours do and in part on the communal services without which effective use of the land by separate owners would be nearly impossible.[45]

An uneasy postscript to this book explains why Hayek is not a conservative: because conservatives lack any fixed view of how the social order operates. Conservatives are not opposed in principle to government control – only to the particular aims of particular governments. Conservatism also shows a fondness for authority and a lack of understanding of economic forces. 'In general, it can probably be said that the conservative does not object to coercion and arbitrary power so long as it is used for what he regards as the right purposes.' Like the socialist he 'regards himself as entitled to force the value he holds on other people'.[46] In the light of this postscript it is even more difficult to understand why Hayek thinks that 'socialists' have been responsible for the growth of the welfare state. The role of such conservatives as Bismarck is not discussed. The reasons for the growth of the welfare state remain at this stage obscure.

Hayek's Third Phase

In this most recent (but even at the age of 82 it would be rash to assume the last) phase, Hayek has recaptured public attention but again more for his political stance than for the finer details of his scholarship or system. In part this – as in the first phase – can be blamed on the coarseness of public opinion. But Hayek himself must take some of the responsibility. Although there are elements of great interest in his thought to all camps, his interventions in more topical affairs have always been in support of the Right in the political spectrum. However if we try to look at the work of Hayek the thinker in this phase, we find the following main elements of change.

1. Hayek's theses about knowledge, freedom and law have been translated into a new set of concepts. The main distinctions are between 'taxis' or made order and 'cosmos' or spontaneous order. The economic order is one part of a sphere of decision-making called a 'catallaxy'. We also have the distinction between 'nomos' and 'thesis'; general rule and specific regulation.
2. Hayek's main concern has come to be with the rule of law in the sense of 'nomos' – general rules known in advance.
3. The evolutionary strand of Hayek's thought becomes more prominent. The case for the free order comes even more to be made in terms of its role in a process of social selection.
4. Hayek has developed his thoughts on distribution and his defence of the individualist approach much more strongly.
5. Hayek has a different view of the main motive force behind destruction of the spontaneous order. It is no longer to be sought in the writings of intellectuals but in the development of democracy.
6. Hayek has now begun to make positive proposals ranging from an elaborate scheme for constitutional reform in the third volume of *Law, Legislation and Liberty* to his scheme for the denationalisation of money. The prophet of spontaneous orders would appear to have fallen for the attractions of paper schemes.

The three volumes are of intimidating length and suffer perhaps from Hayek's tendency to spread his fire over several subjects: this time the minor key being law rather than psychology.[47] But in many ways they are more attractive works than *The Constitution of Liberty*. That book had a pontifical quality. These are more attractive in their style: more inventive in their presentation of the ideas and more personal. Hayek's thought in this third phase has rightly received careful attention from people well beyond his usual range of admirers. Above all, however, the books have come into a world which is now much more receptive to Hayek's thirty-year-old messages. In 1960 *The Economist* in a most hostile review of *The Constitution of Liberty* wrote that 'Professor Hayek's certainty remains astonishingly unshaken by the failure, over fifteen years of so many mixed economies and welfare states to progress even a single step down the predicted road to serfdom.'[48] By the mid-1970s there was a much more receptive climate.

The starting points are familiar ones. No one person can ever master more than the smallest amount of information needed in a society. Hume and Mandeville are given their usual places in the pantheon. On the one hand we have the fragmentation of knowledge; on the other we have the synoptic delusion that one mind can know everything.

Hayek's new task is to rework the theory of social Darwinism. Hayek reclaims the theory of evolution for the social sciences. But the theory provides for the selection of customs, institutions and practices rather than individuals.

The concepts of 'cosmos' and 'taxis' play a key part in this theory of social Darwinism. A cosmos is a spontaneous order: a taxis is a constructed one. These concepts have a life of their own in Hayek's thought, giving it a direction that it has never had before. The spontaneous order begins to take on a more 'social' cast in spite of the best intentions of its author. By order Hayek means 'a state of affairs in which a multiplicity of elements of various kinds are so related to each other that we may learn from our acquaintance with some spatial or temporal part of the whole to form correct expectations concerning the rest, or at least expectations which have some chance of proving correct'.[49] A spontaneous order or 'cosmos' is very different from a made order – or organisation – or 'taxis'. The spontaneous order included organisations as well as individuals: it even includes government, although in a stand-by role rather like that of a maintenance department in a factory. Only the spontaneous order will be able to use the information dispersed in society.

To protect the spontaneous order Hayek turns in old age to the lawyers rather than to the economists. He is attacking the key point of decision in the 'taxis', the point of legislation. Lawyers have been corrupted by false economics but Hayek is hopeful of improving them. The 'cosmos' will in fact develop its own forms of judge-made law or 'nomos' which Hayek contrasts with the 'thesis' or law of legislation. The idea of nomos is closely linked to the concept of natural law and quite opposed to the idea of legal positivism – that each law requires a sovereign. The spontaneous order or 'catallaxy' depends on abstract rules of a general kind. These rules help us to deal with unknown contingencies. The human mind can in fact work only within these abstract rules because it cannot generalise about a great many particular cases. A spontaneous order operating without interference will be the order best fitted to increase the opportunities for any one unknown person picked at random.

The smooth ordering of day-to-day life depends, in Hayek's view, on the observance of rules of just conduct which are deep in the minds of individuals. The cosmos with its rules implies a particular conception of justice. Justice is usually negative and procedural. The rules of just conduct would seem to include essentially freedom of contract, the inviolability of property and the duty to compensate another for damage due to his fault. This is a procedural approach to justice. It has nothing to do with conceptions of social justice, which concentrate on results. Hayek's discussion of the concept of social justice is a subtle one. Value to society depends solely on the unpredictable outcomes of many independent decisions. Incomes earned in the market by different persons will normally not correspond to the relative value of their services to any one person. The enemy now has become not central planning or the welfare state but the moral deception of social justice, which leads to egalitarian policies. This idea of social justice has some consequences which will worry the more sentimental. It is quite wrong in Hayek's view for governments to intervene to compensate people for losses of accustomed positions. 'The frequent recurrence of such undeserved strokes of misfortune affecting some group is, however, an inseparable part of the steering mechanism of the market.'[50] Hayek then elaborates his definition of the best society as one in which 'we would prefer to place our children if we knew that their position in it would be determined by lot'.

Social justice has become the elixir for the leviathan. The old welfare state denounced in *The Constitution of Liberty* now begins to take on an almost benevolent look. It was concerned with abolishing destitution. Social justice has become the slogan with which any threatened group tries to protect its position. We are moving towards a new tribalism and a revolt against the spontaneous order and the discipline of abstract rules.

In the third volume, Hayek comes to a more specific diagnosis of the disease and prescription of the remedy. 'With some regret' he does not consistently use the neologisms defined in the first volume. The theme is that 'this threatening development towards a totalitarian state' now is brought about not by the hubris of the planners but by 'certain deeply entrenched defects of construction of the generally accepted type of "democratic" government'.[51] More particularly the defect is a legislative assembly with unlimited powers. 'Political parties in these conditions become in fact little more than coalitions of organised interests whose actions are determined by the inherent logic of their mechanics rather than by any general principles and ideals on which they are agreed'.[52] He has taken over the economics of politics – but in a fairly extreme version. The domination of government by 'sinister' organised interests is stated as a self-evident truth rather than argued. Legislative assemblies are no longer concerned with general rules. They are much too concerned with administration. However Hayek maintains his more subtle view of the role of government – going well beyond Adam Smith or Friedman. Government has the exclusive right of taxation – but there is no reason why service should usually be provided by public monopolies. 'What is generally described as the public sector ought not thus to be interpreted as a set of functions or services reserved to the government; it should rather be regarded as a circumscribed amount of material means placed at the disposal of government for the rendering of services it has been asked to perform.'[53] We need a stronger independent sector – the 'two-fold division of the whole field into a private and a public sector is somewhat misleading'.[54] Hayek praises organisations such as Alcoholics Anonymous.

In Hayek's view the '. . . real exploiters in our present society are not egotistic capitalists or entrepreneurs, and in fact not separate individuals, but organisations which derive their power from the moral support of collective action and the feeling of group loyalty'.[55] He finishes with a model constitution designed to reduce the power of organised groups. Under this general rules would be set by an assembly based on suffrage exercised once in a lifetime by people who had reached the age of 45. They would elect some of their peers to sit for fifteen years. There would be a lower chamber concerned with day-to-day administration within this framework of general rules. It would be elected by universal suffrage on party lines and could not issue any orders to private citizens which did not follow directly and necessarily from the rules laid down by the legislative assembly. Civil servants, old age pensioners and the unemployed would not have the vote. There would be a strengthening of local government and a move away from state monopolies. Democracy is to be tamed by middle age and a Swiss constitution, with the denationalisation of money as the complementary element.

Having escaped from the 'American fashions' of which he complained in his inaugural lecture at Fribourg to the more congenial atmosphere of Vorder-Österreich, (Hither Austria)[56], Hayek seems to have taken on a new cutting edge. Although *The Constitution of Liberty* is dedicated to the 'unknown civilization that is growing in America' there are few signs of American influence on much of the book. After ten years in Chicago the first reference to Friedman comes on p.381 and to Stigler on p.508. In his latest phase Hayek too has moved away from the heavy emphasis on thought of the eighteenth and nineteenth centuries which had never in fact been his forte. His tendency to fit every thinker into the Hayekian mould had drawn some heavy criticism from

Harrod (1946)[57] and even from Robbins (1961)[58]. Robbins, in particular, took issue with Hayek's attempt to muster Hume into the ranks of the Hayekians.

Even in this latest phase Hayek the politician continued to command greater attention than Hayek the social thinker. Unlike his close friend Popper, Hayek's reputation was never mainly scientific and his scientific reputation suffered from his forays into more topical matters. Occasionally Hayek surprised by a revival of a theme from the past. His Nobel Prize lecture marked a return to earlier themes about the hubris of economics and the worship of quantification.[59]

Side by side with the restatement and development of Hayek's main themes on society, government and knowledge, went a considerable series of writings on inflation. It is Hayek's 'despair' about this problem which has led him to abandon the restraint of a lifetime and to produce reform plans. The causes of inflation are to be found for Hayek in the social, political and trade union pressures which push up wages. The increase in wages is accompanied by pressure on the monetary authorities to increase the money supply. This reinforces the inflation and sets expectations which ensure continued inflation. *The Constitution of Liberty* has in two pages an uncanny anticipation of the whole expectations theory of inflation, although Hayek clearly believes at this stage that expectation will always be adaptive, and never rational.[60] This part of Hayek's analysis has passed into conventional economics. He has found many fewer to follow him in his view of the real effects of inflation. Inflation makes certain types of output more profitable and certain types of employment then expand. As the tide of inflation drops back so the jobs created by inflation are stranded.

The use of monetary measures to deal with inflation is seen by Hayek as an evasion of the real issues. These are to do with changes in the structure of relative prices and relative demands for labour. 'The illusion that maladjustments in the allocation of resources and of relative prices can be cured by the manipulation of the total quantity of money is at the root of most of our difficulties. Such a use of monetary policy is more likely to aggravate than to reduce these maladjustments.'[61] Hayek's thought is marked by a considerable pessimism.

> We now have a tiger by the tail: how long can this inflation continue? If the tiger (of inflation) is freed he will eat us up; yet if he runs faster and faster while we desperately hold on we are *still* finished. I'm glad I won't be here to see the final outcome . . .[62]

Hayek is by no means in agreement with Friedman and the monetarists on the theory of inflation. They, in Hayek's view, suffer from exactly the same fatal fascination for simple aggregates as do the Keynesians. He also takes issue with their use of the most mechanistic version of the quantity theory. This theory assumes that changes in the quantity of money come about through government action.[63] But given that there are many close substitutes for money the changes in private liquidity can completely offset government-induced changes. Nor does Hayek like the vagueness of the monetarists' view of the real effects of inflation. He is suspicious of Friedman's schemes for monetary rules and for indexation. Here Hayek returns after 45 years to many of the themes which he took up in *Prices and Production*, his first major book in English.

References

1. M. Friedman, Foreword in F. Machlup (ed.), *Essays on Hayek*, London; Routledge and Kegan Paul, 1977, p.xxi.
2. F.A. Hayek, *The Road to Serfdom*, London; RKP, 1944.
3. The Mont Pelerin society is an international group of economists and others which first met in 1947. Hayek also seems to have been part of the inspiration for the Institute of Economic Affairs (IEA). After reading a summary of the *Road to Serfdom*, Antony Fisher, founder of Buxted Chickens and early patron of the IEA, sought out Hayek and was encouraged by him to set up an economic research organisation. The reference to Beatrice Webb is in Hayek's review of *Our Partnership*, reprinted in *Studies in Philosophy, Politics and Economics*, London; Routledge and Kegan Paul, 1967, pp.341–2.
4. F.A. Hayek, *The Constitution of Liberty*, London; RKP, 1960.
5. The best discussion is Norman P. Barry, *Hayek's Social and Economic Philosophy*, London; Macmillan, 1979. S. Brittan's article in *Encounter*, 'Hayek, The New Right and The Crisis of Social Democracy', does something for the honour of the economists and related species.
6. F.A. Hayek, *Prices and Production*, London; George Routledge, 1931, p.3.
7. *Prices and Production*, p.4.
8. *Prices and Production*, Lecture IV, pp.89–112.
9. *Prices and Production*, p.1.
10. Beatrice Webb, *Diary*, 1 May, 1937, p.6323.
11. *Diary*, 5 August 1938, p.6519.
12. F.A. Hayek (ed.), *Collectivist Economic Planning*, London; Routledge, 1935. This includes Von Mises' earlier classic essay.
13. F.A. Hayek, 'Economics and Knowledge', reprinted in *Individualism and Economic Order*, London; Routledge and Kegan Paul, 1949, pp.33–56.
14. *Studies in Philosophy, Politics and Economics*, 1967. p.91.
15. *Individualism and Economic Order*, p.54.
16. F.A. Hayek, 'Scientism and the Study of Society'; Part I, *Economica*, N.S. 9, 1942; Part II, Ibid. 10 (1943); Part III Ibid. 11 (1944).
17. F.A. Hayek, *The Counter-Revolution of Science*, Glencoe, Ill.; Free Press of Glencoe, 1955, p.23.
18. *The Counter-Revolution of Science*, p.24.
19. *The Counter-Revolution of Science*, p.24.
20. *The Counter-Revolution of Science*, pp.29–30.
21. *The Counter-Revolution of Science*, p.31.
22. *The Counter-Revolution of Science*, Chapter VII.
23. *The Counter-Revolution of Science*, p.98.
24. F.A. Hayek, 'The Use of Knowledge in Society', reprinted in *Individualism and Economic Order*, pp.77–91.
25. F.A. Hayek, *The Sensory Order*, London; Routledge and Kegan Paul, 1952.

26. *The Sensory Order*, p.7. Professor Peter Herriot, Professor of Psychology at Birkbeck College, comments on this:

It's amazingly good – for its time. He comes up with a theory of neuro-physiology almost identical to that of D.O. Hebb who gained a world wide reputation in the 40s and 50s for his 'cell assemblies', 'phase sequences', etc. These theories have been long since discarded, since technological advances have made closer examination substitute for the inferences Hayek and Hebb had to make. However, for its time it is an outstanding piece of work, indicating a wide-ranging knowledge of the psychological literature.

I am most grateful to Professor Herriot for discussing the book with me.

27. F.A. Hayek (ed.), *Capitalism and the Historians*, Chicago; University of Chicago Press, 1954.
28. *The Road to Serfdom*, pp.150–62.
29. J.M. Keynes, *Collected Writings: Activities 1940–1946 Shaping the Post-War World Employment and Commodities*, London; Macmillan and Cambridge University Press, 1980, p.386.
30. *The Road to Serfdom*, p.156.
31. *The Road to Serfdom*, p.158.
32. F.A. Hayek, *The Constitution of Liberty*, London; RKP, 1960, pp.20–1.
33. *The Constitution of Liberty*, p.12.
34. *The Constitution of Liberty*, p.13.
35. *The Constitution of Liberty*, p.27.
36. *The Constitution of Liberty*, p.63.
37. *The Constitution of Liberty*, p.40.
38. *The Constitution of Liberty*, p.84.
39. *The Constitution of Liberty*, p.123.
40. *The Constitution of Liberty*, p.124.
41. *The Constitution of Liberty*, p.130.
42. *The Constitution of Liberty*, p.109.
43. *The Constitution of Liberty*, p.259.
44. *The Constitution of Liberty*, p.259.
45. *The Constitution of Liberty*, p.341.
46. *The Constitution of Liberty*, p.401.
47. F.A. Hayek, *Law, Legislation and Liberty: Vol.1, Rules and Order, Vol.2, The Mirage of Social Justice, Vol.3, The Political Order of a Free People*, London; Routledge and Kegan Paul, 1973–1979.
48. 'Manifesto of a Whig', *The Economist*, 25 June 1960, p.330.
49. *Rules and Order*, p.36.
50. *The Mirage of Social Justice*, p.94.
51. *The Political Order of a Free People*, p. xiii.
52. *The Political Order of a Free People*, p.13.
53 *The Political Order of a Free People*, p.47.
54. *The Political Order of a Free People*, p.50.
55. *The Political Order of a Free People*, p.96.
56. F.A. Hayek, 'The Economy, Science and Politics', in *Studies in Philosophy, Politics and Economics*, pp.251–69.
57. R. Harrod, 'Professor Hayek on Individualism', *Economic Journal*, Vol.LVI, 1946, pp.435–42.
58. Lord Robbins, 'Hayek on Liberty', *Economica*, February 1961, pp.61–78.
59. F.A. Hayek, in *Full Employment at Any Price?*, London; IEA, 1975.
60. *The Constitution of Liberty*, pp.331–2.
61. F.A. Hayek, 'The Outlook for the 1970s: Open or Repressed Inflation?', in F.A. Hayek: *A Tiger by the Tail*, London; IEA, 1978, p.118.
62. *A Tiger by the Tail*, p.112.
63. F.A. Hayek: *Denationalisation of Money*, London; IEA, 1978, pp.76–7.

3 Friedman

Hayek has been a totem of the New Right, though little attention has been given to the details of his work. Friedman has been more fortunate. His detailed contributions both in social policy and in macroeconomics are read by students all over the world: and some of his concepts have passed into common circulation. He has received both esteem in form of the Nobel Prize and detailed attention. There are many minor problems in assessing Friedman's work, not least the tendency to intellectual exhibitionism and the habit of introducing qualifications and conditions into statements. But the major problem is how to fit together the three main phases of his work. The chameleon-like quality of his views on macroeconomics has been remarked before with the transition from being deeply affected by the 'Keynesian temper of the times' in the 1940s to the monetarism of the 1970s.[1] But there have been other wider changes both in the content and in the public impact of his professional work. The 'economist's economist' of the mid-1950s is always an underlying part of the Friedman persona;[2] but by the mid-1960s the main point of the impact on the world was very different. The main note for that decade was struck by the publication in 1962 of Friedman's manifesto for *laissez-faire* in *Capitalism and Freedom*, which was to come to even greater attention during Goldwater's campaign for the US Presidency in 1964. In the last phase of Friedman's career the interest in detailed microeconomics is less prominent and his name becomes ever more closely associated with certain theses on macroeconomics.

There are three Friedmans: the positive economist, the campaigner for *laissez-faire* and the macroeconomist. But it is easier to distinguish shifts in the kind and quality of attention which the various Friedmans have received than to make divisions in time of Friedman's own work. There are leads and lags in Friedman's work. Thus between 1955 and 1957 Friedman published his essay on the quantity theory, his theory of the consumption function which harks back to Friedman's work in the 1930s and a paper advocating educational vouchers.[3] In 1962 and 1963 he published his lecture notes on price theory many of which go back to the late 1940s, his monetary history of the USA which gave him the confidence and the professional reputation to launch his much more speculative essays in monetary analysis, and *Capitalism and Freedom*.[4]

The three Friedmans differ substantially in intellectual method and have had to face differing degrees of critical attention. The most obvious contrast is between the unwavering constancy of views on social policy and the developments and changes in his work on monetary topics. There is little change between *Capitalism and Freedom* (in substance dating from the mid-1950s, although not published until 1962) and *Free to Choose* published in 1980 in the handling of social topics.[5] However, the Friedman monetary doctrines of the mid-1950s are very different in kind from those of the mid-1970s. There is a contrast between the empirical basis of much of the work on monetary topics and the much more dogmatic cast of the work on social issues. Even within the monetary work it is difficult to reconcile Friedman the monetary historian with Friedman the econometrician.

A final complication is that of political impact. The Friedman of his own writings carefully construed is one thing; the Friedman who has lodged in the crania of politicians, and particularly of British conservative politicians, is something else. Yet the academic Friedman has not really repudiated the Friedman broadcast by the politicians. The allegiance from the head has been welcomed, but that from the gut has been an acceptable substitute.

Friedman the Positive Economist

Before moving to Chicago in 1946 Friedman had done little work on price theory. But in the next few years he was to establish a reputation as an 'acute and agile theorist',[6] and to add to his earlier reputation for empirical research. From this phase there are two sides to Friedman's work which need more detailed treatment. One is Friedman's work on economic methodology which has remained an underlying theme throughout. The other is Friedman's extensive work on distribution and on labour markets which seems to have contributed little to the later Friedmans. The failure of development has had important consequences for the cast of Friedman's work on social policy giving it even less a mooring in positive economics and more of a political flavour.

Friedman's celebrated essay 'The Methodology of Positive Economics' could perhaps be seen as the first encyclical of a new Pope. It marked the end of the somewhat confused post-war period in the American economics profession when unorthodox ideas received a greater hearing than at any time before the 1970s.[7] In addition to its attempt to tidy up loose ends such as the 'theory' of imperfect competition and attacks on the orthodox theory of labour markets, it provided the base for what was to be a characteristic combination of theorising and econometric testing which was to dominate post-war writing. The essay is also notably at odds with the whole thrust of Hayek's work with Friedman's emphasis on the close companionship between the natural sciences and economics and its stress on statistical testing.

The essay is a proclamation in favour of a body of 'positive economics . . . in principle independent of any particular ethical position or normative judgements . . .'[8]. Its performance is to be judged by the precision, scope and conformity with experience of the predictions it yields. In short positive economics is or can be an 'objective' science, in precisely the same way as any of the physical sciences. The fact that economics deals with human beings makes for difficulties but not fundamental differences. Differences about economic policy can be resolved by appeals to the facts. Differing views on the effects of minimum wages legislation: of the appropriate role and place of trade unions, of tariffs and of monopoly policy could be resolved through appeals to positive economics.

Positive economics is about theories and about their empirical testing. Friedman did not say that assumptions made in theories can be as unrealistic as the author likes. Rather a good theory would have a certain robustness in the sense that it would not be falsified by large amounts of evidence, by exposure to a mass of 'complex and detailed circumstances'.[9] A theory was to be judged by the robustness of its predictions rather than by the complexity of its assumptions. Friedman tried to illustrate this with examples. One is of the standard formula for working out the velocity of a falling body. In a vacuum all bodies fall at the same rate. In the atmosphere a ball falls faster than a feather – but this does not disprove the theory. Friedman advances more ingenious arguments in his defence of orthodoxy. Firms that maximise returns will prosper. Natural selection will validate the theory. The survival of the theory over a long period of time also is evidence in its favour. If there is no challenge to the theory from an alternative, this is indirect testimony to its worth.

Assumptions can help in defining a theory in an economical way. But the models are then applied to a complicated real world. It is half true that 'there is nothing new under the sun'. This half truth makes the model acceptable but it is also half true that history never repeats itself and this has to be borne in mind in applying the model. Friedman quotes with approval Marshall's approach to competition. The ideal type of perfect competition was highly useful, but 'at one extreme are world markets in which competition acts directly from all parts of the globe; and at the other those secluded markets in which all direct competition from afar is shut out, though indirect and transmitted competition may make itself felt even in these; and about midway between these extremes lies the great majority of the markets which the economist and businessman have to study'.[10]

The essay looks forward to 'progress in expanding this body of generalisations, strengthening our confidence in their validity and improving the accuracy of the predictions they yield.'[11] This is a programme for a self-confident profession with all the trapping of a science. Yet the problem of balance between contingent circumstances and the model remains. Even a strong theory such as the one about the velocity of falling bodies can mislead in certain circumstances. But are the underlying models of economics any stronger? The quantity theory is described by Friedman as a strong theory – but how likely is this to be altered by circumstances? Positive economics was a rallying point for the profession, but it left open the possibility that economics would oscillate between dogmatic abstractions and inconclusive statistical testing.

The oscillation can be tracked down in a number of detailed areas of Friedman's work. Least known is his work on issues relating to distribution, and to labour markets.[12] Here is tension between Friedman's view of the 'long run' in which the full strength of market forces will work themselves through and the series of short runs in which qualifications and exceptions abound. Friedman begins from a standard exposition of the basic theory of demand and supply. On the demand side most of the emphasis is on the individual firm. Market forces operate strongly in the long run, but in the short run there may not be a very clear relationship between changes in demand for goods and demand for labour. Unions may have some long-run influence by restricting entry to occupations, but their main effect is in creating confusion in the short term by taking credit for things which would have happened anyway.

Friedman also discusses briefly the ethical implications of existing demand-side theory. He argues that orthodox marginal productivity theory is in fact widely and unthinkingly accepted: the 'ethical proposition that an individual deserves what is produced by the resources he owns'.[13] However the implications of this for policy are not entirely straightforward. As an ethical guide, Friedman believes that 'it can neither be wholly accepted nor wholly rejected'. For two individuals in comparable circumstances and equal opportunities the proposition is entirely reasonable: but

> for two individuals with unequal opportunities, the principle seems much less reasonable. One man is born blind, another with his sight; is it 'just' that the former receive less than the latter because his productivity is smaller? The difficulty is that it is hard to see any other principle to apply. The fundamental 'injustice' is the original distribution of resources – the fact that one man was born blind and another not. It is clear that in such cases we do not in fact apply the principle of payment according to product.[14]

The supply part of the market shows even more ambiguities than the demand side. In the very long run competitive forces might prevail, but there are complications arising from the peculiarity of labour as a factor. Because human capital cannot be bought and sold, the scope of market forces in stimulating investment in human capital is reduced. This may lead to under-investment. On the other hand family pride may encourage over-investment in human capital. 'Hence there may readily be either under-investment or over-investment in human capital relative to non-human capital.'[15] It seems doubtful whether market forces will work fully here even in the long run, particularly as Friedman accepts that there is some degree of division in society into non-competing groups. This means that even across generations there is not free entry to occupations.

Friedman has also developed a case on theoretical grounds that 'one cannot rule out the possibility that a large part of the existing inequality of wealth can be regarded as being produced by men to satisfy their tastes and preferences.'[16] Friedman shows how different attitudes to risk could produce different distributions of income. However, this is simply a presumption. There is no actual empirical evidence. This theory was originally developed from an influential article published in 1948 and Friedman has been prepared to make quite high claims for it.[17] People are unequal because they have chosen to buy different kinds of tickets in the lottery of life. We should be careful of moral judgements about the unfairness of income distribution. 'Inequalities resulting from deliberate decisions to participate in a lottery clearly raise very different normative issues than do inequalities imposed on individuals from the outside.'[18]

Friedman's work on labour markets had oddly little coherence for the prophet of positive economics. It is difficult, too, to fit together the early empirical work on professional incomes with the later Panglossian speculations about risk and the happy harmony in the labour market. The Friedman–Kuznets study of income from professional practice in America before 1939 showed quite clearly that restrictions on entry into medical schools had raised medical incomes well above the level that could be explained by market forces.[19] It was not just that the economic and social stratification of the population limited the number of able people who could apply to medical training in the first place, but that professional vested interests limited the number of places. The picture was of a society in which both class divisions and private vested interest greatly interfered with the way in which markets operate. There is certainly rather little empirical testing apart from some evidence on medical salaries and on the limited effects of union bargaining power. Nor is there any coherent theory of distribution. The chapter in *Price Theory* on the relation between the functional and personal distribution of income is rambling and inconclusive:[20] at the end the reader is little more clear on what the relation is than he was at the beginning.

In *Capitalism and Freedom* all the ambiguities and qualifications that surround Friedman's treatment of labour markets in his lectures on *Price Theory* have disappeared. 'Most differences of status or position or wealth can be regarded as the product of chance at a far enough remove.'[21] However, Friedman also develops here a further thesis: that capitalism has led to less inequality than other systems. 'The chief characteristic of progress and development over the past century is that it has freed the masses from back-breaking toil and has made available to them products and services that were formerly the monopoly of the upper classes.'[22] But, as Friedman goes on to say, 'detailed statistical evidence on these phenomena, in the form of meaningful and comparable distributions of income, is hard to come by', although in his view 'such studies as have been made confirm the broad conclusions just outlined'.[23]

Friedman the Campaigner for *Laissez-Faire*

Friedman's social views were put forward in his 'manifesto for *laissez-faire*', *Capitalism and Freedom*. He has later repeated many of them in *Free to Choose*. Although in essentials there has been little change, there has been some change of emphasis. We take here the statement in *Capitalism and Freedom* as the authoritative one and then examine the changes in emphasis.

The book begins with a statement of faith and then continues to abstract principles and their concrete applications. Its major theme is that of the beneficent results to be expected from competitive capitalism. Its minor theme is that of the role of government – and of the policies needed to limit that role. But first comes the statement of faith.

> The preservation of freedom is the protective reason for limiting and decentralizing government power. But there is also a constructive reason. The great advances of civilization, whether in architecture or painting, in science or literature, in industry or agriculture have never come from centralized government. Columbus did not set out to seek a new route to China in response to a majority directive of a parliament though he was partly financed by an absolute monarch. Newton and Leibniz; Einstein and Bohr; Shakespeare, Milton and Pasternak; Whitney; McCormick; Edison and Ford; Jane Addams, Florence Nightingale and Albert Schweitzer: not one of these opened new frontiers in human knowledge and understanding, in literature, in technical possibilities, or in the relief of human misery in response to governmental directives. Their achievements were the product of individual genius, of strongly held minority views, of a social climate permitting variety and diversity.[24]

This is the stuff of myth and rhetoric with little close relation to reality. If we were to examine each one of these figures in turn we might well find that their relationship both to the social climates around them and to government action were a little more complicated than Friedman has allowed for. Thus Newton lived in fear most of his life of a 'social climate' which would have reacted strongly against his unitarian views. Florence Nightingale spent much of the later part of her life campaigning for a stronger government action to improve health services. But Friedman's own belief is that government can never duplicate the variety and diversity of individual action. Government for him imposes uniform standards and mediocrity.

After the statement of faith come the principles. Freedom is defined in the negative sense: as freedom from coercion by others. 'Society' is made up of individuals who have freedom and then have to decide what to do with it. The most important issue is what the individual does with his freedom. The major aim of the liberal is to leave people free to decide what to do with their freedom. People venture out into the wider society mainly for economic reasons. The basic problem of social organisation is how to coordinate the economic activities of large numbers of people. In advanced societies 'the scale on which coordination is needed, to take full advantage of the opportunities offered by modern science and technology is enormously greater'.[25] This raises certain difficulties in reconciling interdependence with individual freedom: but these are difficulties which give little pause to Friedman. The private enterprise exchange economy can resolve most of the problems. The market acts to protect others from coercion: the consumer has choice and so does the seller: so does the employee because he has other employers for whom he can work. The role of government is simply to set the rules of the game. But the market greatly reduces the range of issues which have to be resolved within the political system. The contracts made between individuals and organisations in a modern economy raise no special problems. They are free in the same way as contracts between individuals in a simple exchange economy.

Friedman propounds the theory that the market disperses power and makes it easier to resolve decisions – while the political process tends to concentrate power. 'Economic power can be widely dispersed. There is no law of conservation which forces the growth of new centres of economic strength to be at the expense of existing centres.'[26] Friedman believes that political power is more difficult to decentralise. 'There can be many millionaires in one large economy – but can there be more than one outstanding leader'. The market also preserves political freedom. Its role in doing this is illustrated by the experience of the McCarthy era. Most of the victims went into small business, trade and farming. 'No one who buys bread knows whether the wheat from which it is made was grown by a Communist or a Republican, by a constitutionalist or a Fascist, or for that matter, a Negro or a white.'[27]

Friedman then turns to the role of government. He emphasises again that widespread use of the market reduces the strain on the social fabric. But even in this ideal world, there would still be some conflict between the freedoms of different people. The need for government arises from these conflicts. In matters of the use of physical force, this need is obvious: but Friedman accepts that difficulties may also arise from the possible different interpretations of property rights. He accepts the case for some government action to regulate private monopolies and to deal with external effects. Government has some role in producing public goods: but this is much more limited than even Adam Smith would have wanted to see. City parks are included, but there is no reason why national parks such as Yellowstone National Park should not be run by free enterprise. Friedman discusses the possible case for action on paternalistic grounds. Parents do not have complete power over children and there is some case for public provision. His remaining chapters work out these detailed principles in various areas of welfare and economic policy. The detailed analysis of the perverse or pernicious effects of government action is followed by a single proposal which cuts the knot and re-establishes freedom. These policies can be listed as follows:

- An 'automatic' increase in the money stock at a 'specified' rate;
- Floating exchange rates;
- Vouchers in education;
- Negative income tax.

The chapters on monopolies and on licensure have no such clear policy prescriptions.[28] It is notable that Friedman's criticism here of the activities of the American Medical Association does not lead to specific proposals for dealing with their restrictive policies. His plea for diversity is one which most people are likely to be sympathetic to – but how is it to be achieved?

The same ingenuousness about social pressures is displayed in the chapter on racial discrimination. We are told that the market will provide a natural force to eliminate discrimination. This is supported historically with the thesis that the development of capitalism has been accompanied by a major reduction in discrimination. The maintenance of the general rules of private property have made it possible for black people to make more progress than they would have done. This is because discrimination involves a cost. 'A businessman or an entrepreneur who expresses preferences in his business activities that are not related to productive efficiency is at a disadvantage compared to other individuals who do not.'[29] Such an individual is in effect imposing higher costs on himself than are other individuals who do not have such preferences. Discrimination is a taste and in a 'society based on free discussion, the appropriate recourse is for me to seek to persuade them that their tastes are bad and that they should change their views and their behaviour and not to use coercive power to enforce my tastes and my attitudes on others.'[30] But this ignores the problem of private social controls. If there is a very strong social taboo in favour of discrimination, then the employer or worker who does not discriminate may well have to pay dearly for breaking the taboo.

The same ambiguity about private power affects Friedman's arguments about unions. He is against legislation banning the closed shop. He believes that competitive conditions will produce a variety of contracts, some with the closed shop and some with the open shop.

How have Friedman's views altered in *Free to Choose* published in 1980? The solutions have changed little, but his view of the pervasiveness of the evil has changed. Government is even more villanous than it was in 1962 and the 'Great Society' programme gives him even more ammunition. The power of the market for good is still as great as ever, but government intervention has become more pervasive and more destructive.

Friedman the Macroeconomist

There are some elements in Friedman's thought on monetary issues which have been consistent, particularly his views on the general stance of policy. He has always advocated automatic rules for assessing government policy. The paper written in 1948, 'A Monetary and Fiscal Framework for Economic Stability', advocated automatic changes in budgetary stance depending on the nearness of the economy to full employment.[31] His proposals were designed to serve the long-term aim of a monetary framework which should operate under the rule of law rather than the discretionary authority of administrators. 'The main plank of the proposals was to "eliminate" both the private creation or destruction of money and discretionary control of the quantity of money by central bank authority'. He was later to evolve a different form for the rule – that there should be an automatic and moderate increase in the total money supply year by year. But the search for automatic rules was always there, and Friedman seems to have evolved the present form of his rule by the mid-1950s.

The basic values produced a certain stance of policy. Over the years neither the values nor the policies have changed very much. Friedman's monetary policy was the same in 1981 as it was in published form in 1962 and apparently in unpublished form in the 1950s. But his analysis of the world economy, the empirical results and the conceptual range have changed.

We can distinguish three main periods in the development of Friedman's monetary thought. In the first lasting up to the mid-1950s, he was deeply influenced by the 'Keynesian temper of the times'. There was the yearning for automatic rules, but within a basically Keynesian framework.

The main market solution advocated in this period was that of flexible exchange rates. In the second period from 1956 to 1971 he was principally preoccupied with establishing the stability of monetary relationships within the general framework of the new quantity theory. Since the early 1970s he has been more concerned with broadening the monetary system to take account of the problem of inflation, and he has given prominence to the important new concept of the natural rate of unemployment.

Friedman's views of monetary policy have certainly been influenced by his values – as he has been candid enough to admit.

> My own policy position has undoubtedly been affected by these inter-connections between value judgements and scientific judgements. Certainly the monetary policy I have come to favour – a steady rate of growth in the quantity of money – is highly congenial to my preference for limited government and, where government is essential, for limiting government so far as is possible by clearly specified rules rather than granting wide discretionary powers to government officials.[32]

However, it is fair to say that some of Friedman's scientific explanations do not always fit in so nearly with his basic value judgements. He has always attributed little importance to ways in which government deficits help to cause inflation: nor does he think unions cause it. It would be wrong to see Friedman's views as originating in a single-minded drive in which all 'positive' considerations were subordinated to values. Nevertheless the attack on Keynesianism has at times taken on the quality of a crusade. In 1970 Friedman gave a lecture on 'The Counter-Revolution in Monetary Theory'. He explained in a footnote: 'I chose this title because I used it about a dozen years ago for a talk at the London School of Economics', and went on to say, 'At that time I was predicting. Now I am reporting'.[33]

As with Hayek, there is a major difference between the real Friedman and the version of monetarism that has become popular in Britain. There are three main differences. One is that British monetarism has taken over Friedman's earlier version of the inflationary process rather than his more sophisticated later version. In his earlier version, Friedman stated without qualification that inflation was always and everywhere a monetary phenomenon. By 1980, this view had changed. The monetary approach to inflation is now only 'the beginning of an understanding of the cause and cure of inflation, not the end. The hard questions are why the quantity of money expands more rapidly than output and how the difference can be eliminated.' We need to understand the political pressures that cause governments to expand the money supply. Secondly, the modern British version has not incorporated the greater concern that Friedman now shows for the short-term effects of a slowing down of monetary growth on real output. His experience of the 1968–71 period of policy-making in the USA was chastening. He admitted to being subdued by the failure of tight monetary policies to affect prices and their rather large effect on output.[34] Thirdly, British monetarism has never incorporated Friedman's views of the relative unimportance of deficits in the short-term. Friedman's view is that the long-term goal of lower spending is the critical one.

> Deficits have often been connected with inflation, but they need not be. Deficits were large in 1931 and 1932 when prices were falling drastically. There was a surplus in 1919–1920 when prices were rising rapidly. Whether deficits produce inflation depends on how they are financed. If, as often happens, they are financed by creating money, they unquestionably do produce inflationary pressures. If they are financed by borrowing from the public, at whatever interest rates are necessary, they may still exert some minor inflationary pressure. However, their major effect will be to make interest rates higher than they otherwise would be.[35]

Deficits are the lesser evil: a short period of high interest rates is to be preferred to a long spell of high taxes.

In the middle period dominated by the new quantity theory the 'positive economics' of Friedman's thought is strongest. It is during that period that there was the most characteristic mixture of theory and statistical testing. The major themes are the elusiveness of reliable theory and his emphasis on the importance of statistical results. We first set out the development of the theory and then examine how far the theory and Friedman's monetary thinking is compatible with his evidence in the *Monetary History of the United States*.

In 1956 Friedman made a clear and elaborate restatement of the theory of the demand for money.[36] This led on to the conclusion that the demand for money was, as an 'empirical hypothesis', quite stable. But he was somewhat diffident about how this could affect other variables in the economy. The theory pointed at most, 'even under the most favourable conditions', to a theory of money income, but 'it tells nothing about how much of any change in [income] is reflected in real output and how much in prices'.[37] Money mattered. But how was still unresolved. There was a missing equation. He still had to show how changes in the quantity of money affected money income.

For a number of years Friedman concentrated on strengthening the empirical results, finally set out in most detail in the *Monetary History of the United States*. In fact his later general empirical results were already well anticipated in a piece published in the *American Economic Review* in 1952 on 'Price, Income and Monetary Changes in Three Wartime Periods'. Here Friedman had concluded that 'price and income changes during the three wartime periods seem more readily explicable by the quantity theory than by the income expenditure theory'.[38] The article went on to say that the 'implications of our results for policy are, I think, no less clear than for economic theory. . . . Our conclusions favour the proponents of monetary policy. If you want to control prices and incomes, they say, in about as clear tones as empirical evidence ever speaks, control the stock of money per unit of output.'[39] These historical results were later developed over the whole history of the United States by Friedman and Schwartz with particular emphasis on the monetary explanation of the Great Depression.

During the 1960s Friedman used the new quantity theory as a base for further empirical tests of the effects of monetary as against fiscal policy. The argument had moved away from the stability of the demand for money – an argument which the Chicago school had won – to the question of whether changes in the money stock determined money income. Friedman's main research with Meiselman contrasted with Keynesian efforts by Ando and Modigliani and others. Little is heard of this literature nowadays and, significantly, Friedman did not reprint any of these contributions in his collection published in 1969.[40] The whole exercise has an embarrassingly Keynesian flavour with its implication of the ability of government to shift money income through various policy instruments. Nor was it all easy to reconcile with the developing Chicago theory of inflation.

The position at the beginning of the 1970s was well summed up by Hahn in a severely critical review of the *Optimum Quantity of Money*.[41]

> The most obvious point to be made at once is that Friedman neither has nor claims to have a monetary theory. His strong and influential views are not founded on an understanding of 'how money works' but on what his empirical studies have led him to believe have been the course of monetary history. He himself at least in this book claims no more. His celebrated policy recommendations themselves depend on a plea of ignorance.[42]

Hahn's basic position is that the formation of a satisfactory model incorporating money 'remains to be accomplished', particularly where such a model involves notions about long-run equilibrium. Friedman is criticised for producing a 'lazy man's theory' by which he does not really analyse how household behaviour affects the demand for money. He is also criticised for the casualness of his statistical tests.

Even more serious and fundamental are the criticisms made by Patinkin.[43] The debate between Patinkin and Friedman has become trivialised into the issue of whether Friedman did or did not misrepresent earlier Chicago thinking. The really important issues are not to do with Friedman's personal good faith, but with the soundness of economic thinking on the issues. Friedman's representation of Chicago may well have put into circulation a very different version of monetary economics than was really justified. The Friedman view of the economy was one in which the private sector is naturally stable in a long-run equilibrium which will emerge quite soon if government intervention is limited to certain automatic rules. Much of the stability arises from the demand for money and from the stable relationship between the money stock and money income. Changes in velocity have some importance at extreme points of the business cycle and also some long-run significance, but such changes are predictable. There is little chance of major offsetting shifts in velocity in the short term because of changing expectations and other factors. Friedman's Chicago has a mechanistic view of the economy.

In Patinkin's telling this was a complete travesty of the real Chicago position between the wars. First it showed little interest in the demand for money at all and consequently the stability of the demand function for money was not at all the central tenet which it later became with Friedman. Second, velocity is not constant in the short run. Patinkin sums up the Chicago tradition as follows:

> Velocity is not constant; on the contrary, a basic feature of economic life is the 'danger of sharp changes on the velocity side' or in other words the danger of 'extreme alternations of hoarding and dishoarding'. These sharp changes in turn are due to anticipations of changing price levels as well as to the changing state of business confidence as determined by earnings. Thus if individuals expect prices to rise and earnings to be good they will dishoard – that is increase the velocity of circulation. But the crucial point here is that these expectations will be self-justifying: for the very act of dishoarding will cause prices to rise even further, thus leading to further dishoardings, and so on. In this way a 'cumulative process' of expansion is set in operation which 'feeds upon itself' and which has no 'natural' limit. Conversely an indefinite 'cumulative process' of hoarding, price declines and depression, and further hoarding is set into operation by the expectation that the price level will fall and/or that earnings will be poor. Thus the economic system is essentially unstable.[4]

From this basis the earlier Chicago school argued for contra-cyclical policies to offset these devastating changes in velocity.

The most important point about the real Chicago tradition is that it had little to say about the concept of long-run equilibrium: it stressed instead that a monetary economy influenced by expectation could be subject to very great swings. It could have an inherent volatility so that change in one direction would reinforce itself.

In 1970–71 Friedman in fact met his critics' requests for a further elaboration of his theoretical framework. Out of the deepest hat in the history of economics was brought the white rabbit. Many critics found it a pitiful and emaciated animal; nevertheless, it was there for all to see. Unusually too there was a much fuller debate between Friedman and his critics. After a long prolegomenon on the quantity theory and the demand for money, Friedman finally comes to define his simple common model.[45] This is presented in an opaque manner with many reservations and qualifications. It has found few takers.

There remains an enormous contrast between the tentative quality of Friedman's statement of the basic model and the stridency of some of his day-to-day comments on various topics. But it is noticeable that the stridency is greatest on the issue of inflation and on social topics. Friedman has had less and less to say about macroeconomic policy.

His approach can be summed up as that of making certain simple, almost mechanical, changes, such as his rule for the money supply and flexible exchange rates. Once these are made, then the economy will move towards the underlying long-run equilibrium. This mechanistic view of the economy can be expressed either through single equations linking the money stock or money income or through rather more complex models. But it does not easily allow for two sets of pressures which exist in the real world. One is the existence of swings in confidence, mood and expectation which can influence economic behaviour. The other is the possible conflict between internal and external equilibrium. As a penetrating critic with great practical experience quoting Keynes put it, 'If we are dealing with a closed system so that there is only the condition of internal equilibrium to fulfil, an appropriate banking policy is always capable of preventing any serious disturbance to the status quo from developing at all . . . but when the condition of external equilibrium must also be fulfilled then there will be no banking policy capable of avoiding disturbance to the internal system.'[46] We turn now to Friedman's view of history.

The relationship between money and money income is complicated in practice by changes in velocity. 'Velocity tends to rise during the expansion phase of a cycle and to fall during the contraction phase.'[47] This is rather different from the Friedman of the models. But more significant is his treatment of wider confidence factors. This is most strikingly shown in his discussion of the silver agitation from the mid-1870s to the mid-1890s. It is difficult to reconcile Friedman's account of monetary history with his usual mechanistic view of the economy. Here Friedman and his collaborator Anna Schwartz laid a great deal of stress on the influence of pressure groups and swings of political opinion. They concluded that 'The ebb and flow of political agitation during those two decades were an important source of short-term monetary uncertainty which affected the links between internal and external prices'.[48] After the development of the South African gold reserves in the 1890s the price of gold fell and mankind descended from the cross of gold. People's opinions and attitudes affected policy. 'The entire silver episode is a fascinating example of how important what people think about money can sometimes be. The fear that silver would produce an inflation sufficient to force the US off the gold standard made it necessary to have a severe deflation in order to stay on the gold standard.'[49]

However Friedman's treatment of the 1929–31 collapse is rather different. It stresses the importance of monetary policy rather than of confidence factors. Here the policy of the Federal Reserve was responsible and an injection of high-powered money at the right moment could have avoided the depression. If additional high-powered money 'had been made available', the trigger – the low quality of loans in the 1920s – would have discharged only a blank cartridge. However the Canadian evidence quoted by Friedman suggests that it was possible to get a big decline in income without any large decline in the money stock.[50] In the face of circumstances of panic it seems hard to believe that a mechanical change in the amount of high-powered money could really have avoided the Great Depression, let alone stimulate recovery once it had come about.

These sections from the monetary history bring us back to the central issue: the mechanistic approach. This is also illustrated by Friedman's advocacy of flexible exchange rates. Certainly these have not proved the important remedy that Friedman seems to have expected.

Friedman has written little about the actual experience with floating exchange rates in recent years. These have come under increasingly heavy criticism from Buchanan, Hayek and others who see them as having provided a more permissive environment for inflation.[51] Thus Buchanan and Wagner write 'Until 1971 the monetary policy of the [Federal Reserve Board] . . . was constrained to an extent by the international system of fixed exchange rates among separate major national currencies . . . the fixed-rate constraint offered a means through which the direct political pressures on the monetary authority could be forestalled.'[52] Floating exchange rates may have made it rather easier to run foreign exchange markets from day to day, but they have had major effects in changing the pressures on policy for the domestic economy. The fate of floating exchange rates shows some of the difficulty of seeing the economy as a range of separate markets in which a few simple changes simply bring about greater freedom in each market.

In this last phase Friedman has begun to rely even more heavily on the idea of an underlying long-run equilibrium in the economy. The idea of the natural rate of unemployment first appeared in 1967. This is the rate which will emerge out of the free play of markets when governments learn to leave well alone in demand management. It is a rate which will be compatible with a stable price level so long as past government policy has not entrenched expectations of future inflation. In his important 1967 presidential address to the American Economics Association Friedman explained his view that government policy could not shift this natural rate of unemployment. It could cause disturbances, but it could not change the real outcomes in the economy.[53] His Nobel Prize lecture in effect presented a more precise view of the costs if government tried to shift the economy away from the natural rate of unemployment.[54] The costs would be in terms of an accelerating rate of inflation so long as expectations adapted to the realities of an inflationary economy. The natural rate of unemployment could be lowered if markets became more efficient, but government would only cause accelerating inflation if it tried to do this. Friedman's actual advice to governments has often been a lot more qualified and cautious than might be expected from this theory. His experience in 1969–71 had been a sobering one. In 1972 he wrote that 'I made overly optimistic predictions in 1969 about how soon inflation could be expected to respond to the monetary slow-down.'[55] The decline in output was more than he had expected and the decline in prices rather less. But the main public and professional impact was by the long-run theory, rather than by the qualifications. In fact the concept of the natural rate of unemployment came to be a major stimulus to a whole new school of even truer believers in long-run equilibrium.

Friedman has often been identified with certain views on inflation. Yet curiously little of his writing has been about inflation. The balance of Friedman's own writing has been strongly on the links between money and the rest of the economy. The rise in the American inflation rate came late in his career, and he is not one of the generation whose whole approach has been shaped by it. The theory of inflation developed in his Nobel Prize lecture has gained an enormous hearing but there is little in his previous work to support it. Even the concept of the natural rate of unemployment was first coined in relation to the very different set of issues to do with the effects of monetary policy. The struggle for a theory to underlie the simple model did not even begin in the case of inflation.

Friedman now qualifies the pure monetary approach to inflation. It is not just about the quantity of money but about the political pressures which lead to increases in that quantity. Yet he has never developed in any detail what those pressures might be. Nor does he accept Hayek's view that such pressures are so important that they do invalidate the simple cure of restricting the growth of the money supply. The Friedman approach may have been qualified but the simple solution remains.

Conclusions

In a moving tribute to a colleague who died young, Friedman wrote that he might have lived to be one of 'that small band who make economics'.[56] Friedman has certainly been one of these, perhaps even more with the public than with professional economists. But there are questions. One is the lack of positive content to his work on social topics. He lacks a developed theory of man in society such as Hayek has; nor does he deal much in evidence. His prestige as a positive economist has been used to support venerable propositions about the virtues of the market. Within macroeconomics the programme of positive economics has been carried out more fully but with far less than total success. It has not produced an ever-growing body of reliable theories and generalisations. Increasingly it has had to fall back on broad approaches to macroeconomic aggregates which Hayek would regard with the greatest suspicion. My main conclusion on Friedman's macroeconomics is a negative one: it does not give a reliable base for dogmatic assertions about the right lines of policy for any long period of time in the future. It suggests rather the need for caution and for an attempt to relate different instruments more pragmatically to circumstances that may rapidly change.

References

1. Leonard Silk, *The Economists*, New York; Avon Books, 1978, p.59.
2. 'As some artists are painters' painters, so Professor Milton Friedman is an economists' economist.' The *Economist*, 8 May 1954, p.450 (in review of *Essays in Positive Economics*).
3. Milton Friedman, 'The Quantity Theory of Money: A Restatement', in M. Friedman (ed.), *Studies in the Quantity Theory of Money*, Chicago; University of Chicago Press, 1956; Milton Friedman, *A Theory of the Consumption Function*, NBER/Princeton University Press, 1957. Friedman's work in the 1930s is mentioned in the Preface; Milton Friedman, 'The Role of Government in Education', in R.A. Solo (ed.), *Economics and The Public Interest*, Rutgers, New Jersey; Rutgers University Press, 1955.
4. Milton Friedman, *Price Theory: A Provisional Text*, Chicago; Aldine Publishing Co., 1962 (2nd edition 1976); Milton Friedman and Anna Schwartz, *A Monetary History of the United States 1867–1960*, NBER/Princeton University Press, 1963; Milton Friedman, *Capitalism and Freedom*, Chicago; University of Chicago Press, 1962.
5. Milton Friedman and Rose Friedman, *Free to Choose*, London; Secker and Warburg, 1980.
6. P. Newman, 'Review of *Essays in Positive Economics*', *Economica*, August 1954, pp.259–60.
7. Milton Friedman, 'The Methodology of Positive Economics', in *Essays in Positive Economics*, Chicago; University of Chicago Press, 1953.
8. *Essays in Positive Economics*, p.4.
9. *Essays in Positive Economics*, p.14.
10. *Essays in Positive Economics*, pp.34–5.
11. *Essays in Positive Economics*, p.40.
12. This makes up of about half of *Price Theory*, namely Chapters 7–15.
13. *Price Theory*, p.199.
14. *Price Theory*, p.200.

15. *Price Theory*, p.204.
16. *Price Theory*, p.277.
17. M. Friedman and L.J. Savage, 'The Utility Analysis of Choices Involving Risk', *Journal of Political Economy*, August 1948, pp.279–304.
18. *Price Theory*, p.278.
19. M. Friedman and S. Kuznets, *Income from Independent Professional Practice*, New York; NBER, 1945.
20. *Price Theory*, Chapter 14, pp.251–61.
21. *Capitalism and Freedom*, pp.165–6.
22. *Capitalism and Freedom*, p.170.
23. *Capitalism and Freedom*, p.170.
24. *Capitalism and Freedom*, pp.3–4.
25. *Capitalism and Freedom*, pp.12–13.
26. *Capitalism and Freedom*, pp.15–16.
27. *Capitalism and Freedom*, p.21.
28. *Capitalism and Freedom*, pp.119–60.
29. *Capitalism and Freedom*, p.109.
30. *Capitalism and Freedom*, p.111.
31. Milton Friedman, 'A Monetary and Fiscal Framework for Economic Stability', reprinted in *Essays in Positive Economics*, pp.133–56.
32. Milton Friedman, *Introduction to Dollars and Deficits*, Englewood Cliffs, New Jersey; Prentice Hall, 1968, pp.8–9.
33. Milton Friedman, *The Counter-Revolution in Monetary Theory*, London; IEA, 1970, p.7.
34. Milton Friedman, 'Have Monetary Policies Failed?', AEA Papers and Proceedings, *AER*, 1972, p.14.
35. Milton Friedman, 'Fiscal Responsibility', in *An Economist's Protest*, New Jersey; Thomas Horton, 1975, p.91.
36. 'The Quantity Theory of Money: A Restatement', in *Studies in the Quantity Theory of Money*.
37. *Studies in the Quantity Theory of Money*, p.15.
38. Milton Friedman, 'Price, Income and Monetary Changes in Three Wartime Periods', in AEA Papers and Proceedings, *AER*, 1952, p.621
39. 'Price, Income and Monetary Changes in Three Wartime Periods', p.623.
40. Milton Friedman and D. Meiselman, 'The Relative Stability of Monetary Velocity and the Investment Multiplier 1897–1958', in *Stabilization Policies*, Commission on Money and Credit, Englewood Cliffs, New Jersey; Prentice Hall, 1963.
41. F.H. Hahn, 'Professor Friedman's Views on Money', *Economica*, February 1971, pp.61–80.
42. 'Professor Friedman's Views on Money', p.61.
43. Don Patinkin, 'The Chicago Tradition, the Quantity Theory and Friedman', *Journal of Money, Credit and Banking*, February 1969, pp.46–70. There is a further article by Patinkin and a reply by Friedman in M. Friedman *et al.*, *Milton Friedman's Monetary Framework*, Chicago, University of Chicago Press, 1974.
44. 'The Chicago Tradition, the Quantity Theory and Friedman', p.50.
45. M. Friedman, 'A Theoretical Framework for Monetary Analysis', *JPE*, March/April 1970, pp.193–238. Reprinted in *Milton Friedman's Monetary Framework*.
46. Director's comment by A. Hettinger of Lazard's in *A Monetary History of the United States, 1867–1960*, p.812, quoting J.M. Keynes, *A Treatise on Money: Vol. X, The Pure Theory of Money*, London; Macmillan, Royal Economic Society, 1975, p.314.
47. *A Monetary History of the United States, 1867–1960*, p.302.
48. *A Monetary History of the United States, 1867–1960*, p.91.
49. *A Monetary History of the United States, 1867–1960*, p.133–4.
50. *A Monetary History of the United States, 1867–1960*, p.352.
51. J.M. Buchanan and R.E. Wagner, *Democracy in Deficit*, New York; Academic Press, 1977; F.A. Hayek, *Denationalisation of Money*, London; IEA, 2nd edn., 1978.

52. *Democracy in Deficit*, p.122.
53. Milton Friedman, 'The Role of Monetary Policy', *AER*, March 1968, pp.1–17.
54. Milton Friedman, *Inflation and Unemployment: The New Dimension of Politics*, London; IEA, 1977.
55. Milton Friedman, 'Have Monetary Policies Failed?', AEA Papers and Proceedings, *AER*, 1972, p.14.
56. 'To Miguel Sidrauski', in *Milton Friedman's Monetary Framework*, p.vii.

4 The Economics of Politics

The economics of politics (EP) has been a gradual development with changes in the protagonists, the political stance and the direction of interest. The protagonists begin with Schumpeter in the 1940s, through to Downs in the 1950s, and lately to Buchanan and Tullock of the Virginia School. In the last phase EP has become strongly identified with the New Right in its political stance. Nearly all the main practitioners are of the liberal school, and their findings have been used to support the crusade against big government. However, at one time, the economics of politics was far from being the sole property of the Right. Neither Downs nor, later, Breton can be fitted into that category. Lately there has been a major shift in the direction of interest from the demand side of the political market to the supply side. The main interest was once in how voters and parties make choices about public goods; now it is in the economics of bureaucracy, and in the supply-driven momentum to the growth of government spending.

The literature on EP has come to take on an evangelistic tone. The Institute of Economic Affairs has been the main centre for missionary publication in Britain. Its efforts have found few converts. EP has had little effect on mainstream teaching of economics and even less on the wider body of thinking about government problems. Even the political Right shows only intermittent interest. Such critical attention as EP has lately received among economists has been given to its conclusions about the rising share of government spending in GDP. Even further back, most of the major critiques of EP have come from political scientists, such as Macpherson, and philosophers, such as Barry.[1]

EP has, in a sense, been a casualty of the polarisation between Right and non-Right economists. There are elements in its analysis of problems of choice in government that need to be taken very seriously. The case for constitutional reform to improve the quality of choice in democracy deserves a far wider hearing. It would be more likely to get that hearing if it were not attached to the automatic assumption that any constitutional reform would certainly lead to a great reduction (as opposed to alteration) in the role of government. EP argues that we should seek better methods of arriving at the true preferences of voters, but it seems to have a priori ideas about what those preferences might be. Similarly, its view of the economics of bureaucracy has become one-sided. Niskanen has moved on from his early model of bureaucracy to practical proposals for increasing the effectiveness of bureaucracies.[2] For the Virginia School, the only real choice remains between bureaucracy and the market. It has shown little interest in the possibility of reform.

Nor has EP resolved a major contradiction in its view of the state. In one sense, the state is seen as driven by pressure groups, especially producer groups. In another, the rolling back of the state is seen as a change of great significance, and one which can be achieved by constitutional means, by Buchanan's plan for a new fiscal constitution to ensure balanced budgets or by voting rules to enforce two-thirds majorities for important changes.[3] Yet is is not clear whether the EP economists believe that constitutional change can work where the underlying social conditions do not support it. It is possible to argue that decisions in politics depend far more on the underlying social and economic balance than they do on forms of constitutions. Dahl has argued that 'in so far as there is any general protection in human society against the deprivation of one group of the freedom desired by another, it is probably not to be found in constitutional forms'.[4] Yet the New Right remains strongly Madisonian in its belief in checks and balances through constitutional means.

Within the ranks of EP's own theorists are many who have not faced the full implications of Olson's work.[5] This suggested that there would be very strong tendencies for large groups to form organisations which would only remain in being through an element of compulsion. Small groups can combine and work together through voluntary means as each member can see the link between the costs to himself of group action and the benefits achieved from it. For large groups, the results of collective action are public goods. There will be every incentive to evade the costs. Free riders will get the benefits anyway. Large groups will only survive with an element of coercion. This analysis suggests that powerful pressure groups held together by coercive means will usually be a strong force in society. It is difficult to fit this in with the strong underlying individualism of most of EP. The implication of Olson is that even if government were to be reduced, the coercive forces of large private pressure groups would still find other ways of influencing society. The Federal Government might decline, but the American Medical Association would remain.

In the old theory of democracy, well-informed voters were believed to make choices among proposals in the light of the public interest. Schumpeter was the first economist to suggest this was an unrealistic view of the demand for policies.[6] It was impossible for voters to become well informed about the whole range of policies: nor could they have the same sense of responsibility in dealing with political issues as they had in dealing with those in which they, the voters, had a direct personal stake. Informed choices are possible on local issues, which are much closer to home, but not on the wider issues. 'The reduced sense of responsibility and the absence of effective volition in turn explain the ordinary citizen's ignorance and lack of judgement in matters of domestic and foreign policy.'[7] Democracy was a system in which the actual decisions were taken by representatives. In Schumpeter's well-known definition it was 'that institutional arrangement for arriving at political decisions in which individuals acquire the power to decide by means of a competitive struggle for the people's vote'.[8]

Schumpeter thought that the political elite would only show real sense of direction under certain very rare circumstances. They would tend to be like the prime ministers of the French Third Republic.

> Where governments are as unstable as they have been in France from 1871 to the breakdown in 1940, his [the prime minister's] attention must be almost monopolised by a task that is like trying to build a pyramid from billiard balls. Only men of quite unusual force under such conditions can have had any energy to spare for current administrative work on bills and so on; and only such exceptional men can have acquired any authority with their civil service subordinates who like everybody else knew that their chief would be out before long.[9]

Downs' theory takes over Schumpeter's view of voters but gives a much more refined model of how the political elite would behave.[10] Schumpeter had been rather censorious about voters, but for Downs ignorance is rational. Why should voters incur costs in acquiring information when their influence on outcomes was likely to be small? 'Any concept of democracy based on an electorate of equally well informed citizens presupposes that men behave irrationally.'[11] Only people who can expect to get benefits out of the political process will take a systematic interest in it. Nonetheless, voters choose between potential governments and they have to take a very broad view of how their future will be affected by governments.

The aim of governments is to get re-elected. Parties 'formulate policies in order to win elections rather than win elections in order to formulate policies.'[12] Parties represent coalitions of differing views and they have to arrive at compromises, under conditions of uncertainty. All this might seem to be a recipe for exploiting the ignorant and gullible by what Adam Smith described as 'that insidious and crafty animal vulgarly called a statesman or politician'.[13] All the same, the voter has a certain gut feeling for consistency and a certain sense of value for money. He is groping, from a base of near-zero information, to get a grasp on the unmeasurable of future utility income. But Downs seemed surprisingly optimistic about how the system would actually operate. This is partly because in conditions of uncertainty and possible internal conflict parties will tend to reach for consistency. Parties have an incentive to adopt a simple and consistent set of policies which change slowly over time and which are easily recognisable by voters. Parties will tend to converge in their policies within a two-party system, particularly on issues about which the majority feels intense agreement.

This model would suggest a political system dominated by gradualism. Party policies will change only slowly if a party has recently been successful in an election. Voters will be suspicious of innovations. When a government evaluates possible changes in spending so that the marginal vote gain of the marginal dollar spent equals the vote loss of the marginal dollar of financing it will tend to look carefully at potential losses as well as at gains.

The Downs model will predict major increases in the role of government only under two assumptions. One is that fiscal illusion is extremely important and pervasive. 'Fiscal illusion' is a state in which partly through inadvertence and partly through deliberate manipulation by government, voters are not fully aware of the real costs to them of government spending. If the voter is in fact more conscious of the benefits of extra government spending than of the costs of extra taxes, the model could produce major increases in state spending. The other assumption is that producer groups would come to exercise a disproportionate influence on the political process. But if benefits to one producer group could be made only by imposing costs on other producer groups, one political success would tend to lead to counter moves by other aggrieved groups. Producer groups in this model could only gain ascendancy and permanent advantage if their gains were not very noticeable and did not impose obvious costs on others.

Downs made some early attempts to use his theory to make predictions about the size of the government budget.[14] He argued that the government budget would always be too small in a democracy. Every citizen believes that the government budget is too large in relation to the benefits. Benefits are remote and difficult to measure, while people are well aware of the costs. In effect, fiscal disillusion is much more prevalent than fiscal illusion. Such brave speculations, however, have a somewhat dated look in face of much evidence that voters underestimate the costs of public services.

Buchanan and Tullock in *The Calculus of Consent* (1962), developed an early view of the demand side which had quite different implications for the size of the public sector.[15] They looked at the effect of majority voting where the underlying intensities of preference differ and where there could be overlapping coalitions. Intense minorities could put together a series of coalitions which would 'cause a relative overinvestment in the public sector if the standard Paretian criteria are accepted'.[16] This was illustrated by an example of the bargains that will be struck on the repair of feeder roads in a community with a hundred isolated farms. Overlapping coalitions will drive up the total cost of road repair compared with what would have been chosen by the median voter. 'Each voter pays enough in support for the repair of other roads to attain a position of equivalence between estimated individual marginal costs and individual marginal benefits, but the payments included in his private calculus make up only a part of the costs of total road repairs that he must as a tax-payer in the community support.'[17] The constitutional rule of majority voting has profound consequences for the balance of public spending.

At this stage most of the analysis concentrated on the demand side. Buchanan, however, also spent some time on the supply side, mainly drawing on the work of Italian writers on fiscal illusion.

One of Buchanan's earliest papers was on the Italian tradition in fiscal theory.[18] He was especially warm in his praise for Puviani, whom he saw as

> above all else, a political realist. He looked at the world around him and saw no sign of genuine democratic participation in the process of making collective choices. Such choices appeared to him to be made by the ruling or governing class, and he entertained no illusions about these choices being made in accordance with any vague criteria of general interest. The choices were not even conceived to be rationally made for the benefit of the governing class itself. Decisions as such were usually made on pragmatic grounds and each was reached on the basis of causing the minimum of social friction.[19]

From this approach, Puviani constructed his hypothesis. He stated that the actions of government could best be explained by the hypothesis that the government always acts to hide the burden of taxes from the public and to magnify the benefits of public expenditure.

In the five years after the publication of *The Calculus of Consent* in 1962, there was a major increase in public spending and in the size of the Federal Government. These changes greatly increased the influence of EP on opinion and shifted its balance towards the supply side. The suddenness of the change in spending did not fit in well with the early explanations of the demand side which, in one way and another, stressed that any increase would be gradual. Even in the view of Buchanan and Tullock, the size of the public sector would increase only through a long drawn out process of negotiation. The theoretical models of bureaucracy were yoked together with conspiracy theories of the political process to form a more relevant supply-side analysis in this new situation. EP also acquired, in these years, a growing interest in the macroeconomic phenomenon of the share of public spending in GDP.

Increasingly, the economics of politics has come to stress the supply side and the role of bureaucracy in pushing up public spending. Tullock's pioneering book saw bureaucratic growth as the inevitable result of the difficulties of control and supervision.[20] The limit of any one man's ability to supervise others is very soon reached: and so is the limit of any subordinates' desires to follow instructions.

Large bureaucracies must lead to internal empire-building and to increasing amounts of bureaucratic free enterprise. One remedy is to create an imperial system of bureaucracy – such as that of the former British Colonial Office or the Chinese mandarinate – in which people of similar cultural background are given responsibility and left to exercise it. The general upshot is a high degree of coordination among the separate aspects of a task or set of tasks which could not be achieved without the mechanism of an organised hierarchy. The market mechanism can, however, achieve such coordination and Tullock gives a long comparison of the US Army's difficulties in supplying spare parts for its vehicles and the relative success of the market in organising supplies of spare parts for civilian trucks.

Tullock's theory could help to explain the growth of managerial slack. However, like Parkinson's law, it was derived from observation of foreign services and colonial bureaucracies. It seems to be chiefly a theory of muddle rather than of dynamic growth. The decolonisation of the theory of bureaucracy was mainly the work of Niskanen. He developed a theory which allows more specific predictions about the output and size of bureaux. The bureau negotiates over budgets with its sponsor. It offers a promised set of activities and the expected output(s) of these activities for a budget. Unlike the open market where the adjustment is marginal and where units of output are offered for a price, a bureau offers a total output in exchange for a budget. This gives the bureau a kind of monopoly power.

Bureaucrats have aims of their own. They attempt to maximise their own utility – a bureaucrat is interested in a number of things: higher salary, reputation, and a quiet life in managing the bureau. He is more likely to get these things if he tries to increase the size of the bureau. Even his own paymasters expect him to advocate expansion.

> Both the executive and the legislative officers reviewing the bureau fully expect the bureaucrat aggressively to propose more activities and higher budgets. In fact these officers would not otherwise know how to perform their review role. They lack the time, the information and the staff necessary to formulate new programmes. . . . The total activities and budget of most bureaux are beyond comprehensive understanding, so the executive and legislative officers focus most of the review on the proposed *increments* and reveal their priorities by approving differing proportions of these.[21]

The model suggests predictions that a bureau's output will be up to twice that of a competitive industry faced by the same conditions of cost and demand. However, many of the worst outcomes can be avoided if bureaux operate in a competitive environment and if the gains from spending and the costs are more clearly brought together.

The advocates of public choice became more secure in their conclusions about the inefficiencies of the public sector during the 1970s. They quoted in support evidence on the growth of the public sector in the USA. From 1947 to 1960 the budget was in balance overall: seven years of deficit were matched by seven years of surplus. From 1961 to 1976 there was only one year of surplus and the cumulative deficit was more then $230 billion. Public spending of all kinds amounted to 32.8 per cent of national income in 1960; this percentage had increased to 43.4 by 1975. The conclusions also found support in evidence of the lower efficiency of various kinds of public sector enterprise, ranging from airlines to health care and refuse collection. In Buchanan's view 'Governmental financing of goods and services must be divorced from direct governmental provision or production of these goods and services.'[22]

The evidence against large public sector monopolies seems clear: however, there are important signs that public enterprises can achieve different results depending on their size and the degree of competition that they face. Niskanen's study of students' performance in Californian public schools indicates that median scores on standard reading and mathematics tests at both the sixth and twelfth grades are a significant negative function of the school's district size for districts larger than 2000 students. In Niskanen's view 'Inefficiency is not a necessary characteristic of the supply of government services. For a given output, these studies suggest that costs can be reduced by contracting with private firms, by reducing the size of bureaux and by increasing the competition among bureaux.'[23]

The debate on the public sector's share has covered three separate issues: whether there has been any increase at all; causality if there has; and the effects. On the first issue, the opposition argues that the increase has been moderate, even negligible, by proper definitions of public spending. Thus, Chrystal and Alt argue that public spending should be defined as spending on real goods and services, and that such spending has only risen from 17 per cent of GDP in 1955 to 20.5 per cent in 1974.[24] These definitions contrast to the wider definition which includes transfer payments. A related argument has been about whether the public sector debt should be measured in real or nominal terms. The real public spending borrowing requirement (PSBR) is much lower than the nominal one.

On this first issue of whether the increase is negligible, the New Right has had rather the better of the argument. The rise in public spending on goods and services may have been modest, but the overall rise in the public sector share, including transfer payments, surely cannot be neglected. The possible diversion of output from the private to the public sector has been only part of the issue. The pressures set up by the claims of higher taxation, leading not least to higher inflation, surely cannot be neglected. The wider definition of the public sector is surely relevant, particularly when seen in conjunction with the shift towards direct taxation. The cumulative effect of rising public spending, together with the shift to direct taxation, has been to increase the income tax taken from medium incomes sharply.

It is not just the New Right which would regard this change as one likely to add to inflationary pressure, as people struggle to maintain real net earnings. As well as extra taxation, the change in the public sector share has implied extra debt. Debts have to be financed in nominal terms, and in such terms the PSBR now represents about 90 per cent of long-term debt in the British economy. The problems of underwriting this large block of debt have begun to be onerous and to have major implications for the general level of interest rates.

The second issue, about causality, accepts that the change has taken place, and asks why? Here the New Right has not had any one line of explanation. In the past, the main cause was seen on the demand side in the bias towards intense producer groups who had the incentive to dominate the political process. Now some would locate the main cause on the supply side in the activities of bureaucracies. Buchanan, on the other hand, would see the change mainly as a result of Keynesian methods of financing deficit combined with democratic politics.[25] There is an inherent bias towards deficits and away from surpluses.

The main theory of the growth of the public sector outside the New Right stresses the demand side. O'Connor, in *The Fiscal Crisis of the State*, suggests two main reasons for the growth of the public sector.[26] One is the desire of large firms to externalise certain costs – to impose costs such as those of social security, health services and care of the environment which might otherwise have fallen on themselves, on the state and the tax-payer. The other lies in the need for social balance. These social expenditures grow in order to buy social peace.

The third issue has been the effects of the change. How far is the growth of the public sector mainly responsible for the lower rates of growth in GNP which have been common to all Western countries? Has there been coincidence rather than causation? A lower rate of growth in GDP, given the inflexibility of the public sector in the short term, would in itself have produced a significant rise in the public sector share. A public sector of unchanged size would take a bigger proportion of a smaller economy. But did the enlargement of public sector cause the downturn or impede the recovery?

The tax effect of an increasing public sector has clearly been profound politically. It has changed voter attitudes to public spending from Spitzbergen to the Rio Grande. It has also added to inflationary pressure. But it seems highly doubtful whether the rise in public spending has been critical in determining real growth rates. Can Britain's low growth rate over the last fifteen years really be attributed mainly to the growth of the public sector? It seems difficult to fit this conclusion to what is known about Britain's past difficulties over a much longer period. The size of the public sector has grown almost everywhere, and yet some countries have still managed a respectable rate of economic growth. There can be many legitimate differences about the role of the public sector: the conclusion of Smith, in the most reliable research on the issue, was that the answer lay between the extremes.[27] The rise in public spending has had some effect on growth but far less than that suggested by the New Right. The strong view of causality remains a purely British and American phenomenon. In continental Europe and Scandinavia there is no similar concentration on the size of the public sector as a major factor in economic policy. A reasonable conclusion might be that the size of the public sector has added to the difficulties of getting an acceptable combination of unemployment and inflation in the weaker economies: but that difficulty would still have been quite considerable even without such an increase.

Starting from coherent models of political behaviour EP has moved on to much more intractable issues to do with the growth of government spending. In a sense, the move has been from a microeconomic version of EP to a macroeconomic one. On the side of the new macro-EP is the voters' powerful concern about rising taxation. Yet the case for the strong view of causality – that the growth of the public sector has been the major determinant of economic performance – remains unproven. It is also difficult to explain the rise in transfer payments in terms of the New Right's theory of bureaucracy.

The Olson Problem

Collard has wondered how it is that Mancur Olson has become a leading member of the 'rogues' gallery' for the New Right.[28] The main reason is that his theory of organisations completely undercuts the New Right's view of government; that it develops a momentum of its own which takes it away from the true preferences of voters. A mixture of political will and constitutional change can bring about the fall of big government and restore freedom.

By Olson's theory, big government is likely to be the prisoner of powerful private interests. If they cannot have their way through government, they will simply use other channels. Reductions in public coercion will simply lead to increases in private coercion. Olson begins from the proposition that it will often be in people's interests to form groups. Small groups will form through free association. They can be kept together through voluntary means as each member can see how his own costs relate to future benefits. For large groups, however, there will be an incentive to evade costs. The benefits of large groups are public goods which cannot be fenced off from free-riders.

In an economy with occupational specialisations and a society with cultural, ethnic and regional differences, there will be many benefits to be had from large organisations. Yet a large organisation will only hold together through voluntary means when there is an unusually strong sense of solidarity. It will either have to maintain itself through compulsory membership or it will have to offer private goods as an inducement. Trade unions have long offered some of both. The closed shop is an old practice and so is the friendly benefit scheme. Some of the gains from membership are now made through lobbying government and through manipulating government agencies. But if the role of government is reduced, the incentive to organise will not go away. If anything, it will be stronger because direct bargaining becomes more important. Some of this bargaining will have purely economic ends in searching for informal methods of restricting the market. Bargaining will also reflect the sense of solidarity of various cultural, ethnic, and regional groups. All these loyalties will still be there, and if they cannot influence government they will seek other means of advancing their interests. The force of the private organisation which had previously been directed at the State would not work itself out through other channels. Olson raises the possibility that these large organisations held together by compulsion will exert coercion of others. The reduction of government will simply clear the way for an increase in private coercion.

The New Madisonians

The Buchanan school has drawn a great deal of inspiration from the American constitution. The model of politics in *The Calculus of Consent* would fit well in 'a nation of small freeholders perhaps roughly similar to the United States of 1787'.[29] The Buchanan school retains an admiration for a constitution in which voting systems and constitutional rules reduce the power of the executive. The American constitution is usually seen in terms of checks and balances between executive, legislature and the judiciary. But it also introduced deviations from simple majority rule by the method of selecting the Senate. Buchanan's proposals for a new fiscal constitution draw on this earlier inspiration. He would wish to see a 'constitutional requirement that the federal government balance outlays with revenues except in extraordinary times'.[30] Tullock has suggested a greater use of the two-thirds majority for making decisions, and Hayek would limit the franchise to the middle-aged.

The alternative view of Dahl and others is that constitutional rules will only be as sound as the underlying willingness to accept them.[31]

Political order depends on various prerequisites: more directly, government depends on the consent of the losers as well as the authority of the gainers. Consent is more likely to grow where there is tolerance. Tolerance depends on shared values and respect for rights. Political rights have little meaning in the face of inequalities which go beyond a certain point. Thus a free political order presupposes certain attitudes which are more likely to grow in certain social and economic conditions. This type of approach to politics can inconveniently trace its pedigree to the great de Tocqueville who devoted many hundreds of pages to the thesis that constitutional rules are only one lesser part of the political order. The spirit of democracy affects every area of life in the United States. This has been well set out by Dahl and illustrated from the history of the United States since Madison – not least by disasters such as the Civil War which the constitution did not avert.

Collective Choice

The EP theorists have surely done a service in their critique of how collective choice is actually made. Such phenomena as fiscal illusion, muddle, waste and bureaucratic inertia would seem to be all too real in any honest account of how government actually operated. There is a tendency to underestimate the real costs of government services. There are also difficulties about the responsiveness of services to consumers. The New Right has made a case against monopoly, but it has not proved that there could not be reforms in ways other than dependence on market forces. There are many differences between public services in their efficiency and responsiveness. Niskanen has brought some of these out for the United States, and they exist in Britain too. For EP economists, the faults on the supply side of the public sector mean that almost any other arrangement would be better. For others, another way is possible.

From its criticisms of the demand side, and of the difficulty of weighting preferences, the New Right jumps to the conclusion that under different methods voters would always vote for less public spending. The New Right wants more open procedures, but they also assume results. The argument for an improved choice on taxation and public spending is a strong one – one possible method is set out in the last chapter of this book. But the New Right is dogmatic about the actual results that would materialise. A balance sheet on EP after forty years might be as follows:

1. It has failed to reconcile its individualist approach with the problem that large private organisations may be permanent centres of power in society.

2. It has shown a curious faith in the constitutional rather than the social determinants of political stability.
3. It has shown clearly that there are major problems in organising collective choice and that existing methods of doing so are far from ideal. Yet it has moved easily from arguments about procedure to assumptions that a different procedure would inevitably show a large swing towards private spending.

References

1. C.B. Macpherson, 'Market Concepts in Political Theory', essay in *Democratic Theory Essays in Retrieval*, Oxford; Oxford University Press, 1975; B.M. Barry, *Sociologists, Economists and Democracy*, London; Collier-Macmillan, 1970. Another good critique is J.F.J. Toye, 'Economic Theories of Politics and Public Finance', *British Journal of Political Science*, Vol. 6, Part 4, October 1976, pp.433–47. D.C. Mueller, *Public Choice*, Cambridge University Press, 1979 is the best survey by an economist.
2. W.A. Niskanen, *Bureaucracy and Representative Government*, Chicago; Aldine Atherton, 1971; 'Bureaucrats and Politicians', *Journal of Law and Economics*, December 1975, pp.617–43.
3. J.M. Buchanan and R.E. Wagner, *Democracy in Deficit*, New York; Academic Press, 1977.
4. R.A. Dahl, *A Preface to Democratic Theory*, Chicago; University of Chicago Press, 1956, p.134.
5. M. Olson, Jr., *The Logic of Collective Action*, Cambridge, Mass; Harvard University Press, 1965.
6. J.A. Schumpeter, *Capitalism, Socialism and Democracy*, London; George Allen and Unwin, (5th edition 1976.)
7. *Capitalism, Socialism and Democracy*, p. 261.
8. *Capitalism, Socialism and Democracy*, p.269.
9. *Capitalism, Socialism and Democracy*, p.286.
10. A. Downs, *An Economic Theory of Democracy*, New York; Harper and Row, 1957.
11. *An Economic Theory of Democracy*, p.221.
12. *An Economic Theory of Democracy*, p.28.
13. Quoted in T.W. Hutchison, *Markets and the Franchise*, London; IEA, 1966, pp.7–8.
14. A. Downs, 'Why the Government Budget is too Small in a Democracy', *World Politics* xii, 1960, pp.541–63.
15. J.M. Buchanan and G. Tullock, *The Calculus of Consent*, Ann Arbor, Michigan; University of Michigan Press, 1962.
16. *The Calculus of Consent*, p.201.
17. *The Calculus of Consent*, pp.139–40.
18. J.M. Buchanan, '*La Scienza Delle Finance*, The Italian Tradition in Fiscal Theory', in *Fiscal Theory and Political Economy*, Chapel Hill, North Carolina; University of North Carolina Press, 1960.
19. '*La Scienza Delle Finance*, The Italian Tradition in Fiscal Theory', p.60.
20. G. Tullock, *The Politics of Bureaucracy*, Washington, D.C.; Public Affairs Press, 1965.
21. *Bureaucracy and Representative Government*, p.40.
22. J.M. Buchanan, 'Why does Government Grow?', p.17 in T.E. Borcherding (ed.), *Budgets and Bureaucrats*, Durham, North Carolina; Duke University Press, 1977.
23. W.A. Niskanen, 'Bureaucrats and Politicians', pp.637–8.
24. K.A. Chrystal and J. Alt, 'Endogeneous Government Behaviour: Wagner's Law on *Gotterdamerung?*', in P.M. Jackson and S.T. Cook (eds.), *Current Issues in Fiscal policy*, Oxford; Martin Robertson, 1979, p.136.
25. *Democracy in Deficit*, Chapter 12.
26. J.O'Connor, *The Fiscal Crisis of the State*, New York; St. Martin's Press, 1973.

27. D. Smith, 'Public Consumption and Economic Performance', National Westminster Bank *Quarterly Review*, November 1975, pp.17–30.
28. D. Collard, 'Market or Government Failure', in *The Emerging Consensus?*, London; IEA, 1981, p.130.
29. *The Calculus of Consent*, p.14.
30. *Democracy in Deficit*, p.178.
31. The case is eloquently made by Dahl in *A Preface to Democratic Theory*.

5 The Institute of Economic Affairs

The Institute of Economic Affairs has been the main publishing source in Britain for the shorter works of Friedman, Hayek and the Virginia School. Its role as a publishing house for internationally known authors with independent reputations grew in the 1970s. There have been fewer fundamental contributions by relatively unknown British authors. The work of Lees on the National Health Service, of Seldon on pensions, and of West on education stood out as landmarks in the 1960s: publications which changed the balance of argument.[1] In the 1970s native contributions have not been so distinctive, and the IEA abandoned its earlier self-denying ordinance against macroeconomics. It asserted an early belief in the superiority of microeconomics, though increasingly its publications have been at odds with this belief.

The IEA does not have a corporate view: nevertheless through its choice of authors and through the work of its full-time staff, Lord Harris and Arthur Seldon, it has made a distinctive contribution to the thinking of the New Right. It has stood out for the strength of its attack on the so-called 'welfare state' and for its surveys of preferences, carried out in 1963, 1965, 1970 and 1978.[2] The main propositions in this Harris/Seldon case against the welfare state have been as follows:

1. State-financed monopoly services will not be related to the true preferences of consumers. They suppress the incentives and the information which comes from the demand in a market.
2. State financed services tend to be under-financed or inefficient.[3] They are inflexible and bureaucratic. 'Not least the welfare state has developed as IEA authors said in the early 1960s into an uncontrollable monster with an insatiable appetite for tax finance and incestuous administrators'.[4] The supply side will go its own way: bureaucratic momentum will carry it even further from the consumers' preferences.
3. The gulf between supply and demand will create many problems. There will inevitably be a gap of this kind in a free service where price is not serving its rationing function. Consumers will demand service up to the level at which its marginal utility to them is zero and tax-payers will not willingly supply this. There will have to be rationing and in a free service such rationing will be by social and political pull. This form of rationing will be much more objectionable and unfair than rationing by price. It will be particularly unfair to working-class consumers.

Harris's and Seldon's contributions have mainly been on the demand side. Here they can point to twenty years of gathering evidence which cannot be ignored. The IEA has been a net importer in its pronouncements on the supply side and on the process of rationing.

Most surveys of consumers' opinions on social services simply ask whether people are generally satisfied. They usually produce results which suggest that two-thirds or more are satisfied and that the remaining third, for a variety of reasons, is not. The IEA has done a service in gently pointing out the inanity of this kind of exercise. It has tried to introduce considerations of cost and price. The four surveys carried out from 1963 to 1978 presented three options for financing service for health and education.

1. The state should take more in taxes, rates and contributions and so on to pay for better or increased services which everyone would have.
2. The state should take less in taxes, rates and contributions and so on to provide services only for people in need and leave others to pay or insure privately.
3. The state should continue the present service, but allow poeple to contract out, pay less contributions and so on and use the money to pay for their own services.[5]

Harris and Seldon interpret the first as the arrangement then existing by which most of the services would be financed by taxes. The second would create two-tier services with the state services concentrated on the poor. The third might be considered a half-way arrangement, although in the Harris/Seldon view it is in principle 'the more libertarian alternative'.[6]

The pattern of answers is clear enough. There has been a distinct swing away from (1) and towards (3). The answers can be analysed as follows:[7]

	Health		*Education*	
	1963 (%)	1978 (%)	1963 (%)	1978 (%)
(1) Keep present system	41	20	51	15
(2) Concentrate on poor	24	18	20	17
(3) Allow contracting out	33	54	27	60
Don't know	2	7	2	8

Harris and Seldon interpret this as a ringing and triumphant endorsement of the IEA's ideas. It is a clinching piece of evidence in favour of a free market on the demand side. These surveys have been widely used and quoted, both in the IEA's own more general indictments of the welfare state and by other people. A crucial question then about the IEA concerns the reliability of these surveys. Do the results really allow the conclusions drawn by Harris and Seldon?

Ironically, the IEA's position as expounded by Harris, Seldon and others over the years would seem to be option (2) rather than option (3). Again and again they have argued that the state should take less in rates and taxes so that the penalty of double taxation does not apply to those who choose to buy privately. They have also called for a more rigorous definition of need than the one used by social administrators. Option (3) would seem to be inherently ambiguous. It calls for continuing the present services. This implies that the present level of taxation would continue with, at best, a small reduction. It also implies that the present non-market system on the supply side would continue. The pattern of answers suggests an increasing amount of public support for having our cake and eating it too. People want to keep the present system, tax-financed and free at the point of consumption, but they also want the freedom to contract out for certain kinds of health care and education. This is hardly useful as a guide for policy unless we knew much more about the practical effects on services of option (3).

In Chapter 11, on the National Health Service, we will look in more detail at this basic issue as to whether (3) is a realistic option. Can we have a two-tier NHS which is the same in its essentials but which is different in that people will pay more for one type of service rather than another? The pattern of answers suggests that people do not want differences in standards of important services depending on ability to pay – yet they want the freedom to choose to pay for better services. It is certainly true that there is a large majority, as shown by another question in the Harris/Seldon 1978 survey, in favour of allowing people freedom to buy health and medical care;[8] but there is some doubt about how people would react if the actual consequences of that freedom were that those who could not pay had a very different standard of service from those who could. The IEA authors could argue that they do not intend any such difference in the essentials of the service. Those who paid would only be buying more convenience, earlier treatment and more choice of doctors. But even if the unessential elements of the service could be separated as clearly as that, there remains the question of why people would be willing to pay substantial extra amounts for them. There must be incentives in terms of a better service for those who pay, yet these incentives – if they were strong enough to attract a really significant amount of private payment – would produce results which would approximate option (2), so heavily and consistently rejected.

Insurance schemes work well where risks are evenly spread; but the risks of prolonged illness are not even. Some groups within the class system are much more prone to illness than others. Harris and Seldon include a detailed factual assessment in the potential market for medicine with choice. 'Generally buyers of the BUPA-type insurance must be in good health and below 60/65.'[9] The main market for private health insurance has been middle-class, middle-aged men in the home counties. It is difficult to see how it could be extended to people who are much more likely to be ill. Seldon has dealt with this in another commentary. 'It is true that half of the 450,000 hospital beds are occupied by long-term chronic cases of old and mental patients who are not all poor but whom it may be administratively simplest to finance by taxes.'[10] They seem to skate over some very important problems such as the standard of service for those whose income and life chances have been permanently reduced by illness.

There is also doubt about whether the pattern of answers would not be different after a period of discussion. This is part of the usual case for representative democracy in which certain standards of discussion and the presentation of information are aspired to. Harris and Seldon would have no difficulty at all in answering this doubt. Representative democracy stands totally condemned both by its methods and by its results. Harris and Seldon indeed write as if representative democracy was a kind of conspiracy created by pundits and politicians. They believe that the machinery – Parliament, the ballot box, representative democracy – has never worked effectively. The machinery of representation does not represent individual members of the public but the organised groups that claim to speak for them. As a result the institutions have increasingly diverged from the wishes or preferences of the people as individuals. The implication is that government by national opinion survey is a better way of taking decisions. However, this might in practice raise even more difficulties than government by representative democracy.

Government by opinion survey is a strange choice for those who have such high standards for government. A difficulty begins to appear as soon as we try to translate option (3) into policies: to specify courses of action that in time would not result in outcomes that would have been those of option (1) or (2).

More recently Harris and Seldon have extended their use of opinion surveys to the more general issues of choice between taxation and public spending. Here the results have even more ambiguity. Respondents were asked: 'In California recently two people out of three voted to reduce taxation and accept fewer services. If there was a vote in this country on the same issue would you vote for or against?'[11] Thirty-three per cent voted for and 63 per cent against the reduction in services. However, Harris and Seldon argue that the question should have been rephrased to take account of the fact that reductions in services are only 'possible'. 'A deterioration in services is a possible (though eventually probable if tax cuts are big) but not a necessary consequence of reduced taxation'. They go on to suggest that 'it has been argued by the American economist Professor Arthur Laffer that lower tax rates could yield more tax revenue by sharpening the incentive to earn so that taxable income rises'.[12]

Harris and Seldon then commissioned a new survey to find out voters' opinions on the assumption that reductions in services were only 'possible'. Thirty-three voted for lower taxes, 27 per cent against; 34 per cent said they didn't know and 6 per cent would not vote. This hardly amounts to a ringing British endorsement of the Californian proposition.[13] The don't knows win by a short head. The conclusion of Harris and Seldon that 'There seems little doubt from these results that the voting on a Proposition 13 in Britain would be' would seem to be highly debatable.[14] Their surveys hardly suggest intense support for large reductions in government spending.

We turn now to the IEA's views on the supply side. Here the central theme has been constant – that pricing and the market can do the job. The medium in which this theme is expressed has changed. At the beginning the theme was worked out through very detailed analyses of particular services such as Seldon's pamphlet on pensions and Lees' work on the NHS. Later the denunciations became more sweeping and more related to a general phenomenon called the 'Welfare State' than to particular services. The five main propositions are as follows:

1. State health services and state education are monopolies.
2. They have used their monopoly power to suppress innovation. The opportunity cost of the welfare state is the 'voluntary, private, organic welfare institutions that the state supplanted and suppressed'.[15] The monopoly welfare state is stagnant compared with less centralised, more flexible, systems of welfare where change is welcomed and rewarded.
3. The survival of the monopoly depends on a number of illegitimate means, apart from sheer apathy and ignorance. The chief one is the double payment of those who elect for private provision. People are unwilling to pay twice, through taxation and through private payment, for health care and education. Even so, the monopoly will become more difficult to sustain and will be backed up by coercion if necessary. This degree of coercion is already quite considerable. 'The welfare state has gradually changed from the expression of compassion to an instrument of political repression unequalled in British history and in other Western industrial societies.'[16]
4. It is very difficult for the consumer to bring about any adjustment of the services provided by the state. 'Even when politicians and officials

do their best to provide good schools, hospitals and so on the man whose wife is not comfortable in the hospital ward or the parent whose child is not happy in school cannot change conditions except by the lengthy business of persuading hundreds or thousands or millions of other husbands and parents, a task which daunts most especially the inarticulate.'[17]

5. The introduction of direct pricing to consumers would be feasible and a major step to improving services.

The argument takes for granted that both the NHS and education are centralised monopolies; but this can be challenged. Within the NHS, people are free to shop around between various hospitals, doctors and kinds of treatment. Different units and departments are in competition, and this leads to the growth of some and the decline of others. The NHS could not have survived if it had been run as a centralised monopoly; it would, as the New Right's own theories of bureaucracy suggest, have been impossible to provide such a complex range of services on a centralised basis. In fact there is a high degree of professional autonomy within the NHS and many doctors and nurses are trying to organise their care in personal ways. The family doctor service could least of all be described as a centralised bureaucracy. This is not to say that the NHS does not have problems with *local* growth in bureaucracy: but to ignore the fact of consumer choice between different local health services is to distort reality.

The double taxation of those who pay privately is certainly one influence in maintaining clientele for public services; but it is hardly credible that the services would have survived without a reasonable degree of consumer satisfaction. If double taxation is a factor, so is the potential for growth in private provision. It perhaps operates with a threshold for state service; but a poor state service which imposed costs on individuals in terms of time or discomfort would lead to the growth of private alternatives. This has, in fact, happened in the case of the abortion service; in places where the NHS has not given the service, voluntary agencies and private organisations provide it.

The assumption that the public has no voice in public services can also be challenged. People are bringing voice to bear every day of the week on their local schools and on their local hospitals and health services. The suggestion that you have to persuade millions of people in order to get a change in a local public service is far-fetched. It is difficult for the poor and the inarticulate, but it would remain just as difficult for them to change a privately financed service through spending power.

Harris and Seldon argue for the immediate introduction of direct charging for health and other social services against a rather large amount of evidence that such charging is found almost nowhere.

Health care is not paid for by the consumer at the point of use: nor is the producer finding his own budget. The discipline of price is not to be found even in the American or Australian systems which the IEA so admires. In no major country is there a market for health care in the sense that there is a market for cars or stereos. Nor is there a market for education in any country. It could no doubt be attributed to a world-wide political conspiracy, but unless this is the explanation the non-existence of the market is difficult to fit in with a Hayekian view of the world. If price really is the answer why has it not been adopted anywhere in the world? Here the philosophy of social evolution conflicts with the constructivist tendency in the New Right which led Hayek to declare that he was not a conservative.[18] Hayek's disapproval was of those conservatives who simply wanted to control the machinery of the state and to strengthen centralisation in order to impose their own solutions. The IEA's advocacy of price has come dangerously close to this kind of constructivism in seeking to impose a market where it has not been the predominant form anywhere.

The Financial Basis of the Welfare State

IEA authors have also had a good deal to say about the perverse financial basis of the welfare state and how it could be reformed by negative income tax. Seldon has taken a leading part in the trench warfare over the meaning of the *Economic Trends* surveys of the costs and benefits of public spending.[19] His main contention is that the welfare state is not redistributive because people are paying as much or more in taxes as they are getting in benefits.[20] There are flaws in this argument. The first is the implication that if state-financed health and education services were greatly reduced, the tax–benefit ratio for families would be much more favourable. This is doubtful because tax revenues finance many things other than health care and education. If all spending on education and the health service were stopped, this would cut only 20 per cent of the family's tax burden while eliminating all the benefits. The tax–benefit ratio would be much worse rather than better. Before the family was paying about the same amount in taxes as it was getting in benefits. Afterwards, it would be paying 20 per cent less tax, but would be under obligations to pay for compulsory schooling and for some minimum standard of health care.

The critique of *Economic Trends* is also misleading in its implication that public spending is not in any sense redistributive at present. It is first of all clearly redistributive through the social security system. Families in the bottom three groups in the distribution of household income depend largely for their income on the social security system. It is also redistributive horizontally between single people and families. Both types of household pay about the same amounts of taxes – but get very different amounts of benefit. It is certainly true that for households of non-retired people, the welfare state is not vertically redistributive. Rich families do as well or better than poor as Le Grand has argued as well as Seldon:[21] but it is redistributive between people in and people out of work and between single people and families.

The IEA, through various authors, has also consistently advocated negative income tax. The authors differ in their views of how much redistribution they want to see brought about. Seldon has argued that 'the state should much sooner on a larger scale have redistributed income in the form of purchasing power. . .'.[22] Clark's reverse income tax scheme on the other hand involves a reduction in spending by about a half compared with the current social security system.[23] But there has been agreement on the basic proposition that most of the welfare state could be replaced by negative income tax. Clark's reverse income tax scheme is however very different from Friedman's negative income tax.[24] In Clark's scheme, RIT payments would be made only in particular circumstances such as unemployment, sickness or regular low earnings. 'These claims would have to be checked through something like the present procedures of doctor's certificates and occasional inspector's visits in sickness claims, and in the case of unemployment claims availability for work including the routine signing on at labour exchanges . . . .'[25] The scheme seems to be to replace the social security system with something very like the supplementary benefits scheme under another name. At the same time, health and education would move towards private provision. The case for these schemes stands or falls on the case for abolishing social security which is discussed fully in Chapter 10.

Once the idea of negative income tax is translated into administrative detail it has to be reconciled with the need to preserve labour market incentives. It then begins to look rather like a non-contributory scheme for welfare payments and national assistance.

Conclusions

The IEA began as David and has aged into Goliath. In its early days it was a small brave voice against the complacent orthodoxies of the 1945 welfare state. Now it is in danger of becoming an orthodoxy in itself. It has even shown exactly the tendency towards obfuscation which its theses would have led us to expect from a settled bureaucracy. However the market so far has been rather slow to generate competition.

References

1. D.S. Lees, *Health Through Choice*, London; IEA, 1961; A. Seldon, *Pensions for Prosperity*, London; IEA, 1960; E.G. West, *Education and the State*, London; IEA, 1965.

2. These are summarised in Ralph Harris and Arthur Seldon, *Overruled on Welfare*, London; IEA, 1979.
3. J.M. Buchanan, *The Inconsistencies of the National Health Service*, London; IEA, 1965.
4. A. Seldon, Preamble to *The Emerging Consensus*, London; IEA, 1981, p.xxii.
5. *Overruled on Welfare*, pp.44–5.
6. *Overruled on Welfare*, p.44.
7. *Overruled on Welfare*. pp.44–50.
8. *Overruled on Welfare*, p.58.
9. *Overruled on Welfare*, p.110.
10. A. Seldon, *Charge*, London; Temple Smith, 1977, p.89.
11. *Overruled on Welfare*, p.22–4.
12. *Overruled on Welfare*, p.24.
13. *Overruled on Welfare*, p.24.
14. *Overruled on Welfare*, p.38.
15. A. Seldon, *Wither the Welfare State*, London, IEA, 1981, p.16.
16. *Overruled on Welfare*, p.204.
17. *Charge*, p.40.
18. F.A. Hayek, *The Constitution of Liberty*, London; Routledge and Kegan Paul, 1960, Postscript, pp.397–411.
19. CSO, 'The Effects of Taxes and Benefits on Household Income 1980', *Economic Trends*, no.339, January 1982, pp.97–126 and previous articles annually since 1961.
20. *Charge*. Chapter 10 is the fullest statement.
21. Julian Le Grand, *The Strategy of Equality*, London; Allen and Unwin, 1982.
22. *Wither the Welfare State*, p.25.
23. Colin Clark, *Poverty Before Politics*, London; IEA, 1977, pp.50–2.
24. M. Friedman, *Capitalism and Freedom*, Chicago; University of Chicago Press, 1962, pp.190–5.
25. *Poverty Before Politics*, p.30.

Conclusion

The first part of this book attempted to be a critical account of how the thought of the New Right has developed, somewhere between the works of disciples and the hostile polemics. We began by looking at the system as a whole and then at various individual and distinctive contributions.

There has been a particular shortage of material on how the New Right has changed and developed. It has moved into the age of positive economics without being marked by it. To a surprising extent, the New Right deals in principles and in broad assumptions. It has also been willing to extend its brief well beyond economics as conventionally defined. Its sayings, like those of the Delphic oracle, have been available on a wide range of subjects but have been much less ambiguous. In an age when economists have come to see themselves as operating in a highly technical and scientific way, the New Right seems to have a much older and more traditional style. The individual contributions are all within this framework of political economy; but they vary in quality, with Hayek far ahead.

The New Right has found an increasing audience and following. This is partly because of changes in the social sciences. There used to be writers who dealt with broad issues such as the nature of society and the role of the state. Laski and Wallas in Britain and Lippman in the United States were prominent at one time but are now little read. This species of writer is now extinct. With increasing specialisation has come a retreat from the general. The course of political debate has also become less about general principles and more about detailed policies.

There has been a vacuum on these rather large issues which the New Right has moved into. It has been helped here by the increasing stress on economic aims within politics. Governments have stood, or more usually fallen, by their handling of the economy. Events have conspired to bring economics into greater prominence and to produce a receptive audience for answers more definitive than it was really equipped to give. The main message of the first part of the book is a negative one: economics is not equipped to deal with the wider political issues over which it has shown increasing domination. Helped by the prestige of positive economics and of econometrics, economists have asserted squatter's rights on territory where positive economics is of little use. The social teachings of modern economics show both arrogance and dogmatism.

The tax-payers' revolt is now everywhere, from Spitzbergen to the

Rio Grande. In every developed country rising shares of public spending in GDP have tended to produce greater hostility to taxation. Some of the strongest reactions were in Scandinavia, long before Proposition 13 in California. Yet the intellectual conquests of the New Right have been much less complete. The full case against government has become the dominant view only in Britain and in the United States. Adherence to the theory of sound money and distrust of inflationary finance are claimed as its own central doctrines by the New Right. But the following for such sentiments and policies can be found quite separately from the New Right's views on government. They have found much greater support over the years in Sweden and in West Germany than anywhere else, both countries with extensive government intervention. Caution about Keynesian economics is not only found among the New Right. The really distinctive features of the New Right in Britain and in America have been its criticism of government and its view that the condition required for greater freedom and well-being is a substantial reduction in the role of government.

Why is it that such views have found a much wider following in Britain and in America than elsewhere? The tax-payers' revolt is everywhere but the social doctrines of the New Right are not. The answer might lie partly in tradition. Catholic teaching since the nineteenth century has always been at odds with *laissez-faire*, and countries with a strong Catholic tradition have never been promising territory for the New Right. The robust atheism of the New Right has created further resistances even beyond those arising from its social doctrines. Countries also differ in the degree of influence by social democracy. Scandinavia, for example, has been much more deeply affected than most. This social democratic culture has not been a welcoming one to the New Right. It is possible to see the Keynesian/welfare state periods in Britain and especially in the United States as historical anomalies. Except in special circumstances, the predominant note of peacetime politics, it could be argued, has been some form or other of individualism. Once full employment and the welfare state could no longer be financed painlessly through higher growth, popular support for them weakened. By this thesis, Herbert Hoover and Neville Chamberlain are the archetypal figures and in normal circumstances the political scene will be dominated by their latter-day reincarnations.

The explanations in terms of tradition might look, too, at the different sense of 'society' found in European countries compared with Britain and the United States. In the continental tradition 'society' has claims on the individual and the individual exists fully only in a society. This social sense leads to the development of institutions. The state has been more active in promoting new businesses and in industrial management in France, Germany and Scandinavia than in Britain and the United States. There has also been a keener perception of the possibility of social conflict going back to the nineteenth, and even eighteenth, century.

However such explanations seem rather unsatisfactory. Britain, after all, has a fairly long tradition of welfare state development, even in the inter-war period with its conservative domination. Even the welfare tradition of West Germany seems, on closer inspection, to have rather less substance. The state's corporate activities in social security and other fields simply reinforce a pattern of distribution brought about by the market. German social policies are notably harsh for the poor and for groups such as single parent families – far harsher than in an individualist country such as Britain. Nor do these explanations of tradition fit easily to the suddenness of the change. If there was such a strong effect from different traditions, why did it not show itself gradually during the 1950s and 1960s?

In the case of Britain we have to begin from the brute fact of decline. Britain in the last fifteen years has been through an experience of economic decline. The decline can be charted in rates of inflation, of growth, of unemployment, and in the shifts in the net trade balance of manufactured goods. From 1951 to 1967 the inflation rate was barely above the OECD's average: now it is one of the worst in the industrial world and there have been some particularly damaging periods when it has moved well above even its own high average. Only the United States has had a comparably poor record in growth during the same period. The British unemployment rate has shown an even more worrying deterioration over the last fifteen years. No other country has lost a third of its employment in manufacturing over this period. No other country has suffered such a large change in its net trade balance in manufactures. With the economic decline have come conflicts in industrial relations with a few lulls but little sign of real improvement. There can be real difference of view about causes but the evidence is overwhelming that British economic performance and the British record in industrial conflict has been peculiarly bad during the last fifteen years.

These changes have created a political market for bold solutions of a far-reaching kind. It is in this context that we have to explain the change in aspirations and intentions. The outcome, for example the share of public spending, has in fact been rather different. The changes can be explained as *ex ante* programmes and intentions rather than by outcome. There was a market for something other than the incremental programmes which form the main stock of political parties in successful countries. So far these solutions have been promulgated by the Right. The unstable situation tilted towards the Right. The main Left solutions of the Bennite school have not found many customers, although they may do in the future.

Politicians of the Right might still have continued to market modernised versions of the 'middle of the road' approach of Macmillan's government and the later stages of Heath's government. Their shift in position was influenced by two sets of changes: among intellectuals and among voters. Among intellectuals, and particularly among economists, there was a very marked shift away from Keynesianism in macroeconomics and towards monetarism. American economists were refining and developing Keynesianism. British economics, on the other hand, was dominated for a very long time by a peculiarly crude version of 1939 Keynesianism. British Keynesianism was vulnerable: it fell quickly like Singapore with all its guns loaded with the wrong ammunition. There was also a more diffuse change in attitude to the state, especially to the welfare state. This had come to be considered in a rather vague way as a good thing; now it became more associated with waste and with lost growth. These changes among the intellectuals made it morally and intellectually possible for politicians of the Right to change their stock in the political market and to alter their policies for the supply side.

At the same time changes among the voters were altering the demand side. Voters too were influenced by waning faith in the public sector. The most striking change was in 1979 among council tenants; but even more important was a weakening of the traditional pressures in favour of welfare state policies. Changes in the class system were creating new and more unstable attitudes among voters. The traditional Labour vote was in decline. Specifically, British unions became less effective in influencing their members' votes. It used to be said that union membership was a strong force making for a Labour vote: by 1979 that was no longer so. British unions have shown an almost complete failure to move away from primitive ideas about strength through sectional wage-bargaining. They have rejected the social contract approach to trade unionism by which the trade union movement as a whole wins gains for its members through influencing social policies. Instead they have preferred to put trial by industrial strength at the centre of their activities. The result has been a steep decline in their political credibility, especially with their own members. The political elite in unions has been pushed into certain decisions on strategy and these have had political implications in weakening the coalition in favour of welfare state policies and in making the tilt to the Right even stronger.

The fact of decline created the market for new intentions. In principle, these could have come from the Left just as well as from the Right. In the United States the pattern was rather similar. The change in economic performance was seen most obviously in the rate of inflation. But other aspects of economic performance were also beginning to show signs of the 'British disease'. The market for bold solutions was there. There were changes among the intellectuals, although Keynesians have conducted a fighting retreat and the monetarists have been somewhat more cautious in macroeconomics than in Britain. The failure of Johnson's 'Great Society' experiment and the troubles of New York and other big cities gave edge to doubts about the public sector. More important in America were shifts among the voters. The decline of trade union influence was there too, but the more important influence was the shift in the social and economic balance away from the older industrial states of the North East, Illinois and Ohio. The South and West had always had powerful groups of conservatives. The shift of population and industry gave them a new power. The tilt to the Right was even more obvious among American voters.

Thus, in different degrees economic performance has been worse in Britain and in the United States than in most other industrial countries over the past fifteen years. There are only three other countries with comparably bad records: Belgium, Italy and Australia. Belgium and Italy have social and ethnic conflicts which deflect attention away from mainly economic solutions, and Australia has shown many of the same kinds of development as Britain and the USA. In these countries, and in these alone, there was a market for something stronger than plans for minor modification. The changes in ideas and in voters' attitudes have ensured for the present a tilt to the Right.

Part Two

Introduction

The New Right makes its main public impact through certain macroeconomic doctrines. But there is nothing very distinctive about some of the main features of monetarism in macroeconomics. It is not only the New Right which wishes to discipline the growth of the money supply and to restrain inflation. Nor is it only the New Right which is suspicious of fiscal deficits. Policies for restraining the growth of the money supply and for putting the control of inflation as the first priority have been common to governments of various political complexions in Britain and elsewhere. The distinctive feature of monetarism for the New Right is that such policies are to be merely the beginning of a much more far-reaching plan for reducing the scope of government and for unleashing the market. The New Right's social philosophy is the submerged base of monetarism.

In this second part of the book we look at the critical propositions in social philosophy which are common to all the individuals and schools of the New Right. Underneath the diversity of approach lies certain common elemental propositions which have to be accepted or rejected if the New Right is to be taken at its own valuation as the one reliable guide to the development of modern society. The New Right's propositions comprise:

1. A definition of 'freedom';
2. A view of the role of government;
3. A view of the course of distribution in a modern economy;
4. A strong conclusion about government failure in social services.

Freedom and Government

The discussion here is mainly about principles. The central tenet of liberalism is that the reduction of government to certain very limited functions will be the best way of bringing about the well-being of any individual in society chosen at random. The New Right stresses that there are strong forces promoting rational action and successful results by individuals in the absence of government. The conditions favour rational action, and government is likely to fail if it tries to improve things. But before we look at the evidence on government failure, it is important to see whether the concept of freedom suggested by the New

Right is really helpful and whether there are such strong inherent forces in society which make for successful outcomes. Judgements about the potential role of government might be very different if individual conduct without government showed a high promise of moderation and good sense.

The concept of negative freedom is inadequate, even as set out by the New Right. The growth of responsibility is necessary for this type of freedom to remain socially selected. The New Right maintains that there is only one main prerequisite for this sense of responsibility; that is to reduce the role of government. It argues that there are no other social preconditions.

The New Right also underestimates the risks of private coercion. In some societies, the state has been a countervailing force to private coercion. The state could play a different role: as in South Africa, it could act to reinforce private coercion and to give it a pitiless and relentless quality. But in the United States and in Britain the state has played a much more ambiguous role. A society with less government might not even be free from coercion, even in the Hayekian sense of the term. There is a persistent and serious neglect of the problem of private coercion by the New Right.

Against the New Right's definition we shall set an alternative definition of freedom and another view of the role of government. The conditions of life in small groups will continue to create the need for an institution called 'government'; so will the difference in weight and power between individuals and private organisations.

Is there an Agenda for Distribution?

The New Right's views on the course of distribution form an essential support to its thesis of the role of government. It denies any legitimate agenda for government other than providing a minimum income. This will not be difficult and claims on taxation will not rise because the poor get better off as a market economy develops. We shall argue that there should be a wider agenda for distribution and that the actual course of distribution is not so benign as the New Right would have us believe.

Government Failure

The New Right considers that though government may have good intentions in practice it has been an abysmal failure. This indictment is one of the New Right's strongest themes. But in social security and in health services the evidence of government failure is much weaker than the New Right suggests. In education and housing the government record is much more questionable, but the New Right has been presenting alternatives, especially in education, which would make things worse. The casualty of Friedman's voucher proposals has been serious plans for reform.

In Chapter 13 we turn back to macroeconomics and ask about the social issues raised by the New Right's version of the subject. In the final chapter we look at an alternative.

6 Freedom and Coercion

'Freedom' for the New Right is freedom from coercion. This is what has usually been called the 'negative' concept of freedom: freedom from outside interference by human agencies. There are two important assumptions in this definition. One is that freedom means making one's own decisions. As long as I can make important decisions, I am free. The second is that only specific human agencies can affect personal freedom. In Hayek's definition, I am free so long as no specific human agency is physically forcing me to a course of action other than the one which I would have chosen.[1] The effects of social forces, economic status or psychological conditioning on freedom are ignored.

Other definitions of freedom have various prefixes. 'Positive' freedom, in the sense described by Isaiah Berlin, is the usual one. This carries with it some unfortunate implication that people are only free when they achieve some better self. Bay has written of 'psychological' freedom – a capacity for rational action – and 'potential' freedom which involves absence of unperceived manipulation. Macpherson has written in a similar vein of 'developmental' freedom.[2] These concepts of freedom can be traced back to the idealists of the nineteenth century. The alternative concepts are well-known to the New Right. It is worth considering why it rejects them.

For Hayek, the negative concept of freedom is to be judged by its results in protecting the free ordering of the market. The positive concept of freedom brings about a drift to paternalism and to redistribution by the state. It promotes groups of politicians and intellectuals who set themselves up to judge whether people are achieving their true selves or whether their opportunities are all they should be. Such judgements lead naturally to proposals for government action to redistribute opportunities. The positive concept of freedom implies also an approach to knowledge which is alien to Hayek: that people can get accurate information on the preferences of others and on such complicated and nebulous issues as whether people are attaining their true selves.

Friedman's discussion of freedom is more cursory. By implication, freedom is to be judged by results. A free market will produce economic growth and improved living standards. It will also allow cultural diversity. Friedman has pointed to a 'flowering of charitable activity' in the United States in the nineteenth century.[3] 'The charitable activity was matched by a burst of cultural activity – art museums, opera houses, symphonies, museums, public libraries arose in big cities and frontier towns alike.'[4] So he does not reject the concept of positive freedom as a private ideal. It is simply that positive freedom is not relevant to government.

Hayek denies interest in the quality of particular decisions. These are up to the individual concerned: he will use his freedom as he thinks best. However, Hayek stresses the importance of a sense of responsibility.[5] Although we are not much concerned with the quality of any one person's decision, we are concerned with the quality of the total decisions. If a sense of responsibility is missing, the process of discovery in the free society is not going to work properly. In Hayek's thought it is only the actions of government which can destroy this sense of responsibility. Hayek also believes in the necessary therapy of economic and social stress. Loss of accustomed position is part of the steering mechanism of the market. Public assistance should be strictly limited to the provision of a minimum standard of income. People in small groups can show compassion and use ethical standards of valuation. But such responses are quite inappropriate for society as a whole.

Hayek's concept of responsibility is ambiguous: standing between the positive and the negative concepts of freedom. The central tenet is that the reduction of government to certain very limited functions will be the necessary and sufficient condition for encouraging the growth of responsibility. But this involves two separate propositions. One concerns the conditions and possibilities for rational action. The other concerns the effects of government on individual responsibility and rational action. We shall discuss these two propositions separately. Judgement about the actual or potential role of government might be very different if individual conduct and society without government showed high promise of movement towards a state of grace.

Hobbes saw man's propensity to aggression as the main obstacle to natural harmony. Without a sovereign, society would be a war of each against each. The conditions for responsibility here involved mainly the application of sovereign force to aggressive behaviour. But there are other reasons why the ability to be responsible and the conditions required for negative freedom to produce successful results are difficult to achieve. It is not simply that information is hard to acquire, but that man's capacity to use the information accurately is limited. And there are other impediments on rational action. Dahl and Lindblom have given a good summary of a rather different view of human capacity which they attribute to Freud.

He [man] is autistic; he distorts reality to suit inner needs and then makes his distorted picture of reality the premise of his actions. He is compulsive. He projects his own motives and reality views on others: represses powerful and urgent wants deep into the unconscious for fear of penalties from conscience or the responses of others, only to have his repressed wants unrecognizably displaced on other goals; acquires and displays exaggerated fears; colours the world with emotional tones of forgotten childhood; expresses hatreds and resentments coming from long-buried events; rationalizes all his actions . . . . This is a harsh, grotesque picture, a caricature but let it stand as a warning not to romanticize man's capacity for social action.[6]

Hayek has always dismissed Freudian psychology as an attempt to undermine the sense of individual responsibility. But that still leaves the question of how the human capacity for rational action is to be understood against the emotional side of human nature. The view of Adam Smith, from which Hayek draws so heavily, is in effect a caricature at the other extreme. A more realistic picture might lie somewhere between the two. Man is capable of rational action, but within severe limits set not just by the lack of information but by his tendency to distort reality, his tendency to lapses of memory and attention, and his impulsiveness.

None of this implies any view one way or the other on the role of government. The people who exercise the powers of government may be subject to exactly the same failings in that capacity as they show as individuals. Hayek might also argue that the process of social selection will lead to the development of organisations and cultural practices which will reduce the effects of human waywardness. For example, even without government regulations on the training and fitness of pilots, there would be pressures from insurance companies and surviving relatives to set up a system of accreditation. But the more pessimistic view would suggest that a number of people would dodge the system. A private system of accreditation would tend to have an increasing element of compulsion and would therefore move towards a system rather similar to the one which a government would set up. The pessimistic view of human nature suggests that the capacity for rational action has to be carefully nurtured and supported. This is difficult enough for activities that are mainly technical and mechanical: it is far more difficult when human reactions are involved. The New Right's view would seem to imply a strong inherent rationality. The alternative view would suggest the need for institutions and practices which will protect the individual from himself, particularly because there is a contrast between the relative ease with which impulsive decisions can be taken and their potential consequences both for the decision-maker and for others. Road accidents are only the most obvious daily example.

Our argument suggests so far that the reduction of government is not a sufficient condition for the growth of individual responsibility. The capacity for rational action is fragile and has to be carefully protected. But it is not only vulnerable to impulse and compulsion: it can also be destroyed by changes of circumstance. Economic and social change can be a bracing discipline and can encourage a sense of responsibility. But that depends on age and the existence of other opportunities. Economic change can sometimes be an overwhelming weight which forecloses other opportunities and brings about something like despair and a destruction of the capacity for rational action. Hayek's or Friedman's definition of a coercion is a narrow one. Coercion is practised by definite individuals on others. But in a less extreme definition circumstances could cause so intolerable pressure on individuals as to destroy their capacity for rational action.

It has been accepted by the New Right that there should be some government intervention to deal with 'absolute' poverty; that is, the poverty seen in the late nineteenth century with high child mortality and a short life of drudgery and despair for the poor. It was partly the contrast between the conspicuous consumption of the better off and the unremitting and destructive effects of absolute poverty which led to the beginnings of the welfare state. But it is not simply absolute poverty which can destroy the ability to take responsibility. Economic change can destroy self-respect and create despair. At certain times, economic change can be a stimulus: at others it can simply create pointless destruction which is neither a stimulus to the individual nor an incentive to others. Responsibility requires at least some small amount of self-respect.

It also requires an amount of social integration. Some thinkers of the New Right have touched on this issue directly. They regret the destruction of the sense of community in an impersonal mass society. But without taking an inaccurately romantic view of the past, it is possible to be concerned about the effects of anomie or a lack of norms leading to social disintegration. The number of contacts that have an anomic quality increase for everybody in a mass society. There are still neighbourhoods and extended families, but there are many contacts outside these between people who have no close ties. There are also more individuals who are completely detached from close relationships. The increase in 'anomie' can bring about an increase in irresponsible and destructive behaviour.

The argument is that a sense of responsibility is fragile and requires certain minimum conditions. It implies a pattern of institutions and practices to protect man from his own impulsiveness. It implies a certain level of security and self-respect. It implies a minimum degree of social integration. Freedom in the negative sense will not produce results – it will not be the chosen method for social selection – unless it can be accompanied by a sense of responsibility. The New Right by implication maintains that there is one main and overwhelming prerequisite for this sense of responsibility. This is to reduce the scope of government action. But our argument is that the emotional and social conditions required for freedom, in the negative sense, to work are rather more complicated.

It is also not clear how the emphasis on negative freedom in society fits in with the New Right's view of small groups. Hayek, particularly, has stressed the importance of the small group (the extended neighbourhood) in influencing behaviour. For small groups the concept of positive freedom is important. They can be interested in the well-being of others, and neighbourly support and compassion have a place. But such aspirations and approaches are totally out of place in the national society. It is not at all clear how such a view can be reconciled with the basic theses of individualism. It seems to imply that certain concepts apply for big groups which do not apply to individuals. Nor is it easy to understand how a person could operate with one set of moral attitudes in his individual relationships, but for those to be completely irrelevant beyond.

This conflict between the ideals of the small group and the wider society is most striking where the well-being of children is concerned. The security of the relationship between parents and children would seem to be basic to the development of a sense of responsibility, let alone to more positive concepts of freedom. Unless children develop the capacity to love and to work, unless they develop a moral sense or 'belief in', the outlook for them and for those around them is grim. Children develop these capacities within small groups or close relationships, but it would be odd if such important considerations were not to arouse some concern and interest within the wider society. Leaving aside the question of whether government can do anything effective to support and strengthen the family, one can ask a question of principle. If government can do something to support and strengthen the family relationship, should it do so?

The New Right's treatment of these issues has been cursory. For Hayek, it is all a matter for domestic and neighbourhood life. Friedman had a brief discussion of the issue in *Capitalism and Freedom*.[7] He accepted that the powers of parents over children were limited and that there was some case for state intervention on paternalist grounds. However, this is one of the few issues which was not carried over into his *Free to Choose*. Even when the issue worried Friedman, the argument for intervention only concerned extreme cases of child abuse. The relationship between the family ethic and the wider social ethic remains obscure. How are we to reconcile the overwhelming emphasis on market relationships with the fact that the most basic relationships in life are not market relationships? The ability to act constructively and to maintain cooperation in a market demands qualities and attitudes which are not produced by market relationships but by family relationships.

We have so far been accepting the limited negative concept of freedom. We have seen that the New Right case for this concept is made in terms of results. The 'good' society for Hayek is that one in which the chances of anyone selected at random are likely to be as great as possible. 'The best society would be that in which we would prefer to place our children if we knew that their position in it would be determined by lot.'[8] By implication such a society would be based on a negative concept of freedom. Friedman looks back to the nineteenth century as the golden age of progress. The negative concept of freedom allowed people to take responsibility. We have argued so far that the conditions for the development of a sense of responsibility are rather more than a minimum interference by government. The prerequisites for freedom, in the negative sense, to remain socially selected, are much more complicated than the New Right allows. The negative concept depends ultimately on the results it can obtain. If it does not produce these results it will be rejected by both the rule of reason and by popular fury. It cannot produce these results and guarantee a context of order without certain conditions. Whether government can help successfully in promoting these conditions is a separate question.

The central statements of the New Right are partly about freedom and partly about coercion. We have argued that one possible defect of the New Right's definition of coercion is its concentration on the alteration of the will by direct human agencies. A choice between unpleasant options does not involve coercion. Hayek believes that 'Even if the threat of starvation to me and perhaps to my family impels me to accept a distasteful job at a very low wage, even if I am "at the mercy" of the only man willing to employ me, I am not coerced by him or anyone else.'[9] We have argued that the pressure of adverse circumstances could become so intense as to amount to a form of coercion. But there is another weakness in this definition of coercion. This is its assumption that coercion, even in the narrow sense, usually arises from the actions of governments. The New Right's argument is that society with little government will show strong tendencies towards both economic competition and cultural pluralism – private coercion will be rather exceptional.

Past argument on this has concentrated on whether the free order is likely to maintain economic competition. There has been a good deal of discussion about trends to monopoly and the possibility of managers in large firms exercising discretionary power. The New Right has had slightly the better of the argument because with free trade and the range of substitutes made possible by technological change, competitive pressures have increased. But large firms still have enormous power compared with particular individuals, small firms and communities at any one time. In this sense, Galbraith's concerns find support. Large firms have less protection against competitive pressures and shifts in the world economy than they used to have. However, when the dinosaur keels over, it tends to be replaced by a beast of the same large size but better adapted to its environment. Even though a particular large firm is under stronger competitive pressure, the species continues to exist and to increase its hold on the economy.

The debate over the coercive role of the large firm has tended to be a dialogue of the deaf. The New Right has pointed to the fact that large firms collapse or have to face the unexpected. The Left has argued that large firms amount collectively to a concentration of power which threatens the individual and the smaller community. At the very least, there is a difference between the importance of some decisions to the large firms compared with their importance to those on the receiving end. A small decision by a large firm may have fearsome consequences for small groups of people. In that sense there is good cause for concern about the possible exercise of coercion by large firms.

The conduct of large firms and other organisations is not dictated simply by economic variables. It will reflect the cultural environment. There has been some discussion on whether monopolies can act coercively in a purely economic sense, but very little about the likely extent of private coercion by big organisations other than firms. The theory of organisations suggests that there will be strong pressures to organisation by vested interests. These interests could act indirectly by shaping opinion and thus indirectly controlling action, as well as by direct coercion.

Private coercion could be either indirect or direct, and it could be brought about either by vested interests or as a result of friction between people with differing convictions, beliefs or prejudices. We will look first at the case of private coercion by vested interests. The New Right's main assumption is that private vested interests will have little power in the longer term; they will cancel each other out. How sensible is this assumption?

Vested interests could include professions as well as the more informal and local activities of clans, dynasties or extended families. The status of professions has some rationale in the protection of the public, but the gradual accumulation of preference usually goes far beyond anything that could be justified as in the public interest. The activities of clans and extended families could not even have that degree of defence; but in many societies their influence is pervasive. Even in British and American society it is quite considerable. The theory of organisations would suggest that such groups have strong incentives to secure their positions locally and nationally. Some of them will have advantages not just of income and security but of preferential access to debate and the power to deny unpopular opinions a hearing.

Such exercise of private power may be important enough to be serious impediments to the free society, even in the New Right's sense of the term. Private power is at best complacent and self-perpetuating. Experiment and innovation may seem highly desirable in the abstract but may not find such a warm welcome if they threaten established positions. The contrast between a spontaneous order and the dead hand of state prescription is an unreal one. It completely misses out the possibility that private power can be a very serious barrier to experiment and to innovation.

Vested interests will show great energy and inventiveness in pursuit of their prime aims. But there will be some loss of momentum because their aims are limited and particularistic. People driven by strong beliefs or prejudices do not have this saving boundary of inertia. Here the exercise of private power may become, at worst, tyrannical. The New Right rightly shows concern about some activities of trade unions: but it has little to say about the activities of some cultural and religious groups. It seems to imply that people of differing convictions and prejudices will show a tender respect for one another. But people driven by strong prejudices tend to show increased energy and expansive force as their hold on society grows. The open society with free competition and tolerance has been the exception. Much more common is the intolerance shown by religious and cultural interests.

Friedman's discussion of discrimination is a good example of how the New Right minimises the problem of private coercion.[10] It is a curiously contradictory approach in its details. He argues that discrimination imposes a cost on the discriminator because it means that he would have to pay more than he normally would. But he also argues that Fair Employment Practice Laws impose an unfair burden on employers. They would have to shoulder enormous costs through lost custom if they did not discriminate. The employer is simply reflecting the community's tastes for discrimination. But the most serious flaw in the argument is the notion of how these tastes are going to be changed: '. . . in a society based on free discussion, the appropriate recourse is for me to seek to persuade them that their tastes are bad, and that they should change their views and their behaviour'.[11] However the existence of serious discrimination must suggest that the society is not really free to start with and that the appetite for rational discussion may be rather easily satisfied. It is not quite clear, for example, that Friedman's remedy would have been applicable to rural Mississippi. There and elsewhere in the South rational discussion has followed experience which was brought about by coercive legislation such as the 1965 Voting Rights Act.

The New Right's definition of coercion concentrates on direct actions by government. We have criticised it for its neglect of possible private coercion. But it also neglects the possibility of coercion through the pressure of opinion and conditioning. The emphasis seems to be on physical action. But the denial of information about alternatives could also be coercive. There could be unperceived external restraint which would take away a person's ability to make choices. This could arise from lack of information or from distortion of information. Propaganda, conditioning and prejudice could all have some of the same effects as direct physical coercion. The existence of negative freedom implies that different approaches will get a hearing; it implies a degree of cultural pluralism. The New Right's concentration on physical coercion is in a sense curiously old-fashioned.

The argument about concepts of freedom is an old one with supporters of the positive concepts going back to the nineteenth-century idealists and beyond. Green argued for example that 'Freedom of contract, freedom in all the forms of doing what one will with one's own, is valuable only as a means to an end. That end is what I call freedom in the positive sense; in other words the liberation of the powers of all men equally for contributions to the common good.'[12] The doctrine got a bad name because of its association with the idea that the individual could and should be coerced in order to find his true self. It is a high-risk doctrine. It might lead to a situation in which the potential of individuals had been truly fulfilled. It might, on the other hand, lead to oppression. It could be taken to imply an exercise in paternalism in which some have power to assess the progress of others towards their better selves.

We may not be able to define the better self and real potential, but the idea of a right to participation in society remains attractive. Under the regime of negative freedom, participation depends on the ability to compete in the market. Supporters of this regime have had little difficulty in demolishing the more extreme case for positive freedom. But it is also possible to argue that freedom is not the only value even if we accept the negative concept. The idea of human rights has usually gone beyond liberty to equality and fraternity. Hayek has made the most full and courageous case for the view that, in effect, the only human right should be the right to personal liberty. Equality and fraternity will lead to misguided and counter-productive interventions by government. Can there be a defence of such ideals?

The traditional defence has been the ethical ideal of a common humanity; that there are certain basic human needs which should be met outside the market. The argument is for a minimum level of security, income and worldly resources required for self-respect and participation in society. The claims of this minimum ought to be met for everybody in society before consumption beyond it is allowed. Such a minimum could even find support from the idea of equality of opportunity. It is not possible to adjust for all differences in family background, but there is some minimum in potential or life chances which should be assured. It could be well argued that full equality of outcome would not be in the interests of the poorest given the need for growth and incentives, but this is not to say that any level of inequality however great is tolerable. The critical issue is partly one of values: how much weight do we give to this ethic of a common humanity? But it is also one of fact: is it possible or feasible to provide a minimum of income, resources and life chances for everybody?

The old argument about positive freedom and about whether the ideals of equality and fraternity had any place, began at a time when society was thought of as a collection of mature adults. The importance of early experiences in the family and of the stability of family life has only become a major theme in social thought since 1918. We now have a rather different view of the importance of dependence. The main responsibility rests with parents, but social policy can in various ways both relieve stress and add to opportunities. Evidence on the dependence of children and the importance of early family life gives some new weight to the old arguments about common humanity. Social policy can relieve stress through raising the income of households with dependants. It can also create opportunities through day nurseries and play groups for young children as well as through the education system for older ones. There is no reason why all this should be undertaken only by public action – there is plenty of room for voluntary groups – but some element of subsidy will often be required.

The idea of positive freedom has an attractive element: that there is a wider social interest in the fulfilment of potential by the individual. We argue that such an interest can be served in another way by introducing values other than freedom. The ideals of liberty and fraternity can be supported ethically as the ideals of common humanity. They justify at least collective effort to provide a minimum core. The other question, however, remains: is government effective in providing this core? We might be able to make an ethical case in principle: we might even be able to establish that such a core could be financed without serious damage to growth and incentives. But will government inevitably fail in its attempts to guarantee this minimum through social services? The New Right differs in its view of the principle. Hayek believes that it is wrong in principle for government to try to provide this core, while Friedman believes that government aims are in principle acceptable and even noble. But the New Right is at one in asserting the strong case for government failure. Government may mean well, but it always fails in practice. Its activities will threaten the life chances of the less well-off and the market will do better in providing the minimum. In this chapter we have looked at the principles; in later chapters we shall turn to the practice.

References

1. F.A. Hayek, *The Constitution of Liberty*, London; Routledge and Kegan Paul, 1960, Chapter 1.
2. Isaiah Berlin, 'Two Concepts of Liberty', in *Four Essays on Liberty*, London; Oxford University Press, 1969, pp.118–72; C. Bay, *The Structure of Freedom*, Stanford, California; Stanford University Press, 1979; C.B. Macpherson, 'Berlin's Division of Liberty', in *Democratic Theory: Essays in Retrieval*, Oxford; Oxford University Press, 1973, pp.95–119.
3. M. Friedman and R. Friedman, *Free to Choose*, London; Secker and Warburg, 1980, p.36.
4. *Free to Choose*, p.36–7.
5. *The Constitution of Liberty*, pp.71–84.
6. R.A. Dahl and C.E. Lindblom, *Politics, Economics and Welfare*, Chicago; University of Chicago Press, 1976, p.60.
7. M. Friedman, *Capitalism and Freedom*, Chicago; University of Chicago Press, 1962, p.33–4.
8. F.A. Hayek: *Law, Legislation and Liberty: Vol. 2, The Mirage of Social Justice*, London; Routledge and Kegan Paul, 1976, p.132.
9. *The Constitution of Liberty*, p.137.
10. *Capitalism and Freedom*, pp.108–18.
11. *Capitalism and Freedom*, p.110.
12. T.H. Green, *Works: Vol. III, Miscellanies and Memoir*, London; Longman, Green, 1888, p.372 (as quoted in Bay, *The Structure of Freedom*, p.55).

7 The Role of Government

The New Right is identified with a view of the role of government which could more properly be attributed to Milton Friedman than to any other economist. We have seen that Hayek would be prepared to allow quite a wide field for government so long as it was not operating through centralised monopoly. However, even Hayek in his later writings seems to have moved towards Friedman's view that the functions of government should be greatly reduced.

This view is usually supported by the well-known passage in *The Wealth of Nations*. There is no doubt about the enormous influence of Smith's discussion on modern economics:

> According to the system of natural liberty, the sovereign has only three duties to attend to; three duties of great importance indeed, but plain and intelligible to common understandings; first the duty of protecting the society from the violence and invasion of other independent societies; secondly, the duty of protecting, as far as possible, every member of society from the injustice or oppression of every other member of it, or the duty of establishing an exact administration of justice; and, thirdly, the duty of erecting certain public works and public institutions which it can never be for the interest of any individual, or small number of individuals, to erect and maintain, because the profit could never repay the expense to any individual or small number of individuals, though it may frequently do much more than repay it to a great society.'[1]

This passage represents those functions of the state on which nearly all economists would agree. But it leaves them in some difficulty to justify most of the functions of the modern state. There have been attempts to find justification for these functions within a framework of welfare economics. State intervention may be justified where there are differences between social and private costs. The state may be able to ensure that social costs or social benefits are taken into account, although the New Right can legitimately complain that the welfare economists have said little about the possibility of government failure. Recently there have been attempts to use the welfare economics to justify state action in changing the distribution of income.

These attempts to justify specific government activities have done little to alter a powerful undercurrent of feeling in economics that government is at best a necessary evil. Economists always seem to believe that the age of less government is just round the next corner. This belief has been reinforced by the growing literature on government failure. We shall discuss this in later chapters. In this chapter we deal with the general feeling that government is in some sense unnatural and even possibly created by malign forces in politics. We shall argue that the growth of government is not due to conspiracy. Government is defined here in a general sense as state involvement in a wide range of actual or potential decisions made by individuals and enterprises. The New Right believes that such interference can and should be made to disappear. Our approach suggests in contrast that certain pressures make for third party intervention and that we should concentrate on reform and not on an illusion that it could all be made to disappear. This general consideration of government may also help to explain the very big range of government activity, going far beyond the traditional welfare state.

The New Right is a philosophy of action, the essential effect of which would be to create a greater freedom of action by various kinds of agent. But there is a difference in force between motives and consequences. Motives count for a great deal: consequences for rather less. Consequences weigh especially lightly in the balance where they are likely to appear only far in the future. Action is often easy: the consequences can be severe and permanent. There can be a separate argument about whether government would do better than private agents. It may be that government will simply bring into being a new class of agents who will be as impulsive as the private kind. But in this submission the difference in force between motive and consequence remains a major problem of life. Any philosophy of the virtues of speedy action has to explain how it proposes to deal with this problem.

Action is subject to impulse. A decision can be taken very suddenly to move a car a few feet over on a road with possibly devastating consequences for others. However, we are dealing here mainly with the kind of actions that are based on reason and reflection rather than on reflex. Even in these actions, motives have far greater weight than consequences, and the further away the consequences the less weight they have. Motive is the overwhelming reason for undertaking an action. Consequences may not simply be discounted – they may be unknowable and in the future. There were sufficient motives for the outbreak of the First World War, but the consequences were not predicted at the time.

The existence of uncertainty has often been used to bolster the argument for market solutions. Hayek would argue that uncertainty makes it more important to concentrate responsibility for decisions and to give the maximum incentive to turn that uncertainty into calculation of risk based on information. Responsibility gives the incentive to collect accurate information. But this argument only fits when all possible consequences are being borne by the person making the decision. When the consequences are borne by others and also when they are far in the future, the incentive to take account of them may be very weak. It will be more sensible then to provide the third party (government) with the role of making sure that possible long-term consequences are taken into account. This may reduce the speed at which decisions are made, but it may be the only way of ensuring that consequences are taken into account.

There are other reasons why consequences may be ignored in a society made up of small family groups. Action and reaction are affected by our limited capacity to be sympathetic and involved outside our own circle of family, friends and neighbours. An accident to somebody in this circle is a catastrophe; an accident in the next town is forgotten in half an hour. It may well be that a vague sense of altruism will not be an adequate link between these small groups and the wider society; the long-term interests of small groups requires practices and institutions which will provide such a link.

We have yet to establish that government could supply the link in a useful way. It could be that government failure would be so certain and so total that it would be better to do without government. We are simply arguing at this stage that there is an inherent instability in society which is no more than a collection of family-based small groups. Each group is capable of impulsive action which takes little account of long-term consequences. The motive for such action would show a much greater regard for the well-being of the small group itself than for any vague collectivity. The conditions of life in this social order will continually create pressure for an institution called 'government' or for a certain kind of third party.

Our argument so far has gone little beyond that of Hume in his essay 'Of The Origin of Government', an essay which has had little attention from economists.[2] Men are governed by interest: 'even when they extend their concern beyond themselves, it is not to any great distance; nor is it usual for them in common life to look much beyond their nearest friends and acquaintance'.[3] Men therefore undertake to set up an institution called government which will ensure that the rules of justice are observed. Hume not only presented the case in principle; he also maintained that government could in fact carry out useful functions. Some men are given the particular role. This makes the 'observance of justice the immediate interest of some particular persons'.[4] Hume was not specific about the range of decisions which would involve the attentions of magistrates or government. Apart from the rules of justice it seemed to extend to various kinds of public works; however, the discussion of consequences would seem potentially to open a wide agenda.

The usual discussion in economics about the role of government has a curious timelessness to it. Much of it, as we have seen, is based on assertions made two hundred years ago. But there are a number of changes since Adam Smith's day which have strengthened the case for a third party. One obvious one is the greater potential for damage and unpleasant consequences which may arise from actions. When speed was limited to that of a galloping horse and damage to that of gunpowder or a cannonball, a philosophy of action raised fewer doubts. But technology has changed the potential. The force of motive remains but the consequences may be very much greater. The development of technology raises more doubts about a philosophy based on making it easier for private agents to take action with far-reaching consequences.

There is also a greater contrast today between the power of the individual and the small family group and that of the big organisation. Production is organised in firms and other large enterprises, some of them run by government. Households are vulnerable to these and poorly informed about them. Debate in this area has concentrated on the issues of competition between firms – whether large firms are under more or less competitive pressure than slightly smaller firms. But if, as seems likely, large firms are under rather more competitive pressure than the Galbraithian view allows, there is still a vast difference in power between the household and even a small corporate enterprise. The household is vulnerable to misfortune, to its lack of information and to economic risk. It is limited in its mobility. The difference in power means that transactions in markets are often not between independent and roughly equal contracting parties. The individual household is not striking a free bargain with the corporate enterprise. There is often a strong possibility that private coercion will replace free market outcomes. The imbalance in power further strengthens the case for a third party to which households can turn.

The last feature which has to be taken into account is the effect of urbanisation. The conditions of city life are such that one person's action affects many others. As Hayek has stressed, the concept of privately owned property rights will be drastically modified in cities.[5] But this interdependence goes far beyond building regulations to almost every aspect of daily living. In urban life, there is a major problem in making a social order from the activities of individual households.

We have argued for the need for a social order wider than the household. This case can be made by the traditional argument on neglect of consequences which has gained force from changes in technology and corporate power and the growth of cities. All these changes create pressure for the intervention of third parties in a wide range of decisions, including those to do with family welfare and with the protection of the environment. This wider social order could in principle come about through culture or through markets, rather than through government action. But because the difference between the power of the corporate enterprise and the fragility of the household is at the root of the problem, the market cannot do the whole job. There will be pressures towards intervention by a third party of the government type.

The New Right would argue that government would simply become mainly a prisoner of vested interests. Where it was not, it would engage in activities set by the interests of bureaucrats. Certainly the New Right has made an important point about the fiction of omniscience with which state action used to be discussed. The idea of an all powerful, all wise government setting to right all the mistakes made by the market was a travesty. But the New Right has now swung to the other extreme of denying any role of government beyond the Smithian minimum. It is true that the actions of government will be greatly influenced by political considerations; but there is also some idea of the public interest which sets some limits to political competition. However falteringly and intermittently, government in western liberal democracies has tried to represent some ideal of fairness; it has tried to establish an order which would reduce the possible frictions between small households and corporate enterprises. Government represents some values which are important to society. Even in South Africa the idea of fairness gives us some standard against which to assess the actions of that country's present government. Beyond family ties and group self-interest has to lie some minimum concept of human rights. People are elected to office as representatives of party or group interest, but they also undertake to judge issues without prejudice and to keep in view some wider sense of the public interest.

Friedman and others also object to a political process on the grounds that it is likely to be more divisive than the market. The market can represent shades of preference while the political process cannot. But this is mainly because those issues that move into the political process are exactly those that cannot be resolved by private means.

We have argued that the conditions for small group life will continually create pressure for an institution called 'government', and that there is an imbalance of power between households and corporate enterprises which adds to the pressure. One of the few assets that households have that is not directly open to corporate enterprise is the right to vote. Thus the main recourse which households have is to the political process. We still have to examine the evidence for and against the hypothesis of government failure in specific areas of policy. We have been concerned with the validity of the New Right's view that there can be major revisions in the amount of government activity, that the amount as it is today is somehow anomalous and the true amount should be something different. It may be that particular activities of government could be reformed or dispensed with, but that does not mean that we can dispense with government as such. Society without government will in part be a collection of small and vulnerable households. It will show the effects of powerful private organisations and enterprises. From these will come constant pressures for a greater role for a third party. There are ways in which the political process could be reformed, but in current social conditions it is inevitable that more and more issues will come to enter that process.

References

1. *Wealth of Nations, Vol. II,* London; Methuen, 1930, pp.184–5.
2. David Hume, 'Of the Origin of Government', in H.D. Aiken (ed.), *Hume's Moral and Political Philosophy*, New York; Hafner, 1972, pp.97–101.
3. 'Of the Origin of Government', p.97.
4. 'Of the Origin of Government', p.100.
5. F.A. Hayek, *The Constitution of Liberty*, London; Routledge and Kegan Paul, 1960, p.341.

8 Is There an Agenda for Distribution?

The New Right has a predominant view on how far society should alter the distribution of income arising from the market. It denies that there is any legitimate agenda for collective choice beyond the issue of absolute poverty. It accepts that government should levy taxation to ensure that everyone has the minimum required for physical subsistence, but any activities beyond that are part of the mistaken collectivist past. The state has undertaken various forms of redistribution which we label 'social security'. These include the payment of pensions to the elderly, measures to raise the income of families through child benefit, and payments during periods of unemployment and sickness when earnings from the labour market are interrupted. All these should, in New Right thinking, be replaced by a simple form of negative income tax with a level of payment just enough to prevent poverty in an absolute sense. The two main propositions are (i) There is no legitimate agenda for society on issues of distribution other than that of preventing poverty in an absolute sense; and (ii) The concept of relative poverty is dangerous and illegitimate.

The New Right also has certain views about how the agenda for distribution came to be somewhat different from this austere minimum. There are many pressures from the political process to interfere with market outcomes. Politicisation has operated strongly. Modern societies contain powerful interests which attempt to bring about equality of outcome.

The New Right has a predominant view about the actual course of distribution. It has argued that under capitalism the real incomes of the poorest will, through the operation of the market, increase. Friedman has even gone on to argue a stronger proposition, namely that capitalism will bring about greater equality of incomes. These positive propositions support the more normative ones about the agenda for distribution. It is possible to have such a short agenda because the course of economic change is not raising new and difficult questions. If economic change were less benign – if, for example, it reduced the incomes of the poor in absolute terms – it would be much more difficult to reconcile the prescriptions on minimum income with those on state spending and taxation. The New Right believes in a minimum income for all. It also believes that state spending and taxation should be reduced. It is quite easy to reconcile these two commitments if the labour market is operating to raise the incomes of the less well off. It would be much more difficult if there was a growing difference between the sum of income provided by the labour market for the 30 per cent less well off households and the amount required to meet a minimum standard.

In this and Chapters 9 and 10 we challenge these views. The main contentions are as follows:

1. There is a fuller agenda for collective choice on issues of distribution, which households face in an industrial society. We look at the case for family allowances as an example of how this wider agenda is made up.
2. The course of distribution in the most recent phase of economic development has been towards reducing the labour market incomes of the 30 per cent less well off households in absolute terms.
3. There is a case for collective action for pensions through social security. The social security system, far from being a conspicuous example of government failure, is the least worst solution to the problem of maintaining real incomes in retirement.

Should There be an Agenda for Distribution?

The classic justification for state action in economics concentrated on the case for providing goods and services. The public good case begins with Adam Smith. Economists have always regarded the distribution of income as an important issue. Most textbooks begin by emphasising that the proper working of a market economy requires a fair distribution of income, but until recently they have said little about possible grounds for collective choice in altering the distribution of income.

Before the 1960s redistribution was justified, if at all, in utilitarian terms. An extra pound was worth more in satisfaction to a poor man than the pound lost to a rich man. The marginal utility of incomes – the gain in satisfaction from a little extra income – was greater to the poor man. In a community with more poor than rich the way to the greatest happiness of the greatest number lay through redistribution.

This type of argument was vulnerable to the criticism that it was impossible to compare satisfactions between people. Since the 1960s there have been attempts to make a stronger case for redistribution through using welfare economics. People may not just be interested in their own well-being but in that of others as well. People's 'utilities' may be interdependent. I may be interested not just in my own level of income, but in whether you have a decent income as well. The play of forces in the market will not take these altruistic concerns into account.[1] Government action may be needed to make sure that such concern for others actually affects the pattern of income distribution. The sum of private decisions left to themselves may not reflect the full span of people's preferences. Some degree of redistribution may be 'Pareto-optimal', i.e. it may leave some people more satisfied without actually reducing anybody's satisfaction.

This debate has caught little attention outside a narrow circle and the whole idea of interdependent utility has perhaps been given too much weight anyway. Even if people do have altruistic concerns there is still the question of how these are translated into policies. Even if such feelings exist within conscience there must be some mechanism for collective choice for translating them into practice. Defence of state action in these terms has to say much more about how collective choice comes about than has usually been the case.

Economists have argued, but while they argued a considerable range of collective choices about distribution were actually made as part of a series of piecemeal administrative decisions. It would, in principle, be possible to establish what preferences about redistribution had revealed themselves through the political process. Collective choices do not necessarily arise from pure principles but from practical problems in an imperfect world. This is not to decry the importance of principles but to suggest that we also have to look at the actual types of redistribution which have been attempted. Some of them may have been the result of undue politicisation, but it may be that some of them would have found favour under more rigorous decision-making systems such as that of a two-thirds majority.

A working definition of a 'legitimate' issue for collective choice here involves three points. The first is that it should bring about a pattern of income distribution different from that which the market alone would have brought about. It has to do something that only government can do. Secondly, it has in principle to bring about a better fit between the distribution of income and the distribution of individual preferences than the market alone would have done. Finally, it has to be a change that would command assent, perhaps a two-thirds majority, even in a rigorous regime for making decisions. Using this definition, we shall argue that there are some issues to do with the distribution of income over the lifetime which have been neglected by economists.

Economic theory and economic research have had little to say about the social aspects of distribution. The main body of work has dealt with how income is divided in the labour market. The classical economists were concerned mainly with the division between factor shares. Relative scarcities of land, labour and capital determined distribution.

Nowadays the focus is more usually on individual labour markets. The demand for labour is determined by its price, the relative price of labour and capital, by the level of output and by the state of technology. On the supply side, the theory of human capital together with Adam Smith's theory of net advantages now holds the field. Workers will choose occupations according to the rates of return which they show; that is net lifetime earnings less training costs, although workers will also be influenced by the non-monetary aspects of the work. All these approaches taken together tend to produce a highly 'economic' view of how the labour market operates. Differences in earnings reflect on the supply side differences in degree of risk and return, and on the demand side differences in the level of demand. Thus, the wage structure mainly reflects the free operation of the labour market. There are some qualifications. Differences in social background and educational opportunity limit access to better paid occupations. Trade unions and professional associations also raise the earnings of some workers but the effect is no more than to make them 10–15 per cent higher than they would have been otherwise.

Against this has to be set the revisionist qualifications to the theory. These would accept that there were certain minimum levels of pay which might affect supply, and certain maximum levels which might affect demand. But within that range there is scope for bargaining and discretion, which is the greater because the external labour market is not open. Large employers fence in their internal labour markets. They hire trainable labour and then go through a training and grading process to fit the workers to the jobs. Once in the jobs, workers tend to be tied to one employer. All these decisions are made on a lifetime basis and, once made, only an earthquake or a major recession will shift them. The external market operates sluggishly within a wide range of discretion. In the face of lifetime commitments, high training costs and high costs of worker mobility, the speed of response on the demand and on the supply side may be slow. The response will be even slower if we admit that social and psychological elements may influence the labour contract. An employer may want to maintain continuity of employment even at the price of short-term loss. Workers may be influenced by loyalty to each other and/or to the employer. The employment contract has sometimes been compared to the tie of marriage. It may not be that, but it is usually more than a casual relationship.

The main new element since 1960 has been the rise of human capital theory to dominate the supply side of the argument. This has tended to give powerful reinforcement to the more economic approach. One strong criticism in the past had been that supply and demand forces seemed to have little effect on the wage structure in the short term. This short-term had no standard definition but was usually seen as a period less than five years. Much criticism had centred on the lack of change of differentials to accompany changes in quantities demanded or supplied. Nowadays interest in the structure of relative wages in the short term has faded because the process of choice is seen as relating to the whole working life. Studies of wage structure are now more confident in seeing differences in earnings as part of a pattern over a lifespan. Differences in education and work experience are now more precisely marked out in their effect on earnings than they were twenty years ago.

Other possible issues of distribution have attracted less discussion. There is a range of issues to do with the more social aspects of distribution on which economics has little to say. The more Right-wing economists would tend to think that they were not legitimate issues at all but simply the result of political machination. The more Left-wing economists would accept that such redistribution could be justified because of the interdependence of utility functions; but apart from this they would have views on these issues as voters rather than as professional economists. The main issues are the distribution of income at various stages during a lifetime, depending on the amount and nature of family commitments, and the distribution of income between those in the labour force and those who are out of it. Apart from a courageous discussion by Harry Johnson in 1961, which he did not carry over at all in his later work, neither the New Right nor the economics profession as a whole has spent much time discussing these issues.[2]

The New Right has had a great deal to say about vertical redistribution but very little about the pattern of income during a lifetime. Its approach, presumably, is that, in the main, people should bear the costs of their own decisions to have children. If they could not support children they should not have them. If redistribution was desirable it could be brought about by voluntary transfers and by the purchase of insurance against children by single people and couples without children. The insurance market could bring into being policies that would allow some measure of redistribution during a lifetime.

It would seem unlikely that the market could do this for a substantial number of families. One difficulty might be lack of foresight. And it might be considered rather unfair that children should bear the whole consequences of their parents' lack of foresight. But an even greater difficulty is that of gaining income now in return for payments made out of future labour income. Many parents would not have been in the labour market long enough with earnings high enough to buy an annuity for their years with dependent children. Their earnings in the future are uncertain and, perhaps, low. It is doubtful whether they would be bankable. This type of redistribution is limited by the fact that future labour income is not a firm security for benefits in the present. Even if there were the market for these transactions, it could only provide for redistribution of one family's income over the lifetime of the parents, not for redistribution between different households with the same income. But the fact of uncertainty about life prospects makes impossible the pure redistribution within one family's income. The family is gaining income early, during the child-rearing stage. There is no guarantee that that family will be intact to repay the income in later years. Maintenance of equivalent income implies some form of horizontal redistribution.

Harry Johnson's further discussion of these issues contains one clear lead towards a policy of family allowances. He argued that control of family size was not within the individual family's power. Our society was rapidly moving in that direction but it still has a long way to go: 'measures such as family allowances and income tax relief for dependents aimed at subsidizing the larger families have a rationale in the imperfect availability and utilization of knowledge in this area of consumer decision-making'.[3] It was also possible that 'a more sophisticated philosophy of capitalism might go further and regard the rearing of children as an investment industry producing human capital for the future and deserving of financial support by society on purely economic grounds'. But he had contributed earlier his much more general discussion of the vulnerability of the family in a highly specialised economy.[4] It is a small unit with a narrow and highly specialised economic base. It cannot deal freely in human capital. The small economic size of the family also makes its welfare dependent to an important extent on the physical and social environment in which it lives and over which it has little control. Finally the narrow economic base of the family, its dependence for income on the sale of the services of its head or heads, renders its income and welfare extremely vulnerable to the human risks of illness, accident and death: and the economic risks resulting from either the freedom for change that the opulent society allows or the inability or incompetence of government to stabilise the economic system. Some of the social risks are possibly insurable but the economic risks are not, and Harry Johnson argued that such risks should be borne by society as a whole. Family allowances are among the possible ways by which society could act to reduce the vulnerability of the family.

There are few discussions of these issues in the New Right's pages. Friedman has a brief discussion of a possible paternal duty of government, but he seems to be thinking more of preventing cruelty than of income support.[5] Yet if a society is rich enough to guarantee a minimum level of income, it should surely define this minimum in equivalent terms. A policy of this kind could also find support because it implies a degree of social responsibility for children. The New Right would certainly accept that parents should not have unlimited power over children. But is it sensible to argue that society's responsibility be confined to the more extreme forms of physical and mental abuse? How far should a child be forced to share without qualification the poverty of its parents? Although some may escape from such a background, for many others it may mean permanent damage to self-respect.

The aim of a guaranteed minimum in equivalent income could also find support from the principle of equality of opportunity. It is not possible to equalise all opportunity and to make adjustments for all differences in family background. But equality of opportunity may have little meaning in the face of poverty. Equality of opportunity implies that all children should have some minimum of resources with which to take their chance.

Finally, the policy of family allowances could find support from concern about the position of women in society. Women with young children will not be able to participate as fully in paid work as others. Their incomes will be more dependent on that of their husbands. There is the possibility here of a great deal of private coercion as well as of danger to the interests of children. There is a case for a guaranteed payment of some minimum level of income directly to the mother while she is taking on most of the work of child-rearing.

These arguments might be used, however, to justify no more than a system of payments to a minority – a policy similar to that of the Family Income Supplement (FIS) in Britain by which a relatively small proportion of the population gets an income supplement. The case for a universal system, such as family allowances, could be made in that it would avoid stigma. However it is not at all clear how far one limited social policy could possibly alter fairly deep-rooted attitudes. More crucially, a policy for family allowances could express a clearer approximation to people's true preferences. Many families would prefer to redistribute their income so that it is higher during periods of responsibility for bringing up their children. As we have seen, it is impossible to do this through the market or without an element of redistribution because of the uninsurable risks facing each family. Such a redistribution could only be brought about by government. It might well be closer to people's real preferences and it would stand a good chance of acceptance even under a rigorous two-thirds decision rule. It is suggested therefore that a system of family allowances should be added to the agenda of distribution beyond the subjects which the New Right would wish to place there.

Sources of State Action on Distribution

Governments are held by the New Right to have created dependency and to have intervened unnecessarily in a quest for equality of income. But this seems to ignore the rather pragmatic reasons which have pushed governments into further action. One of the most important of these reasons has been the decline of the extended family in modern societies. This network of family support took care of some, at least, of the dependent family members.

Even so, many dependent people and children had no families to look after them and had to go to the workhouse. Independence and freedom were mainly for adult men – and then only so long as they were in good health. The extended family declined for many reasons and the decline occurred in societies with differing degrees of government intervention. The direct encouragement of government would seem to have been one of the most minor reasons. Changes in society have made for increasing numbers of old people and single parents who are out of the workforce and are not able to get a share of income through the market. Increased government intervention has come about as a slow and pragmatic response to the decline of the extended family; the alternative would have been increased destitution.

For the New Right, society often seems to be composed of adult men in good health. In its many discussions of income distribution, problems of distribution between adult men in work and women with children who are out of the labour force are rarely mentioned. Yet there is no mechanism within the market economy which will ensure a reasonable share of income for dependent groups. Governments in many countries have had to face these issues both because of the decline of the extended family and because views on the rights of women and children have changed. Government policy on the distribution of income has sprung more from *these* issues of distribution than from the pure redistribution from the rich to the poor which the New Right so dislikes. Thus Joseph writes that 'it is now . . . widely accepted that it is a proper indeed a major function of the state to shift incomes and savings from the richer to the poorer members of society'. He goes on to say that such 'Redistribution is unwise. But it is also morally indefensible, misconceived in theory and repellent in practice'.[6] Yet such judgements are made with no consideration of some issues of distribution which have, in practice, been far more important than that of vertical redistribution from the rich to the poor.

Discussion about redistribution cannot be merely abstract; it also has to take into account the basic requirements for sustaining family life in an economy in which the family is vulnerable to disruption and to economic change.

The New Right would confine definition of poverty to the absolute sense of the term – the minimum required to allow physical subsistence. But there are serious reasons for doubting whether poverty as a relative concept – a standard depending upon what is common in a particular period – can be dismissed quite so sweepingly. It is, for one thing, muddled thinking in that so-called 'absolute' definitions of poverty usually include a 'relative' approach to diet. They hesitate to draw the full logic that people can physically subsist on a handful of vitamin pills, water, three oranges and three and a half loaves a week. They allow for a diet that has a certain amount of variation and that can be purchased in the usual range of shops – that at once excludes many inferior highly nutritious foods that are not widely sold, especially in the United States.

The most serious objection, however, is to the ethical view inherent in the New Right's definition of poverty. It implies that society has an interest in maintaining the lives of its members on a purely physiological or animal basis but does not care about whether people's ability to function mentally and socially is maintained. This would seem to be less than humane to people who are not able to re-enter the labour market – the elderly and the disabled. Life is not merely physiological existence: it is also about relationships, activity and dignity. The stress of dependence may, in any case, threaten relationships and induce depression. But if, as well as being dependent, people have to struggle to maintain even the barest pretence of a normal existence in society, integrity, and even survival, will be further threatened. For people who will re-enter the labour market, an absolute definition of poverty becomes a poor business proposition as well as inhumane. It implies that society should be indifferent to their future potential for independence. Thus, rejection of the relative definition involves a view of human life which is both short-sighted and profoundly dispiriting.

Conclusions

The New Right draws a sharp distinction between the legitimate and the actual agenda for distribution. The legitimate agenda is concerned with the minimum required to prevent destitution. The actual agenda has been set by political forces tending towards equality of results. The New Right also sees the structure of labour market incentives as a very delicate one. Almost any interference with it other than the provision of a minimum could have extremely bad results. This is the other extreme to the view of the Left by which income differentials can be drastically compressed by political decision. Neither Right nor Left views fit very easily to the actual issues about social security or transfer payments.

Family commitments are not synchronised with peaks in lifetime income, and it is impossible for households to organise this redistribution of equivalent income for themselves. The insecurity and vulnerability of households to economic change also cannot be dealt with by the households themselves or through an employer-based system of social security. The agenda for distribution can include, as a minimum, family allowances and a system of income support in face of the uncertainties arising from economic change. The agenda is lengthened because of the problem of long-term disability. What share of income are those in the labour force willing to allow to those outside it?

Economists have said a great deal about the dynamics of distribution in labour markets. They have made a sharp distinction between the economic determinants of redistribution – which are held to have great presence – and government activities to influence distribution which are seen as discretionary and secondary. By one view some redistribution could be justified if there were feelings of altruism. For the New Right there should be only a minimum of interference with market outcomes. By both views government actions are seen as discretionary and political.

There are some very strong reasons why in practice the agenda for distribution should be rather longer. The 'social' issues of distribution arise out of the conditions and experience of households in the course of life. Further issues arise in a society which is divided between workers and those who are outside the workforce, between those who have independence and others who are dependent. These issues are not the product of politicisation or of subjective impulses to altruism, even though certainly such impulses may affect the pattern of policies. These are not less real than the economic issues on which economists have written so much. The actual course of economic change in fact is giving them even greater importance than before.

References

1. H.M. Hochman and J.D. Rodgers, 'Pareto Optimal Redistribution', *American Economic Review*, September 1969, pp.542–57 (also comments by Goldfarb and Musgrave and reply by Hochman and Rodgers).
2. Harry G. Johnson, 'The Social Policy of an Opulent Society', in *On Economics and Society*, Chicago; University of Chicago Press, 1975, pp.45–58. (This was written in 1961.)
3. Harry G. Johnson, 'The Economics Approach to Social Questions', in *On Economics and Society*, p.28–9.
4. 'The Social Policy of an Opulent Society' in *On Economics and Society*.
5. M. Friedman, *Capitalism and Freedom*, Chicago; University of Chicago Press, 1962, pp.33–4.
6. Sir Keith Joseph and J. Sumption, *Equality*, London; John Murray, 1978, p.18.

9 The Actual Course of Distribution

Society has a duty to provide a minimum standard of income for all. As Hayek puts it, 'There is no reason why in a free society government should not assure to all protection against severe deprivation in the form of an assured minimum income or a floor below which nobody need descend'.[1] But this commitment will not be testing because the natural course of income distribution will be towards higher real incomes for the poor. Friedman has even argued that the movement of income distribution in the nineteenth century was towards greater equality. Today 'a society that puts freedom first will, as a happy by-product, end up with both greater freedom and greater equality'.[2] The change in income distribution will also eliminate poverty in an absolute sense.

This natural growth of real incomes means that in a free society government can quite easily discharge its obligation to provide a minimum income for all. It can be done without any increase in taxation. If, however, the natural course of income distribution is not so benign, the New Right faces a much greater dilemma. It cannot easily maintain its commitment to a minimum income for all and at the same time limit drastically the role of government.

The New Right's view depends partly on evidence of the long-term movement in income distribution under capitalism. It also relies strongly, in the case of Friedman, on international comparisons in the present day. Its view of the long-term course of income distribution is heavily dependent on the American example of opening up a vast continent in conditions of labour shortage. But Friedman also has something to say about Britain in the nineteenth century. He concludes that 'Economic growth was rapid. The standard of life of the ordinary citizen improved dramatically – making all the more visible the remaining areas of poverty and misery portrayed so movingly by Dickens and other contemporary novelists.'[3] It is true that the performance of the nineteenth-century economy was impressive – particularly before 1880. But the degree of economic inequality was very great. It was not just Engels but the conservative Disraeli who saw Britain as divided into two nations. The market economy grew in Britain under conditions very different from those in the United States, with a much greater degree of inherited political and economic inequality than was known among white Americans. These inequalities came from the distribution of property which resulted from force and conquest. They were reinforced by that inequality of bargaining power in the labour market on which even Adam Smith had much to say in his own day. It is unlikely that he would have said anything different about the position a century later. It is highly doubtful whether this degree of inequality as it existed in 1870 could have been reconciled with the changes in the suffrage in 1867 and 1884.[4]

The division into two nations lessened during the nineteenth century, but it is a travesty to imply that the remaining areas of poverty and misery were some sort of residual problem. The surveys of Rowntree and Booth showed that a very significant proportion – perhaps as high as 40 per cent – of the population were living in households where income, even if prudently used, was not able to provide the minimum necessary for physical subsistence. Rates of infant mortality were such that one out of four of children in poorer neighbourhoods died in the first year of life. One out of two died before reaching adulthood. Most of the volunteers from towns for the South African War had to be rejected on grounds of physical disability. The early development of social services was as much concerned with national efficiency as with social justice. Early welfare state policies represented a response to a very real and major problem rather than attempts by collectivists to undermine a free society. Poverty at the end of the nineteenth century was seen by many observers – not only on the Left – as a threat both to internal stability and to Britain's ability to resist external enemies.

Another view of the course of income distribution in nineteenth-century Britain was that of the socialist Henry George. Against the argument that there had been great gains in average real income in the nineteenth century, he maintained that there had been a polarisation of society. He wrote in 1886: 'The new forces, elevating in their nature though they be, do not act upon the social fabric from underneath, as was for a long time hoped and believed, but strike it at a point intermediate between top and bottom. It is as though an immense wedge were being forced not underneath society but through society. Those who are above the point of separation are elevated, but those who are below are cast down.'[5] In Britain there was a contrast between workers in white collar and upper-manual occupations and those in sweated trades.

The quality of research done on long-term trends in the distribution of income has in fact been rather high. This has been an area of success for positive economics which has shed new light on conflicting generalisations. The classic work is that of Kuznets.[6] In the early stages of economic development income inequality might well increase: it would then stablise in a middle period and finally decline. The American experience had been of widening inequality up to the Civil War in 1861: of stability from the War up to 1929 and then of increasing equality between the Depression and 1950. The early stages of industrialism were marked by high rates of population growth, and high returns both to new industrial investment, and to scarce skilled labour. The early stages of industrialism would also see a shift away from agriculture with its low but equal incomes to industry where incomes were higher on average but more unequal. In the later stages of industrialism labour's market position would improve relative to capital. A check to population growth would reduce the supply of labour and the returns to capital would fall. The better off might continue to save more but they would get a much lower return on it. Returns to training would also be lower than during the first stages of capitalism.

Kuznets does not confirm the view of one simple trend towards greater equality starting with the industrial revolution and continuing on to the present day. Rather a stage of increasing inequality would only be reversed after many decades of economic development. Kuznets' conclusions have been strikingly borne out by later more detailed research, notably Williamson and Lindert's fine work, *American Inequality, a Macroeconomic History*.[7] The strongest evidence is on the relative pay of skilled and unskilled workers. At the time of de Tocqueville's visit in 1831–2, America was usually seen as the land of equality. Unskilled workers seemed much better placed both in absolute and in relative terms than they were in Europe. By 1861 differentials had widened sharply and they remained wide until 1929. A skilled worker was earning about 40 per cent more than an unskilled worker in 1834: in 1914 he was earning twice as much.[8] There was some narrowing during the First World War but this turned out to be temporary. Differentials were restored in the 1920s, and it was only during the Great Depression and the Second World War that differentials finally showed permanent change towards greater equality with every other indicator of income following suit.

The explanations are very much in the Kuznets idiom though using more sophisticated methods. The basic cause is to be found in shifts between labour-using and labour-saving technology. Agriculture uses labour and especially unskilled labour. From 1840 to 1861 there was a shift to manufacturing and away from agriculture. Manufactuing uses capital and skilled labour. Its growth stretches differentials in favour of skilled workers. The shift to manufacturing was reinforced by its faster growth in productivity. After 1929 technological change was for a time labour-using. Productivity grew faster in agriculture and there has also been less labour saving within manufacturing. Above all lower levels of unemployment improved the market position of the unskilled.

Changes in immigration and in labour supply have also influenced distribution. The period from 1820 to 1860 was one of heavy immigration and it was the stop to immigration after 1918 which prepared the way for the later narrowing in differentials. Periods of rapid labour force growth have tended to coincide with periods of rising wage gaps.

Immigration raised the supply of unskilled labour relative to skilled.

The facts suggest that the period up to 1914 was not one of income levelling: nor was it one in which the real incomes of the poor grew rapidly. In fact the late Victorian period saw for the United States what Williamson and Lindert describe as the 'last great surge' in urban inequality.[9] From 1896 to 1914 the real wages of the unskilled rose by 0.42 per cent a year, and this for the fortunate minority who were in regular employment. The position of the many urban poor who were not in regular employment must have been even worse at a time when food prices were rising faster even than the general price level.

For Britain the Kuznets phases are clearly there but with inequality coming earlier and the swing towards greater equality starting after 1914. The increase in inequality started in the 1790s and continued up to the 1840s. Inequality was little changed for the rest of the century but a trend towards greater equality began in 1914.[10] There were striking changes in the pace of real income growth. This was rapid from the 1840s to the 1880s, but by the approach to the First World War real incomes were static. As in the United States there was particular hardship for the urban poor.

Norway – the other country for which there is detailed evidence – shows a different pattern. Income inequality in pre-industrial Norway was very great.[11] This was not an open economy but one in which mercantilist privileges led to a remarkable concentration of income in the hands of a few merchants. The early stages of industrialism from 1860 to 1890 saw little change. The returns to capital under the new regime of economic liberalism were high and work for employees still seasonal. But from the 1890s a strong shift began. 'The vigorous shift towards equality that began in Ostfold in the decade before the turn of the century can be attributed to the factory revolution, which was based on the pulp and paper, the electrical, and the electrometallurgical industries.'[12] The shift towards equality was reinforced by the beginnings of welfare state policies. Norway's late industrial revolution and its late emancipation from mercantilist privileges helps to create a rather different pattern of phases.

For all three countries the movement has been uneven. The long-term evidence before 1929 certainly does not support any hypothesis that the progress of capitalism has led to steady reductions in inequality. Nor has the reduction in poverty in an absolute sense been a strong continuing trend for Britain and the US. Henry George's generalisation now appears to be nearer the mark than Friedman's. The nineteenth century as a whole saw an increase in inequality in the United States and little change in inequality in Britain. More significantly the period from 1880 to 1914 showed remarkably similar features in Britain and in the United States. They were ones of persisting inequality and of acute pressure on the real incomes of the less well off. Booth and Rowntree and the Settlement House Movement in the United States were right to stress the enormous size and difficulty of the problem of poverty.

Friedman has also made much of current international comparisons. We are told that the United States has a more equal income distribution than that of controlled economies such as India and China.[13] It is doubtful whether such comparison has much meaning, particularly when the ideal type of a free economy is drawn so heavily from a society founded by and still dominated by immigrants. Hong Kong cannot be safely taken as a guide to more settled and diverse societies. It is well known that immigrants can achieve unusual feats and are subject to unusual incentives. It may not be easy to transfer these to more settled societies.

From 1914 in Britain and 1929 in the United States through to 1950 the movement was towards greater equality. Economic forces certainly contributed to this but so did social attitudes. Sentiments about equality had particular effect during the Second World War. After 1950 there is a conflict of view. Some see a movement in reverse towards greater inequality, while for Friedman and Hayek recent history is a time of ever increasing egalitarian pressure. We turn now to the period since 1950. What actual changes in distribution have taken place and how might they be explained?

There are in fact three views to be evaluated. One is that of Friedman and Hayek. The middle position is that of the Royal Commission on the Distribution of Income and Wealth which finds stability.[14] Finally there is the school of pessimists who read the evidence as showing a shift towards greater inequality. They all start under certain difficulties, with sources and with methods of comparison. For Britain there are two separate sources and three sets of figures on household income. There are many possible definitions of equality and different ways of interpreting statistics such as Gini coefficients. None of the available figures take full account of fringe benefits nor do they use a full definition of income in terms of net accrual of spending power.

But there is one greater difficulty. The figures do not really measure directly changes in income inequality of actual people. We would like to see how incomes had changed for particular generations or cohorts over long periods of time; instead we have to look at changes in shares of households taken from different generations. The usual comparisons used by the Royal Commission rely heavily on changes in shares by such large samples of households.

There is another approach to measuring inequality: to take people of the same age at different points in the social structure and to chart their progress over a long period. If we found that at the end of, say, fifteen years their incomes were very different, this would be a significant change but one which would be quite consistent with constancy in the decile shares. This would in a sense be a much truer picture of inequality over a lifetime than changes in shares.

The general finding of the Royal Commission was that the distribution of income in terms of decile shares had been remarkably stable. The stability was most striking for the distribution of pay. Well-known figures for the stability in the distribution of pay for manual workers from 1886 onwards were rehearsed again by the Royal Commission. But stability also showed up clearly from figures derived from Inland Revenue. If anything these showed a slight movement towards more equality.

This stability was subject to various complications and qualifications. It was to some extent the product of various offsetting changes. The share of the top 10 per cent – and most notably that of the top 1 per cent – had fallen. The share of the next 30 per cent had risen. Britain had changed from being an economy with a few large prizes to one with more medium-sized ones. The share of the bottom 30 per cent in income from the labour market had fallen but that change had been offset by an increase in their incomes from transfer payments. The welfare state had acted as a countervailing force to offset the increase in inequality that would have come about as a result of change in the labour market. The share of the top 1 per cent was also affected by the increase in the relative importance of labour income relative to property or other sources of income. The labour income of the meritocracy had become more important compared with the returns on investment income of the rich.

The Royal Commission sought to attribute these changes mainly to demography and to altered patterns of employment. It believed that most of the changes affecting the bottom 90 per cent of the distribution could be explained by increased employment of married women, earlier retirement by older men and reduced participation by younger the population. Earlier retirement and longer full-time education have raised the income share of households in the middle section of the population. Earlier retirement and longer full-time education has reduced the shares of labour market income going to the bottom 30 per cent. Only the fall in the share of the top 10 per cent cannot be explained by these demographic and employment factors.

The Royal Commission's detailed analysis did not shift the overall and overwhelming conclusion – greater stability with some slight tilt towards equality. However, this conclusion was partly dependent on the definition of equality which the Royal Commission used, which put great emphasis on changes within the whole span of the distribution. By this definition, the increased income of a working-class family with two wage packets in Luton, relative to the managing director, pulls the distribution nearer to equality. It more than offsets the reduced income of a middle-aged unskilled factory worker in the North West.

The Royal Commission presented a great mass of figures, but the overall interpretation was of stability with perhaps a slight reduction in inequality. The conclusion in Report No.7 is typical: 'The overall impression from the figures is of a reduction in inequality but if the decline in the top 1 per cent is ignored, the shape of the distribution is not greatly different in 1976–77 from what it was in 1949.'[16] It also implied that such stability is likely to continue on into the future.

The Royal Commission generalised at will about these changes in shares as if they could be taken for a very close proxy for the underlying focus of interest of lifetime income inequality. However given the difficulty of getting this into focus it is surely important to look at circumstantial evidence as well. Some of this points to a very different conclusion to that reached by the Royal Commission.

1. The Royal Commission never managed to crack the mystery of why the share of the top 1 per cent had declined. It did not deal with earlier objections to basing judgements on the economic position of the well-off on 'photographs' of their income at one point in time.[17] Was this in Brittain's phrase simply a 'tax return income revolution' without any clear economic or social meaning?[18] It seems likely that there was some real reduction in relative shares at the top as the share of labour income rose and that of rent and property income which accrues disproportionately to the top 1 per cent fell. The income from human capital of the top third became increasingly important and produced a rise in their share. But the Royal Commission never managed to map the border line between income and wealth so it was impossible to pin down the relative roles of tax avoidance and real change in reducing the share at the top. The difficulty of doing this is certainly great but in the absence of any attempt to do so it is dangerous to label the shift away from the top as an important movement towards equality.

2. The Royal Commission did not put enough stress on the decline in the share of original labour income for the less well off. Its figures do in fact show a rather marked reduction in the share of labour income going to the poorest 40 per cent of households. In 1961 they had 15.6 per cent of labour income.[19] By 1977 this had fallen to 10.7 per cent. Poorer households found their share of income reduced by a third.

3. For many in retirement reductions in labour market income were offset by increased income from social security. Such increases were little help to poorer households with heads of working age.

4. The Royal Commission did not do justice to the difference in impact

of higher unemployment by income level. Layard's study is only the latest to show how people with low earnings are much more likely to be unemployed. 'Even omitting those unemployed who have been out of work for over a year, we find that nearly a half of the unemployed were, when they worked, in the bottom 20 per cent of weekly earnings.'[20] It is also clear that the unemployment rate for manual workers has always been much higher than for non-manual workers. For 1981 the differences are a rate of about 8 per cent for non-manual workers and 18 per cent for manual workers.[21]

The effects of rising unemployment in the British labour market have certainly been very uneven. They must have increased inequality.

5. Some evidence from the New Earnings Survey suggests that the Gini coefficients for pay for men had risen from 0.45 in 1968 to 0.53 in 1980. Numbers of professional and managerial workers have increased and pulled up their share of pay.[22] There has been a sharp increase in inequality.

6. Between 1976 and 1980, the share of original income going to the bottom two-fifths of households fell from 10.2 per cent in 1976 to 9.0 per cent in 1980. 'This was due not only to the rise in the number of pensioner households but also to increases in income inequality within most household types.'[23] There was a large increase in the share going to the top tenth. These changes were not, as in earlier periods, offset by changes in tax and transfer payments so inequality in final income also rose sharply.

7. Further indirect evidence about the pattern of changes in the labour market comes from the Royal Commission's own figures about the balance of occupations. In 1951 one out of ten were in the upper non-manual occupations: by 1978 it was one in three, and most of the change was from 1961 onwards. One in five of men is now classed as a manager or administrator. The figures below show the full scope of the changes.[24]

Percentages of the male labour force by selected occupational groups

	1951	1961	1978
Upper Non-manual	12.8	17.8	31.9
Manual	76.7	69.7	55.0

For women there has been a shift from manual to less well-paid white collar occupations, but there has also been a big increase in the proportion of women in managerial and professional jobs: 11.3 per cent in 1951 to 26.2 per cent in 1978. The big expansion in managerial occupations has brought in many young people with educational credentials and has been accompanied by a reduction in the amount of on-the-job promotion for those without formal qualifications.[25]

At least until the recent recession, new entrants to the labour force with better levels of educational qualification have been well placed in the labour market. Unqualified ones were crowded into the declining areas of unskilled and semi-skilled manual employment. The recession adds to the decline here while increasing the discomfort at the top of the queue. It will reinforce the long-term changes which have already produced a decline in the share of the poorer households. The full effects of the long-term occupational change have in fact yet to work through. Managerial and professional workers may have low earnings at the beginning of their working lives. For those who entered the labour market in the 1970s the real gains may not show up until the late 1980s and 1990s.

Between 1939 and 1950 the underlying pull in the labour market was towards greater equality. Research in the 1950s showed some move towards equality of incomes over the period. This was mainly the result of lower unemployment.[26] Some criticised the adequacy of the statistics and the reasons given for the change, but even critics did not deny that some equalisation had happened.[27] Full employment raises the employment prospects of those at the end of the labour queue: even in the 1930s the prospects of those above the bottom had been relatively good. The pull documented by the Royal Commission is in quite the other direction. The most significant division is between 'primary' and 'secondary' employment. Primary employment offers security and rising lifetime earnings while secondary employment has a high risk of unemployment, low pay and poor working conditions. The division is not a simple one with all manual workers on the wrong side of the line: many skilled manual workers and people doing manual jobs in large firms enjoy the benefits of primary employment except in conditions of extreme recession.[28] The security of primary employment is not absolute – a recession such as the present one brings to some unexpected quarters experiences which are well-known, even in good times, to people in secondary employment.

Both economic and social forces help to create the difference between primary and secondary employment. At the end of the labour queue demand is falling and supply rising. The employer will find it easy to shift most of the inconveniences of the employment onto the workers. At the other end of the market there is rising demand for highly trained workers. Such workers also represent a heavy investment in training for the employer. He will have a strong interest in developing a permanent workforce. Social forces work to strengthen the division. There are differences in bargaining power and in status.

The recession has created new shared experiences in misery: but the long-term trend can be seen if we compare what happened between 1961 and 1979 to a primary worker – such as an ICI manager, a local government officer or a skilled worker for BP – as compared with a secondary worker such as an unskilled worker in the construction industry. The position of the manager or local government officer improved in terms of annual real income, lifetime income and promotion prospects, hours of work, job security and fringe benefits. The position of the construction worker got worse in every respect but one – his hourly pay for hours actually worked. He is more likely to be unemployed, and when he does get work it will be more insecure. His normal working week will have gone down, but he will still actually be working the same number of hours. He is unlikely to have an occupational pension and his working conditions are likely to be poor. Changes in the tax system have reinforced the inequality. The tax yield from the earnings of the unskilled will have risen much more than that from the primary worker. Thus the Royal Commission failed to follow through the logic for shares in income of the changes in the labour market that it documented.

The Royal Commission chose to concentrate on the movement in shares and to conclude from these that there had been a slight movement towards greater equality. The circumstantial evidence suggests that much of this stability may have been spurious as a guide to what actually is happening to 'true' income equality – that of cohorts over long periods of time. Many of the new non-manual jobs are filled by younger workers who have not reached their peak in lifetime earnings. Changes in occupational structure and in levels of unemployment have already helped to produce a rather large fall in the labour market income of poorer households. Until now this has been partly offset by improvements in transfers under social security, but whether this offset will continue in the future is very uncertain.

Against the Commission's confident generalisation about stability could be set a more tentative conclusion that there were substantial forces at work making for greater inequality in labour market income. Inequality is being used here in the specific sense of a change which reduces the share of the poorest one-third of households. Some of this loss of income had been offset for older housholds by improvements in social security, but not for younger ones. For the future the outlook was not for yet more stability but for increasing inequality as the full effects of changes in occupational structure and in levels of unemployment work themselves through.

The evidence from the United States already shows a clear trend towards inequality in labour income. This could be taken as further circumstantial evidence of the real underlying trend in Britain. The distribution of earned income for men in the United States has shown a slow but persistent trend towards greater inequality. Two forces were important here. One was the change in occupational composition which as in Britain favoured professional and managerial jobs. The effect of this was reinforced by a rapid increase in the earnings of the better off. Near the top of the range earnings grew by 207 per cent from 1958 to 1977. Near the bottom they grew by 131 per cent.[29] It seems highly improbable that such changes failed to bring about a widening in differentials in household income and indeed they seem to have done that. The Royal Commission's careful international comparison of income distributions produced as one of its few firm conclusions that there was a trend towards greater inequality in household income in the US between 1967 and 1974.[30]

We turn now to the question of causality. This is important to any assessment of whether future changes in income distribution are likely to be benign. The evidence suggests that mature economies such as the US and Britain enter into a further phase beyond those envisaged by Kuznets. In this phase the pattern of activity and output shifts away from manufacturing and into services. Within manufacturing there is also a shift in the demand for labour. Technology comes to have a bias away from unskilled labour. This mature economy has a strong demand for professional and managerial workers.

On the supply side older unskilled workers cannot compete for these new opportunities. Most will go to younger more highly educated entrants to the workforce. At the top end of the market the shift in the demand curve encourages an increase in supply of eligible labour with trainable characteristics. But at the other end of the market the unfavourable shift in demand leads to a growing labour surplus. The changes which take place are consistent with a labour market which has the following features:

1. Changes in technology and in output mix bringing about shifts in relative demands for labour. Economic development enters into a new phase marked by increasing inequality.
2. Access to new areas of employment by younger better educated workers.
3. Crowding of workers without skill or with obsolete skills into declining areas of employment.

Institutional influences act to reinforce economic advantage. Both employers of trained staff and the workers themselves have a strong interest in developing internal labour markets where there will be commitment on both sides. The worker seeks security rather than the highest possible earnings in the short term. The employer wishes to protect his investment in training. The primary employer so long as he maintains a minimum viability will tend to offer more and more security. Marshall saw cumulative processes at work in labour markets by which higher earners became progressively more able to compete:[31] today in different ways success in the labour market also tends to breed success. The influences of social forces operating in the internal labour market strengthen the influence of the economic forces of supply and demand. It is highly likely that such forces have not fully worked themselves through and that the labour market will continue to show increasing polarisation.

Both the pure economic and the more revisionist theory predict a worsening prospect for workers at the bottom of the labour queue in such a labour market.[32] In the pure economic case earnings will fall and unemployment will rise. If wages are flexible downwards most of the pressure will be taken by earnings. If wages are not flexible there will be more unemployment. In the revisionist theory people will be pushed down the labour queue to add to the supply of labour already there. The wage structure is rigid and all the pressure will be taken by unemployment.

The New Right argues that the problem can be solved through wage flexibility – through stopping workers pricing themselves out of markets. But this will be of limited use in face of falling demand for unskilled labour arising from changes in technology and patterns of output. It simply creates a few more badly paid jobs which are likely to disappear anyway.

With technical change, the demand for labour shifts towards the better educated and more adaptable. These will tend to be younger workers. The demand for less skilled workers falls while the supply may be constant, or even increase. The prescription of wage flexibility has to be seen against the background of a labour market in which there is a surplus of workers who are not highly productive. Both the marginal productivity and the revisionist theory of the labour queue make the same predictions about the fate of people at the bottom of the labour queue in a changing economy. The picture might be different if growth were fast enough to raise the demand for the less skilled; but this has not been so either in Britain or in the United States in the past fifteen years.

These changes in the labour market have increased pressure on people at the end of the labour queue. They have also meant that more people have left the labour market altogether and have to rely entirely on state benefits. The general effect has been to increase the numbers who are in poverty by the usual definition. The New Right tends to discuss the problem of poverty as if it were a small one and a diminishing one. Can this view be reconciled with the evidence?

The first issue has been about definitions. Here the debate has been in general terms as between 'absolute' and 'relative' definitions. In fact the conventional definition is ready to hand and makes this debate rather unnecessary. A household is in poverty when it has an income at or below the appropriate rates of supplementary benefit. These rates currently amount to an income of £5.50–£6.80 per day for a couple or £3.30–£4.20 for a single person, to cover all expenses.[33] It is enough for survival but hardly a lavish level of living, particularly over a long period of time. The number of people at or below these levels of income is certainly of significance and cannot be wished away as an invention by academics dealing in hysteria and false egalitariansim.

The most recent figures for numbers at or below this level of income are for 1979. The figures cover both people who are still in the labour market and those who are outside. In practice about two-thirds of the poor are outside the labour market:

Numbers in households (thousands) dependent on supplementary benefit or with estimated incomes below SB level, Great Britain, 1979[34]

Pensioners:	3,180
Under Pensionable Age:	2,910
Of those under pensionable age	
Unemployed for more than 3 months	980
In full-time work	390
Sick or Disabled	280
Others	1,260
TOTAL	6,090

The numbers in poverty now amount to 6.1 million people or about 11 per cent of the population. This can hardly be described as a small number. The trend over time is not easy to document. However the total numbers dependent on supplementary benefit have much increased and there have been very clear increases in certain groups. Single parent families are probably the fastest growing group in poverty. At present there are about 850,000 single parents bringing up one and a half million children.[35] In 1971 there were 570,000 and twenty years earlier less than 200,000. The effects of higher unemployment have increased poverty among disabled people and among families with the head in full-time work. When the figures for 1981 become available in the middle of the decade they are likely to show a further sharp increase as a result of the recession. There has been some reduction in the proportion of pensioners in poverty; but many of the gains have been by younger pensioners who are more likely to have occupational pensions and who will benefit from higher pensions under the new earnings related scheme. There is still a great deal of poverty among the very elderly. One survey showed in 1972 that over one-third of elderly people had living rooms which were at a temperature of less than 60° Fahrenheit in mid-winter.[36] There are many still living under such conditions. In general the effect of social and economic change has been to increase the numbers in poverty since 1971. It cannot be dismissed as a small problem or one that will fade away. The persistence of poverty means that the provision of even a minimum income will not be an easy proposition. It is difficult to reconcile this commitment to a minimum income with the New Right's commitment to reduce public spending.

References

1. F.A. Hayek, *Law, Legislation and Liberty: Vol. 2, The Mirage of Social Justice*, London; Routledge and Kegan Paul, 1976, p.87.
2. M. Friedman and R. Friedman, *Free to Choose*, London; Secker and Warburg, 1980, p.148.
3. *Free to Choose*, p.35.
4. The case has been well made by Professor T.W. Hutchison in Chapter II, 'The Changing Intellectual Climate in Economics', in *The Emerging Consensus?*, London; IEA, 1981, pp.19–49.
5. H. George, *Progress and Poverty*, London; Kegan Paul, 1886, p.6.
6. S. Kuznets, 'Economic Growth and Income Inequality', *AER*, March 1955, pp.1–28.
7. J.G. Williamson and P.H. Lindert, *American Inequality, a Macroeconomic History*, New York; Academic Press, 1980.
8. *American Inequality, a Macroeconomic History*, pp.307–8. The main movements for the US, GB and Norway in the best available indicators of income dispersion are as follows:

Pay differentials in US

Ratios of skilled to unskilled workers' wage rates in manufacturing and the building trades: urban workers

1830	1.346
1860	1.668
1914	1.989

Skilled workers in manufacturing

1907	2.05
1937–40	1.65
1955–56	1.38

Source: American Inequality, a Macroeconomic History, pp.307–8

Great Britain

Average wage of an agricultural labourer compared with average of wages of building craftsmen and fitters

1793	53
1830	44
1914	45
1930	52

Source: H. Phelps Brown, *The Inequality of Pay*, Oxford; Oxford University Press, 1977, p.90.

Norway

Income coefficients of concentration (males)

	Sarpsborg	*Kristiansand*
1840	—	0.567
1855	0.592	—
1885	0.475	0.531
1900	0.282	0.471
1950	0.295	0.292

Source: L. Soltow, *Towards Income Equality in Norway*, Wisconsin; University of Wisconsin Press, Madison, 1965, p.17.

9. *American Inequality, a Macroeconomic History*, p.105.
10. L. Soltow, 'Long-Run Changes in British Income Inequality', *Economic History Review*, 2nd series, Vol.21, No.1, April 1968, pp.17–29. Soltow's 'Tentative Hypothesis' was that long-run inequality did not change in the eighteenth and nineteenth centuries. However pay differentials certainly widened between 1790 and 1830.
11. Soltow's 1965 study was of income records in eight cities of two countries. This is based on unusually good data.
12. *Towards Income Equality in Norway*, p.30.
13. *Free to Choose*, pp.54–64.
14. The series of reports on the 'Standing' reference published between 1975 and 1979 are especially useful:
RCDIW Report No.1, *Initial Report on the Standing Reference*, London; HMSO, Cmnd 6171, 1975.
Report No.4, *Second Report on the Standing Reference*, London; HMSO, Cmnd 6626, 1976.
Report No.5, *Third Report on the Standing Reference*, London; HMSO, Cmnd 6999, 1977.
Report No.7, *Fourth Report on the Standing Reference*, London; HMSO, Cmnd 7595, 1979.
Report No.8, *Fifth Report on the Standing Reference*, London; HMSO, Cmnd 7679, 1979.
15. RCDIW Background Paper No.3, R. Dinwiddy and D. Reed: *The Effects of Certain Social and Demographic Changes on Income Distribution*, London; HMSO, 1977, is the best account.
16. RCDIW Report No.7, *Fourth Report on the Standing Reference*, London; HMSO, Cmnd 7595, p.17. The stability was of a fairly generous share. The top 40 per cent of households had 68.1 per cent of total pre-tax income in 1949, 68 per cent in 1959 and 66.8 per cent in 1976.
17. R.M. Titmuss, *Income Distribution and Social Change*, London: Unwin, 1962; J.A. Brittain, 'Some Neglected Features of Britain's Income Levelling', AER *Papers and Proceedings*, 1960, pp.593–603.
18. 'Some Neglected Features of Britain's Income Levelling', p.593.
19. RCDIW Report No.7, p.75.
20. R. Layard *et al.*, *The Causes of Poverty*, Royal Commission on the Distribution of Income and Wealth, Background Paper No.5, London; HMSO, 1978, p.72, For the US the effects of unemployment on poverty are discussed in C.E.Metcalf, *An Econometric Model of the Income Distribution*, Chicago; Markham, 1972.
21. Author's calculations from DE data.
22. We lack for Britain distributions of pay on similar lines to those used by Henle and Ryscavage in the US, but the *New Earnings Survey* can be reworked to show income frequencies.
23. CSO, 'The Effects of Taxes and Benefits on Household Income 1980', *Economic Trends*, January 1982, p.105. This article appeared after this chapter had been written. The share of the top tenth in final income rose from 22.2 per cent in 1976 to 23.1 per cent in 1980. The Gini coefficient for final income rose from 30.2 per cent in 1976 to 32.3 per cent in 1980.
24. RCDIW Report No.8, p.20.
25. This is developed in J. Goldthorpe *et al.*, *Social Mobility and Class Structure in Modern Britain*, Oxford; Clarendon Press, 1980.
26. The best study is D. Seers, *The Levelling of Incomes Since* 1938, Oxford; Basil Blackwell, 1951.
27. Titmuss, *Income Distribution and Social Change*, p.41.
28. The definition is further discussed in P. Doeringer and M. Piore, *Internal Labour Markets and Manpower Analysis*, Lexington, Mass., D.C. Heath & Co., 1971, and in N. Bosanquet and P. Doeringer, 'Is There a Dual Labour Market in Great Britain?', *Economic Journal*, June 1973, pp.421–35.

29. P. Henle and P. Ryscavage, 'The Distribution of Earned Income Among Men and Women', 1958–77, *Monthly Labor Review*, April 1980, p.9.
30. RCDIW Report No.5, and extracts in A.B. Atkinson, *Wealth, Income and Inequality*, Oxford; Oxford University Press, 1980, pp.79–99. The Gini coefficient increased from 39.5 in 1967 to 41.8 in 1974 for household income.
31. A. Marshall, *Principles of Economics*, London; Macmillan, 1964, p.466.
32. The best statement of a revisionist view is L. Thurow, *Generating Inequality*, London; Macmillan, 1976.
33. Pensioners and single parents generally qualify for the higher 'long-term' rates. Unemployed people remain on the short-term rate.
34. DHSS Statement, March 1982.
35. Frank Field, *Inequality in Britain*, London; Fontana, 1981, pp.53–4.
36. R.H. Fox *et al.*, 'Body Temperature in the Elderly; A National Study of Physiological, Social and Environmental Conditions', *British Medical Journal*, 27 January 1973, pp.200–6.

10 Government and Social Security

We have so far argued that in principle a stable society requires an institution called 'government' and that the natural course of distribution is not benign. We turn now to the actual activities of government. Much of the New Right's argument has been that whatever principle is adopted, the activities of government are so wasteful and misdirected that we would be better off with much less of it. We now examine the argument as it applies to social security.

It is an old one going back to *Capitalism and Freedom* in 1962.[1] The New Right's case against social security has developed over the years and has changed in its emphasis. The early argument can be summed up as follows:

1. Social security is misleadingly labelled as an 'insurance scheme'. In fact it is nothing of the sort because individual benefits are not related to individual contributions.
2. Social security is an unnecessary interference with freedom. The individual can be left to decide what amount of security he wants for the future.
3. There might be a problem that some people would decide not to save for their old age and to rely instead on welfare payments. This difficulty could be overcome by making it compulsory to purchase annuities.
4. The social security system is paid for by a regressive tax which is particularly hard on those who enter the labour force early and have a short life expectancy. It provides for an arbitrary and unnecessary redistribution in favour of the better off.

To these old arguments can be added two others:

5. Buchanan has maintained that there could be other ways of affecting a transfer between the generations, if this were desired, than through a social security system. This kind of transfer is quite compatible with the denationalisation of pensions.[2]
6. Feldstein has argued that social security has inhibited private savings and economic growth. 'How would our economy be different if the rate of saving were substantially higher? To be specific in my answers let me use the estimate that social security reduces the nation's rate of saving by about 35 per cent. If this asset substitution had not occurred the long-run capital stock would be significantly higher than it currently is. This would imply that gross national product would rise by about 20 per cent.'[3] Further loss could be avoided by changing over to a funded system.

Against these arguments have to be set the traditional defence of the social security system. The alternative is a system of private insurance with some form of payment to those without any resources. Assuming that such payments were set at a subsistence level, there would be a clear disincentive to save. There is also an argument from 'myopia'. People may be short-sighted about a retirement which seems far in the future. Munnell has also looked at the weaknesses of private insurance schemes: that they have had difficulties in providing adequate vesting in protecting the pensions of those who change employers; their provisions for widows have been poor, and, as is generally admitted, they are not able to provide for indexation against inflation.[4]

The arguments have been partly about principles and partly about the practices of existing schemes. There are some issues which, though important, are not fundamental. For example, the presentation and labelling of the American social security scheme has been changed so that it is clearly not presented as a scheme of individual insurance. We shall argue that in principle there are strong reasons why government should have to run social security. The first is that only government can lay claims on future earnings from human capital. Private pensions schemes must invest in physical capital. As the economy develops, the relative importance of physical capital declines and that of human capital increases. Pensions are related to levels of pay – the pattern of returns on human capital. To stake everything on private pensions is to presume that the returns on physical capital would finance payments which are related to the expanding returns on human capital. Only government is in a position to make commitments of future earnings from human capital.

The second argument is about the nature of the social security system and the redistribution which it brings about. A large part of the New Right's case is that it does not bring about a redistribution. But the case concerns mainly those who are still in the labour force – the low-earners as against the high-earners. There is another important kind of redistribution which it does not take into account. This is the distribution between men and women. Because of differential survival, the great majority of those who draw their pensions in old age are women: in Britain, 60 per cent of the population between 65 and 74 are women and of people over 85, 75 per cent are women.[5] Their pensions are not in any way related to either their own or their husbands' contributions. The system is highly redistributive between men and women. It is difficult to see how a privately based scheme could bring this about.

Could private schemes really do as much as the New Right anticipates? It is not clear why, with all the New Right's insistence on the need for economic change, it is sensible to tie pension arrangements to firms which are very likely to change their identity. They will then be forced either to renege on their obligations or to hand over to their successors commitments which are bound to hold back growth.

The social security system in the United States began in 1935. In Britain and in European countries it has a much longer history. Since 1935, the distribution of income has changed quite radically in all advanced countries. There has been a decline in the share of income coming from capital and a rise in the share of income coming from work. There has also been a decline in the share of income from rent. As both Friedman and Johnson have pointed out many times, these changes reflect the increasing importance of human capital as opposed to physical capital. Changes in technology have made training and skills of new kinds more, rather than less, important. Industry increasingly relies more on specialised knowledge than on specialised plant. Old skills may have become obsolete, but there is a strong demand for new ones. In addition, there have been changes in the bargaining power of capital and of labour which have increased the returns to labour. These changes during most of the post-war period have produced an economy with two features: rising per capita real income, and falling returns to capital.

Within this economy, there has been a consensus that people who were past retirement age should share in the real income gains being made by people in employment or at least have their incomes maintained in real terms. The usual arrangement made under 'good' pension schemes is that the pension paid is some proportion (usually one-half) of income in the final or nearly final years of work, and that this should be up-rated by the price index. In both Britain and America, pensioners have tended to do better than this because their net real incomes have risen compared with those of the employed population. The new pensions scheme in Britain will operate on the normal system of 'good' pensions schemes in providing half-pay on retirement. Under these 'good' schemes, pensions are set by the real level of labour market earnings in the years before retirement. For those entering the labour force in 1981, pensions will be set by the amount of pay expected around 2021.

Private pension schemes can invest in a range of assets, from equities through real property to bonds. But none of these assets capture the full extent of the increased return on human capital, which accrues directly to individuals as increased pay. Insurance companies cannot invest in this directly. They have to find the best proxy which may be investment in equities. However, returns on equities reflect the low returns on physical capital as well as the higher returns on firms which rely on the more advanced kind of human capital. It would have been impossible for private pensions schemes to meet the social norm for good pensions schemes for today's generation of pensioners. A pensioner who retired in 1975 has a pension related to the real level of labour market income in the early 1970s. Insurance companies could not have received high enough returns from the declining share of physical capital to pay pensions of this level. Only the state through its taxing power can pay pensions at the level required by accepted social norms out of current labour market income.

What forces will influence the level of labour market incomes in 2020? It could be argued that there will be a rise in the returns on physical capital. It could also be argued, as Feldstein has done, that the social security system could be adjusted to bring into being a larger stock of physical capital.[6] However, this assumes that it is possible to raise the demand for physical capital. It is not enough simply to increase its supply. The new funded social security system might well run into exactly the same problems of declining returns on physical capital that have affected private pension schemes. A funded state social security system is pointless in that it destroys the main reason for having a state financed scheme – its ability to raise levies out of labour market income. It is also highly doubtful whether such a system would achieve its aim of raising investment in physical capital relative to human capital. The change has come for all kinds of reasons and it is highly doubtful whether the addition of another investment fund, however large, would reverse it.

It seems likely that the share of income to human capital will continue to rise and that there will not be an increased return on physical capital to pay higher pensions in 2020. Once we accept that society should meet a certain norm of guaranteed real income for the elderly, it becomes impossible to meet this through conventional investment techniques.

In the last few years the Western world has experienced various degrees of recession. Recession involves a combination of declining or static real incomes together with declining returns on physical capital. A recession makes more difficult the financing of pensions from the returns on physical capital because these have fallen even further. It also would make it more difficult for those at the end of the labour market queue to get adequate pensions through private coverage. Recession brings into play the older argument for social security – it is the only way in which those with low incomes in work and spells of unemployment will get adequate pensions.

It could be argued that government could top up private provision. Feldstein has suggested that government could issue index-linked bonds. Buchanan has made a similar suggestion.[7] But this, particularly with compulsion to buy annuities, as suggested by Buchanan, would bring about a considerable amount of bureaucratic interference and of public expenditure with no redistributive results at all. The New Right has found one weakness of social security systems – that they are financed in ways which are more onerous to the low paid. But this is not the only issue of redistribution. An adverse finding here does not add up to a judgement on all aspects of the system. The New Right ignores the fact that the system has brought about a very considerable redistribution between the generations, between men and women and between retired people who were lower paid and today's higher paid. The New Right claims to be in favour of abolishing poverty. Yet it is prepared to condemn a system that had led to very large reductions in poverty in old age both in Britain and in the USA.

The complaints of the New Right about the lack of redistribution may seem rather paradoxical. It might well be that a state social security system cannot win. If it is financed by progressive taxation it will be condemned as a step towards the dreaded equality of income. If it is regressive it is condemned as being unfair on the poor. The New Right has it both ways. In so far as social security brings about a transfer from young to old, it is condemned for weakening the bonds of the family. 'Children helped their parents out of love or duty. They now contribute to the support of someone else's parents out of compulsion and fear. The earlier transfers strengthened the bonds of the family; the compulsory transfers weaken them.'[8] If it does not bring about such a transfer it is condemned as inequitable.

There are questions of fact and questions of value to be sorted out. We can ask what the social security system actually does and then ask what it should do. Friedman gives the impression that the social security system has been redistributive away from the poor. 'In addition to the transfer from young to old, Social Security also involves a transfer from the less well off to the better off.'[9] He says this about the present, but it could be a hypothetical statement about the future – that the rich may get larger returns on contributions than do the poor. However, that will depend on the future levels of benefit. Experience has shown that all groups, and especially the poor, have made large gains in relation to their contributions. The hypothetical statement should include two qualifications. One that Friedman makes is that the benefit pattern is biased towards the poor. But he does not add the more important qualification that mortality is heavily unfavourable to men in all social classes. 'At the other end of the life cycle, persons with lower incomes on the average have a shorter life span than persons with higher incomes.'[10] This effect has been more than offset in Britain by the differential survival of elderly women.

A truer picture of the effect of social security in Britain and the USA is that of extensive redistribution. The benefits paid to today's pensioners are far greater than the contributions they paid. The tax-payers have been rather more generous than seemed likely either at the time of the 1935 Social Security Act in the USA or the 1942 Beveridge report in Britain. Differences in definition create problems for international comparisons of changes in poverty, but both in Britain and in the United States there is certainly less hardship among the elderly than twenty years ago. In Britain the proportion of elderly defined as poor by the usual supplementary benefit standard fell from a half to a third betwen 1961 and 1979.[11]

The fullest study of the redistributive effects of the social security system in the past is that by Parsons and Munro. They conclude that 'The current social security system has been a profitable venture for workers in past and even current cohorts. . . . For a single male retiring in 1970 at age 65 after 33 years in the system, a substantial 68 per cent of his benefits were (are) unearned. The welfare component for a married man of 65 with a non-working spouse (over age 62) is higher since such men qualify for additional benefits (about 50 per cent) without additional tax liabilities.'[12]

The New Right also argues that the state monopoly in social security chokes private initiative. It limits people's freedom to provide for their old age in their own way and limits the scope for voluntary effort to support the elderly. Friedman implies that in the absence of social security there would be free and voluntary support of elderly people by their children. It is not clear what is likely to happen to those many elderly people who either have no children or are no longer in touch with them. Nor is it clear how the children, even if they wanted to, could make transfers on this scale if they have children of their own to support. The fact of longevity is also against the argument. Some very old people outlive their children or have children who are themselves in retirement. There is also a small matter of the enormous revulsion which most elderly people have at the idea of being dependent on their children. Impractical and unpleasant as the arrangement would be, it lacks historical reality. Old age was never an idyllic time of disinterested support; it was more often a grim period of extreme poverty ending in the workhouse.

More common is the contention that private saving and private pensions could do the job which social security now does. It is hard to fit this in with the facts about the development of private pensions in the USA and in Britain. In both countries private pension schemes have provided inadequate coverage for small firms, have been unable to provide adequate transferability and to compensate for inflation. At most a third of employees in small firms are covered by private pensions. This is partly a matter of the economics of small groups in the insurance market. As Feldstein has pointed out, 'insurance companies generally cannot sell actuarially fair policies to individuals or very small groups'.[13] This is understandable: but what would not be understandable would be to base a social security policy on the assumption that those difficulties could somehow be overcome magically. They are so serious that less than half the employees in the private sector in the USA are covered by private pension schemes. Many of these pensions are of little use because they are incompletely vested. In 1979, 42 per cent of active workers were covered by a private pension but only 25 per cent were vested. The loss of pension can be quite great as a result of incomplete vesting. In 1972 only 72 per cent of retired men and 55 per cent of retired women who had been covered by an occupational pension in their longest job were actually receiving benefits from a private pension.[14] Private schemes have also been unable to provide index-linked benefits.

Private plans have made some attempt to protect existing pensioners. But the American evidence suggests that the attempt has been inadequate. A Banker's Trust study of private pension plans looked at the record for adjusting the pensions of people who retired in the mid-1960s. The average increase in pensions between 1969 and 1975 for a person who retired in mid-1960s was 16 per cent. This only partially compensated for the 47 per cent increase in the consumer price index over the period. The most detailed study of the future outlook for indexation, that of Munnell in the *New England Economic Review* suggests that it is impossible for private schemes to index pensions unless the government issues index-linked bonds.[15] It would be difficult for government to do this without serious disruption to private capital markets. The bonds would be so much more favourable as a long-term hedge against inflation than any other type of asset that there would be a large movement of capital towards them. This might be less serious if the private sector issued index-linked bonds at the same time, but it is unable to do so. The issue of index-linked bonds, as part of an operation to bolster up private pensions schemes or to fund pension schemes, would have the effect of creating more difficult conditions for private investments in real assets. The aim is to encourage growth of capital stock. This is done through funding the public scheme and encouraging the development of private ones. But if we retain the aim of indexing pensions, such funding implies access to index-linked assets. The issue of such assets would disturb savings and investment in the private economy. The swing to private pensions might in practice not have the desirable effect intended on the size of the capital stock.

Apart from all these practical difficulties there is a more general objection to reliance on private firms as the main source of pensions. The New Right has stressed the benefits of a dynamic economy in which competition will bring into being new firms and make the old inefficient or obsolete ones disappear. It would also argue that in the American economy such changes were common. The whole case against the Galbraithian thesis rests on this. Over long periods large firms will change identity. Is it sensible to tie long-term pension commitments to firms which may not exist when the pensions come to be drawn? The new firms could take over the pension obligations of the old; but this would involve a complex bureaucracy and impose higher costs on the new firms. The New Right also stresses the desirability of workers being willing to move between jobs. Private pension schemes would inhibit mobility. If the aim is to create conditions favourable to change, the encouragement of employer-based pension schemes is the least obvious way of bringing this about.

A social security system has the difficult job of meeting various conflicting requirements over a period so long that risk merges into a more generalised uncertainty. It has to provide a minimum income for all, while maintaining income for those in retirement. It is under pressure both to narrow and to preserve income differentials. It has to meet the conventional commitment that pensions will be related to the real value of labour market income in the years before retirement. It has to do this during a time of economic and demographic change. Nobody can predict conditions in 2020 when today's entrants to the labour force will be retiring.

In such uncertainty, a social security system is a better buy than any realistic alternative. It can relieve poverty while at the same time providing for income maintenance on an indexed basis. The system is administered by the agency which can cover the largest group and which has the most stable long-term identity. It is financed by the only agency which can draw directly on the rising earnings of human capital. Many criticisms can be made of the existing systems in the way that they are presented and financed. But these criticisms made by Friedman and others surely do not undermine the fundamental case for state social security.

The case also needs to be set against the arguments for the two most likely alternatives: a minimum level of payment on a welfare or supplementary benefit basis through a residual state scheme combined with reliance on funded private schemes and a minimum level of payment through a negative income tax system combined with funded private schemes.

The choice cannot be made simply in the abstract or on the assumption that there is an immaculate alternative to social security which is completely free of all disadvantages. The choice has to be made in the light of feasible alternatives. The first alternative, the combination of welfare with private funding, is not a stable one if the commitment to index the real level of incomes in retirement is maintained. Privately funded schemes will be unable to meet this commitment. They will also be unable to give adequate cover to people who change jobs or who have breaks in service. They are especially unlikely to provide adequate cover for women. Under this system there is likely to be a gradual rise in the number of people relying on welfare payments. If these welfare payments are set very low, the standard of living for many elderly people will become unacceptably low compared with the average standard. If they are more generous, there will be a disincentive towards relying on private coverage.

The most canvassed alternative to social security has been negative income tax. This scheme sets a break-even level of income. A household with an income below that break-even level will get all or some of the difference between its actual income and the break-even level. A household with an income above that level will pay tax in the normal positive way. The payment is made to those who qualify because their incomes are low rather than on grounds of being sick, unemployed or retired.

The critical problem is that of the size of the 'negative' payment. On a generous scheme the break-even level of income might be set at the level of the supplementary benefit rate. If households are not worse off than under the present system the break-even level would be about 40 per cent of average earnings. The marginal tax rate required to finance this payment together with other government spending would be about 55 per cent, which is above the tax rate on high incomes, under the present scheme.[16] Thus a generous negative income tax system would require very high rates of tax above the break-even level. It would also have effects on labour market incentives. These would be serious both for people who were getting the negative payment and for those who were paying the heavier tax rates.

It would be possible to set a break-even level of income lower than the current supplementary benefit level of payment or to cover only part of the gap between actual and break-even income. Thus if the tax rate were 33 per cent claimants might only get one-third of the difference between their income and the break-even level. But this would produce a much lower level of payment for many people than does the current system. Friedman himself has in fact now admitted that a negative income tax is not possible 'so long as it is not politically feasible to reduce the payments to many persons who now receive high benefits from multiple current programmes'.[17] He hopes that what is politically feasible today may become politically feasible tomorrow, but it seems unlikely that a programme which would involve such major reductions in benefit levels would find much favour.

There have been modified schemes based on much lower levels of payments. One such is Colin Clark's reverse income tax. This also introduces a test so that only those who were sick, unemployed or retired could in fact get the payment.[18] In effect this is a form of welfare payment rather than a negative income tax. In practice it would turn out to be rather like the supplementary benefit system but with lower rates of payment.

The evidence in fact suggests that the present social security system is quite an effective way of helping people with low incomes. About 83 per cent of social security payments were received by households which would have been poor without the payments. In Beckerman's term the 'vertical efficiency' of the system is high.[19] The current system also gives payment only to those who cannot work. It does not raise all the problems of labour market incentive which would be there under negative income tax.

There are certainly problems with social security systems. Both in Britain and in America they have been financed through regressive forms of payroll tax. They are affected by demographic changes and in the long term these suggest that the burden on the state (the tax-payers) may become heavier. But this problem of increasing burden would be there in the two alternative systems – unless funded private pension schemes could provide indexed benefits. If the aim is to preserve the real incomes of the elderly in retirement, state social security is the 'least worst' system. Other systems would be possible only if this aim were abandoned.

References

1. M. Friedman, *Capitalism and Freedom*, Chicago; University of Chicago Press, 1962, pp.182–9.
2. J.M. Buchanan, 'Social Insurance in a Growing Economy: a Proposal for Radical Reform', *National Tax Journal*, Vol.XIII, No.4, 1968, pp.386–95.
3. M. Feldstein, 'Social Security', in M. Boskin (ed.), *The Crisis in Social Security*, Boston; Institute for Contemporary Studies, 1977, p.23.
4. Alicia H. Munnell, 'The Impact of Inflation on Private Pensions', *New England Economic Review*, March/April 1979, pp.18–29.
5. CSO, *Social Trends*, London; HMSO, 1981, p.14.
6. 'Social Security', p.23.
7. 'Social Security', p.19; 'Social Insurance in a Growing Economy: a Proposal for Radical Reform', pp.386–95.
8. M. Friedman and R. Friedman, *Free to Choose*, London; Secker and Warburg, 1980, p.106.
9. *Free to Choose*, p.106.
10. *Free to Choose*, pp.106–7.
11. Author's calculations.
12. D.O. Parsons and D. Munro, 'Inter-Generational Transfers in Social Security', in Boskin (ed.), *The Crisis in Social Security*, p.84.
13. 'Social Security', p.19.
14. Gayle Thompson, 'Pension Coverage and Benefits 1972: Findings from the Retirement History Study', *Social Security Bulletin*, February 1978, pp.3–17.
15. Quoted in Alicia Munnell, 'The Impact of Inflation on Private Pensions', *New England Economic Review*, March/April 1979, p.25.
16. David Collard, 'Social Dividend and Negative Income Tax', in C. Pond, C. Sandford and R. Walker (eds.), *Taxation and Social Policy*, London; Heinemann, 1980, p.192. The difficulties are also well discussed by D. Piachaud, 'Taxation and Social

Security', in Pond, Sandford and Walker, *Taxation and Social Policy*, and in the Report of the Meade Committee, *The Structure and Reform of Direct Taxation*, London; Institute for Fiscal Studies, 1978.
17 *Free to Choose*, p.126.
18. C. Clark, *Poverty Before Politics*, London; ILEA, 1977.
19. W. Beckerman, 'The Impact of Income Maintenance Payments on Poverty in Britain 1975', *Economic Journal*, June 1979, p.276.

11 The National Health Service

The debate among economists about government failure in the National Health Service is now twenty years old. It has been a debate with serious practical impact, and has contributed to the current growth of private health insurance. A Conservative Minister of Health recently set an aim in 1980 of shifting towards a system of health care in Britain which would have 25 per cent in the private sector rather than the current 5 per cent. The debate has often been acrimonious and has ranged widely between first principles and detailed evidence.

We shall begin with principles, asking whether there is a case for an institution such as the NHS. The argument then moves to evidence. We need a serious examination of the weaknesses of the NHS. It certainly has some, but the New Right treatment of the factual issues has been tendentious. Finally, we try to draw up a balance sheet for the NHS. The main propositions are as follows:

1. There is an economic case for the NHS. So far from being a glaring example of government failure, it represents the least worst solution. The 'pure' market solution is not possible and the alternative solution based on subsidies to demand and third party payment is less satisfactory than a system which intervenes on both the supply and on the demand sides. Ironically the advocates of the market have ended up advocating cost-plus systems of payment while the advocates of state action are pressing for a system which forces practitioners to make rather tough choices at the margin.
2. Much of the empirical evidence put forward by the New Right about the NHS is weak. It is far from adequate to prove its unanimous and strong conclusions that the NHS is a bad thing.
3. The balance sheet of the NHS's successes and failures has enough positive results to suggest that it would be doctrinaire to drop it. Some of the failures might be even greater under a market system.

The Economic Case for the NHS

How has the debate on these general issues developed? We begin by summarising the main conceptual approaches of Lees, Seldon and Friedman.[1] They argue that the demand side of the health market has consumers with preferences, that health care is, by and large, a commodity like any other, and that households should be left free to choose the pattern of consumption which suits their own preferences. The supply side of the health market will adjust to this pattern of preferences. Government intervention will ruin the fit between demand and supply. This problem will be most serious where government intervention takes the form of a free service. In such a service there will have to be rationing, probably by social status and political pull. This rationing will be even less fair than rationing by price. The NHS is virtually a monopoly which destroys consumer freedom, reduces the supply of services below what they would be under market conditions, reduces the flexibility and variety of services and is forced into unpleasant forms of rationing.

Against all this has usually been set a range of arguments about the different characteristics of health care. In the 1960s these arguments were usually put in terms of characteristics on the demand side which justified state intervention. The demand for health care was unpredictable. No one can predict when he or she is going to become ill and illness may carry heavy costs. There were possible externalities: my decision on whether to get my infectious disease treated affects your chance of catching it. The market was characterised by a peculiar difficulty in getting information about the quality of care provided by the medical profession. Finally it was possible to assess need separately from demand.[2]

In the late 1960s the defence of the NHS began to stress its role in drawing on altruism. I have an interest in ensuring that you get a good standard of health care, not just in my own demand but in yours as well. There are 'externalities' in consumption. If you lack adequate health care, my impulse is to help you get it. Government in meeting the demand for health care by certain people, is simply giving effect to these altruistic impulses. There might have been other ways in which such altruism could have become effective, but the NHS with its emphasis on the same quality of service for all irrespective of income was the fullest way to give it expression.[3]

The emphasis on the demand side has given way in the last decade to much greater concentration on special difficulties in supply. The case for government intervention now starts from the supply side. Health care is supplied for payment by third parties, whether these are insurance companies or tax-payers. The consumer is not facing a price at the point of consumption. Nor is he seeking a service which can be easily defined. He is seeking something called effective treatment and in the definition of such treatment he has to leave a great deal of discretion to the doctors. Doctors are not the profit-maximising firms found in normal markets. The profession as a whole restricts entry and this restriction leads to an element of monopoly power. This is an old argument; more important today is the effect of the spirit of emulation among doctors. Their true reward lies in the approval and respect of their peers. This usually lies in the development of advanced techniques and glamour medicine. There is a general spirit of service but this is translated into particular kinds of care by a closed group operating outside market constraints. The new supply-side analysis emphasises the importance of medical discretion. It also stresses the sheer difficulty of measuring effectiveness, and the possibility that acute medical care has become increasingly ineffective.

The debate about 'effectiveness' in treatment started outside economics but has been used to strengthen the economic case for state intervention. It has also given more precise content to the old idea that the consumer lacked information. He is now held to be unable to get information about effective treatment. Different amounts of health spending between countries do not seem to make much difference to mortality and to morbidity. Improvements in health status seem more related to social change and to preventive measures. Fees for service systems of payment encourage people to ignore these issues of effectiveness, and they stimulate over-treatment and over medication. This kind of argument suggests a social decision beyond the individual decisions taken by doctors about patients. There should be a social decision on whether a whole pattern of care is effective or ineffective. Short-run individual decisions by doctor and patient must stay within the accepted pattern: but there are long-run collective decisions about whether a pattern of care as a whole is effective or not. There is also the possibility of changing the pattern of incentives for individuals which would alter that pattern.

'The fundamental issue', wrote Lees some twenty years ago, 'is whether the supply of medical care should be based on the principle of consumer sovereignty or be made the subject of collective provision.'[4] The argument turns on whether consumer sovereignty is possible in any true sense when the supply side of the health industry has such particular features. The basic difference of view can be seen most clearly if we relate it to a specific fact. The United States spends a much higher proportion of GNP on health services than does the UK: 9.3 per cent for the US and 6 per cent for Britain. For the New Right this reflects the fact that consumer preferences have more impact in the US.[5] Consumers there have wanted to spend more on health care, while in the UK the amount spent has been rationed by bureaucrats. The alternative view would stress the effects of third party payment and medical emulation in leading to an expansion in glamour medicine which had little beneficial effect on people's health. The fundamental issue here is the pattern of incentives and institutions on the supply side which would best serve the consumer's interest in effective health care. The opponents of the New Right argue that the system should aim to maximise the long-run supply of effective health care within a budgetary framework which forces account to be taken of the opportunity costs of extra health spending.

The New Right also has firm views on how far its market system contributes to equality or to the treatment of those in the greatest need. It is suspicious of the whole idea of need: in practice there will be a big overlap between need and effective demand. Even poor people will make the effort to pay and thus to turn need into demand. If they want treatment they will make the effort to get it. A market system will free the poor from the queues and subservience which are their lot under tax financing. According to Seldon the NHS rations by 'influence and bully power' which is more objectionable than rationing by price.[6] Some kind of state intervention may be needed to help people with medical catastrophes, but even there in Friedman's view philanthropy can do the job.[7] There are 'long-term chronic cases of old and mental patients', but they can easily be taken care of by a residual tax-financed service.[8] In general rationing by price is a fairer system of meeting need than rationing in other ways.

Finally, the New Right believes that the market will show more flexibility on the supply side than the NHS. The NHS is a monopoly or a monolith which impedes innovation.

There are three general economic issues in the debate as it stands today. One is the role of the consumer and how far it is possible to have true consumer sovereignty in health services. The second is about the pattern of need or what degree of inequality in health care would be tolerated. The third issue is about the best way of securing flexibility and innovation. Can any firm propositions be made after twenty years of this debate?

Consumers exercise their preferences in markets by spending money and this brings about adjustments in the pattern of supply. But it does seem clear that direct payment without reimbursement is the exception in health. The consumer is not often paying at the point of consumption. He is paying for insurance or paying income tax. He does not express his preference by an act of payment. This would seem to be a vital difference between health care and the market. The New Right may then argue that non-profit third parties such as Blue Cross or Blue Shield will get closer to the consumer's own preferences than would government. But this takes us well away from the usual set of arguments about the superiority of the market into issues which are highly debatable. We do not have a market system which is driven by the consumer dollar vote, even in Australia or the United States. In France direct payment is followed by reimbursement.

Thus on the demand side the principle of third party payment is inescapable. It is also clear that the pattern of illness has required the introduction of large government subsidies on the demand side. Insurance schemes are not able to guarantee care for 'bad risks' such as people requiring long-term care and people over 65. As the number of old people increases governments have had to introduce subsidies of the

Medicare type. The New Right would argue that such subsidies reflect a process of vote-buying rather than a genuine response to need. It might prefer a programme of help limited to the truly indigent but it has never been very explicit about this, and the fact remains that insurance-based systems have had great difficulty in guaranteeing cover to a large minority. The overlap between 'demand' and 'need' is not as close as the New Right suggests.

The choice on the demand side then is not between a market system and a government monopoly free at the point of consumption. It is between a national system of health care and a system of third party payment with quite extensive subsidies to those who cannot get coverage. Even in insurance-based systems, governments have intervened to bridge the gap between demand and need. The New Right's preferred system has had to be adjusted to secure a more tolerable degree of inequality.

The New Right's view of the supply side stresses the range of experiment and innovation that will come about under a market system. The medical profession will adjust its methods to meet preferences in the market. The New Right has taken part in the older debate about monopoly power restricting entry to the medical profession. It admits the existence of such restrictions but whatever the position revealed by Friedman's own research on the 1920s and 1930s, it would deny their importance today.[9] It has said little, however, about the goals and motivations of the medical profession. It seems to assume that doctors are profit-maximising businessmen serving customers in the same way as garages and supermarkets. It has had little to say about the economics of professions. But there would seem to be some special features about the medical profession. Doctors are not selling a product which is specific but are offering a general undertaking to give service in the best interests of the patient. They have a professional code of altruism and service to humanity. They are also subject to pressures of emulation. Their performance is assessed and weighed by their fellows rather than directly by consumers. There is one more special feature of growing importance: the ambiguity of their role as managers. They are making decisions which affect large numbers of other people and large amounts of money yet they are not responsible for managing the people or finding the money. In a market the producer has to meet the costs arising from his own production decisions, but this is not so in the medical case. The pure market system is not a reality on the supply side. In reality there are only two possible budgetary contexts for medicine. One is a cost-plus system of financing. In this doctors decide what is best for the patient from a peculiar mixture of motives, some altruistic and some self-regarding. Their decisions are partly influenced by the Hippocratic Oath and partly by the spirit of emulation. They then simply send in the bill for the best treatment to the third party. The alternative system is to set an overall budget within which individual decisions have to be contained. This could be done through an institution such as the NHS or through a system like national health insurance in Canada.

The essential choice is between a cost plus system or one that introduces a budget constraint. The reactions of the medical profession to a cost-plus system of financing might well be such that a very large rise in costs ensued. Professional emulation, the patient's anxiety and the spirit of service could all be powerful influences leading to a rapid increase in active intervention, particularly when there is so much uncertainty about the results of medical intervention.

Increasing numbers of doctors in Britain and in the United States now work in hospitals rather than in surgeries or offices. They are more subject to pressures of professional emulation in hospital and more able to turn their aspirations into reality. The doctor-patient relationship was much simpler before treatment came to be given by large teams using advanced technology. For the critics these changes raise worrying new issues. They quote evidence to suggest that much of the increase in treatment has been ineffective and even positively harmful.[10] The New Right, however, takes a fundamentally different view. The question of effectiveness is irrelevant. If people want the treatment they should have it. It makes no more sense to worry about over-medication than about over-nutrition from eating too much steak or about cars being larger than they need be. An affluent society leads to big increases in many kinds of consumption – why not to more open-heart operations and organ replacements?

But there are more important causes for worry about open-heart operations than about conspicuous consumption of T-bone steaks and Cadillacs. Ineffective medical care of a patient also has effects on third parties, relatives and dependants. The supply of medical care cannot respond to demand in the short run. The pressure of emulation may lead to a rise in the price of medical care which may create severe problems for people with lower incomes – a particularly important argument if 'need' can be distinguished from conspicuous consumption. Finally, there is the structure of the industry on the supply side. In a third party payment system the profession is not subject to the same competitive pressures as are producers in consumer goods markets.

We have argued that there cannot be true consumer sovereignty in the demand for health care. We have also argued that the overlap between demand and need is not close. Demand subsidies of an extensive kind have come into existence throughout the world. We turn now to the issues of flexibility and innovation.

What in principle are the main kinds of flexibility that should be sought for health services? The first general aim is to have an effective and efficient service – one which benefits the patients' health at the lowest cost, consistent with the patients' comfort. There are many detailed decisions to be made, but three general considerations will affect these decisions about efficiency. The first will be whether there is scope for substituting less highly trained staff for scarce and expensive medical staff. The second is the extent to which all people working with the patients work together as a team. The New Right tends to see the problem of flexibility and innovation in terms of dramatic advances usually of surgery by the medical profession working on its own. But the day-to-day care of patients also advances and improves through teamwork to which various professions contribute. In Britain the role of nursing has been particularly important and distinct from that of the medical profession. The organisation of health care should allow room for this teamwork: it should not be a hierarchy dominated by the medical profession. The role of the doctor will always be a great one: but other people – physiotherapists and scientific staff – have their own specific contribution to make.

The third consideration in the search for effectiveness and efficiency will be the scope for choice between hospital and primary community care. There is much more scope now for developing care through family doctors and in the community. A system for organising and financing health care should leave room for choice. The balance between primary and hospital care will also affect effectiveness as well as efficiency. The hospital doctor typically has a short or intermittent relationship with the patient: it may be much more difficult for him to get to know the patient's true situation than it is for the family doctor who can really get to know the patient well. There are different models of health care. One puts the emphasis on specialisation and hospital medicine. The other is a more family-based and preventive system. Both kinds of service have a contribution to make. A system for financing and organising health care should not cramp the freedom of choice for local teams or have a bias to one or other kind of service. It should allow scope for substitution: the deveopment of a team approach, and choice between care in hospital and care in the community. The requirements for flexibility are not only about the most rapid introduction of new techniques in surgery. It is much more important to have a framework in which such innovations are not introduced blindly but fully evaluated in their effect on the patient and if proved successful carried out in an efficient manner.

We can assess an insurance-based scheme against the NHS by these general requirements for flexibility. An insurance scheme usually has two characteristics. It is based on fee for service payment for medical services, with other services attached as secondary bills. It tends to increase the emphasis on the medical profession operating in splendid isolation. It certainly does not encourage substitution and, typically, where such substitution has been suggested, the medical profession has made strenuous efforts to limit it. It does not encourage a team approach. Nursing services for example are a kind of overhead like the bill for catering. Lastly, it does not encourage the development of primary care. In Britain private health insurance is hospital-based. As a former General Manager of BUPA has said, 'It must be stressed, however, that after some unsatisfactory experience with providing cover for general practitioner services, the Provident Associations now supply insurance only for consultants in their private rooms or in hospitals, and for hospital services.'[11]

The NHS has shown a greater ability than insurance-based systems to substitute medical time: to make use of the team approach and to provide a framework in which choices can be made between hospital and community care. Substitution can be seen in hospitals in the wide responsibility of the ward sister and outside hospital in the roles of the district nurse and the health visitor. The team approach is also most clearly seen in the role of nursing in Britain. Primary care through the family doctor has survived in Britain when it has disappeared in other countries. Some of these peculiar features of the British health system were developing long before the NHS, but the NHS has allowed further development of a more varied system than would have come about under an insurance based system.

The New Right and Evidence on the NHS

We turn now to the empirical evidence offered by the New Right about the NHS. The New Right has built up an indictment of failure of the NHS. But the quality of the evidence hardly supports any such clear conclusion. It is far from adequate to prove the New Right's unanimous and clear conclusion that the NHS is a bad thing. In fact any end of the stick has done for this dog. If the NHS spent too much this was an example of bureaucratic waste: too little and this was an example of contempt for consumer preferences.

The New Right's discussions about the NHS tend to have been a by-product – cautionary tales to be used to turn opinion away from 'socialised' medicine. In the US the New Right also makes much use of international comparisons, although in any specific comparison there must be mixed up a general comparison of Britain and America. Health services employ a large number of people in both countries, about one in twenty of the working population. Some occupational groups have skills and ethos which are highly specialised: but the sheer size of the health service sector means that it must be deeply influenced by the society in which it operates. It would also be dangerous to attribute everything that had happened in the UK since 1948 to the NHS and everything that had happened in the US to the market. Health services in Britain and the United States were substantially different well before 1948 and would almost certainly have continued to be different even if there had been no NHS. But the questions about the New Right's treatment of the NHS go far beyond such general reservations.

The New Right has attempted to establish a great number of separate 'facts' about the NHS but they can be summed up into a small number of key assertions.

1. The NHS is a centralised monopoly through which government preferences are imposed on consumers.
2. The NHS is a system which wastes resources in excessive bureaucracy.
3. The NHS is inefficient, in the sense that it uses its resources less intensively than it might. For example the number of cases treated per bed has risen more in the United States than in the United Kingdom.
4. The NHS suffers from a major problem in medical emigration.
5. The NHS has adopted systems of rationing through waiting lists which are much more unpleasant and unfair than the rationing that would come about through a market mechanism.
6. The NHS has shown inflexibility and inability to adopt advanced methods of treatment.

On each of these points the arguments and evidence put forward by the New Right writers have a number of weaknesses. We shall take three sources as reasonably representative. These are Friedman's *Free to Choose*, Seldon's discussions in *Charge* and *Wither the Welfare State* and Cotton Lindsay's *National Health Issues: The British Experience*.[12] Finally we look at the inconsistency of the New Right.

1. The NHS as a monolith

Many discussions and especially those of Seldon present the NHS as a monopoly. The 'welfare state replaced choice for consumers between competing suppliers by monopoly from which there is no escape, except at a cost that the rich can bear better than the poor'.[13]

The NHS is not a monopoly in the sense that the consumer must seek service at one point in the system. It retains (with a few exceptions) choice of doctor and choice of hospital. An individual GP or hospital department is not usually a monopoly in that neither can present the consumer with the choice of getting the service from them or not getting it at all. If the NHS had been based on this kind of local monopoly, there is no doubt that it would have been swept away long ago. There is also the possibility of potential entry by private competition. In fact where the NHS has failed to provide an adequate service that service has been developed outside: such as the abortion service where more than half of operations are now outside the NHS.

The NHS does not confer monopoly power on the local practitioners: in fact hospital departments are in competition for custom and their ability to attract patients affects their prospects for growth or survival. Nor is the manner in which decisions are taken on patterns of care highly centralised. The service was twenty-eight years old before the central authority issued any full statement on priorities.[14] Even then, the priorities were a kind of indicative planning. Some were ignored, such as those on the care of the mentally ill, while others were followed up, such as with the care of geriatric patients. To present the NHS as a highly centralised system in which planners' preferences are ruthlessly imposed on the public is a travesty. Decisions emerge from a very long process of professional and public debate and if anything the pace is arguably too slow.

2. *The NHS as a bureaucracy*

Many arguments have been put to the effect that the NHS employs an excessive number of bureaucrats. Sometimes this is done through plain misrepresentation. Thus Seldon writes 'One figure will illustrate the insatiable appetite of a centralised system for bureaucrats: out of 400,000 nurses in England and Wales, approaching 100,000 (above ward sister) are non-nursing administrators.'[15] In fact the number of non-nursing administrators in England was 11,500, in a total staff of about 400,000 in 1977. The NHS has a real problem with increasing bureaucracy, but it shares this with health systems all over the world. An OECD study in fact showed that the proportion of total expenditure for administrative costs was lower in the UK than in either the US or Europe. General administrative costs were 2.6 per cent of total current outlays in the UK, and 5.3 per cent in the US.[16] The administrative overheads of insurance schemes would seem to be far higher than those of the NHS. Bureaucracy is difficult to measure, but on the tangible evidence of how much of the health care pound gets spent on the patient the NHS scores rather well.

3. *Is the NHS inefficient?*

The older charge is that the NHS does not make proper use of its resources. Its output is lower than that of an alternative system. However there is no agreement about quantity. Some writers conclude that the NHS may indeed perform reasonably well in quantity, but that its main problem is quality of output, that it gives a drab service which does not respect the patients' aspirations for privacy and comfort.

Lindsay maintains that it fails both in terms of quantity and of quality.[17]

Friedman has made some of the most definite statements about the output of the NHS. He contends that between 1965 and 1973 'Output, as measured by the average number of hospital beds occupied daily, actually went *down* by 11 per cent.'[18] He took this statement from a privately circulated document by Dr Max Gammon, which takes the view that 'The primary measure of a hospital's output in relation to its resource requirements [input] is the number of days' treatment which it provides [Patient Bed Days]. This is usually represented by the average number of beds occupied daily.'[19] This judgement puts Dr Gammon and Professor Friedman in a very small minority, possibly of two. The more usual measure of output is that of the number of cases treated. This rose by 15 per cent between 1965 and 1973, as compared with an 11 per cent fall in the number of occupied beds. Even this measure does not fully take into account changes in case-mix and in intensity of treatment for which adjustments would need to be made in order to get a true measure of output.

Lindsay argues that the NHS hospitals will not be concerned to produce efficiently. They are run by bureaucrats who are out for visible rather than useful activity and who will be satisfied with high occupancy rates and excessive length of stay. The main evidence for this is that the NHS has a slower rate of growth in number of patients per bed than the US system, and that length of stay has been greater. However in making the case on patients per bed, which unlike Friedman he accepts as an indicator of output, he does not compare like with like. His figures for hospital beds in the US are taken from hospitals accredited to the American Hospital Association which do not include many psychiatric hospitals or hospitals for mentally handicapped people. His figures for beds in Britain cover all types of hospital. By Lindsay's figures the rate of treatment has changed as follows:[20]

In-patients per available bed year

	US	*UK*
1950	12	6.5
1975/6	24.5	11.0

If we take figures for general hospitals however, the rate of treatment for the NHS has risen from 11 to 21.7: a rise of 97 per cent compared with the rise of 104 per cent in the US.

Lindsay also argues that lengths of in-patient stay are much greater in the NHS. The comparison is made between lengths of stay in US proprietary hospitals and in British hospitals.[21] US hospitals are divided between proprietary (or profit-making) hospitals and voluntary hospitals. Proprietary hospitals only treat about 10 per cent of the total cases and their patients tend to be younger and from higher income groups. They are a highly selected group. It should be stressed that these statements about output are not peripheral to Lindsay's study. They form a major part of the study which was financed by Hoffman-LaRoche and of which a copy was sent to every doctor in the US.

The New Right also criticises the quality of services provided by the NHS. In Lindsay's view, medical care is 'a more varied, higher quality, product' in the US, a meal at 'a gourmet restaurant' rather than a 'Macdonalds dinner'.[22] Seldon has argued, 'Because the NHS can be judged only by quantitative indicators, it puts quantity before quality. In this sense the NHS is the worst medical system in the world outside the Communist/Socialist countries.'[23] He believes that there are 'immeasurable elements' such as 'the waiting and the queuing, the choice of doctor or hospital, the timing of treatment, the responsiveness of doctors and nurses' for which the NHS scores very low.[24] He is certainly wrong in implying there is no choice of doctor or hospital for most patients and there is little strong evidence that doctors and nurses are unresponsive. Certainly waiting lists are a serious problem, but the New Right has not made a conclusive case that the NHS provides a low quality service in those aspects of choice and staff attitudes which most affect the patient's care. It is in any case wrong to judge the NHS performance by invisible or quality aspects of care without considering the family doctor and the community services alongside the hospital service. The main argument used by the New Right has been paradoxically that the NHS spends too much time on the social aspects of care rather than too little. There are problems about quality of care, and the surroundings in which care is given often need improvement. But the New Right claims to have made an indictment of great significance for policy.

4. *The problem of medical emigration*

The New Right has often argued that doctors are queuing up to leave the NHS and to seek their fortunes abroad. This argument has gained some credibility from the fact that for most of the 1950s Governments denied any problem of medical emigration – only to be proved wrong by Abel-Smith and Gales in 1964.[25]

Friedman maintains that 'about one-third as many physicians emigrate each year from Britain to other countries as graduate from its medical schools'.[26] This appears to come from figures for gross emigration. But to get a fair picture we have to consider the flow both ways. Net emigration is about 300–400 or 10 per cent of the output of medical graduates. It has been constant over a long period and has fallen as a proportion of the number of graduates.[27] The number does not seem unreasonable for a large medical system with strong international connections. The expected number of emigrants would not be zero, given that some people undertake training to work abroad (medical missionaries) and some people are interested in specialties such as tropical medicine which have most relevance abroad. The proportion of foreign trained doctors employed in the NHS has remained constant between 1967 and 1977 at around 30 per cent.[28] It is not true to say as Friedman does that 'physicians are fleeing the National Health Service.'[29]

5. The NHS and rationing

The New Right argues that the NHS has adopted forms of rationing which are more unpleasant and socially unjust than rationing by price. It is certainly fair to say that long waiting times for some forms of treatment represent a serious failure by the NHS. However even the New Right admits that people who are seriously ill get rapid treatment.[30] Nor is it true that the NHS must inevitably have waiting lists. There are currently no waiting lists for most kinds of treatment in Scotland and in London.

The waiting list problem is often taken to justify a sweeping change to a market solution. But the actual nature of waiting lists suggests this might not be helpful. Waiting times vary between localities and between age groups. It is elderly patients who are often put on waiting lists for long periods. The service to these places and people needs to be improved – but it is far from clear that a market solution would do this.

6. The NHS's failure to adopt new methods of treatment

This has been a theme only in Seldon's writings. No wonder that while 'the British NHS is slow to innovate in methods of organisation and financing, or even to emulate the pioneering advances in other countries, medical care in the USA displays the widest variety and the most advanced innovations in financing and organising medical service – in health maintenance organisations, pre-paid group practices and other experimental techniques unknown in Britain because they would disturb the smooth running of the centralised NHS.'[31]

Ironically Friedman has strongly criticised the American medical profession for their opposition to HMOs (Health Maintenance Organizations) or pre-paid group practice in the past and even in the last few years the opposition has continued. Friedman wrote in 1962 'There is however no doubt that the tendency towards group practice has been greatly retarded by the AMA's opposition.'[32] Pre-paid group practice is hardly appropriate to the kind of GP service such as exists in Britain. These innovations are curiously advocated in the US in order to bring the service closer to the British model. There is hardly a strong case here.

The Inconsistency of the New Right

The New Right has always been troubled by the low proportion of GNP spent on the NHS. Its main explanation has been the Buchanan thesis of an inconsistency between the individual response on the demand side and the collective response on the supply side.[33] There will be substantial excess demand for a service free at the point of access. But 'Responsible *collective*, i.e. governmental, decision-makers have not expanded investment in supplying health services to the levels of expressed *individual* demands'.[34] The main costs of this inconsistency have been borne by the consumer in terms of increased costs in queuing. The individual citizen has a dual role as a demander of health services and as a potential voter. As a consumer he will select his preferred level of consumption. But as a voter he will take into account the fact that most of any output for which he votes will be used by other people. His supply-side decision will be severely constrained by various spending alternatives – more schools, better housing, larger pensions. The individual taking part in the collective choice process has to balance costs against benefits.

The thesis is difficult to reconcile with the New Right's more general view of the political determinants of spending levels in the public sector. In this more common view, as propounded by Hayek and others, powerful producer groups come to exercise excessive influence over the supply of public services. The process of voting gives greater weight to small intense minorities in contrast to smaller, more apathetic groups. The intense minority of producers acts as a permanent pressure to raise spending levels. At the same time, Niskanen and others have argued that there are supply-side forces that act to raise spending levels by bureaucracies. The bureaucrats' power and status are related to the size and growth of their budgets. From all these points of view, a public service such as the NHS should have shown a rather rapid rate of growth. It quite clearly has not so the New Right has had to fall back on a contingent theory.

The NHS: an Evaluation

We ask now what a fair way to evaluate the NHS would be. The main criticisms can be grouped under two general themes:

1. *Efficiency* that the NHS does not use resources in an effective manner.
2. *Sufficiency* that the NHS system has not led to adequate resources being devoted to the NHS – that its share of GNP has been too low. This means that the NHS gives a minimum service in inadequate buildings.

Some of the NHS troubles could equally well come from either of these causes. A service which is too slow and impersonal could be the result of faults in 'efficiency' or in 'sufficiency'. Is the NHS incapable of giving a good service whatever resources it might have – or is it simply doing the best it can with inadequate resources?

Most of the New Right's detailed analysis has concentrated on the sufficiency theme. The NHS's problems come from the underlying shortage of resources. One definite proposition that does seem to emerge both by implication from the New Right's literature and from a range of other evidence is that the NHS could provide a better service if it had more adequate resources. Thus waiting lists respond to increases in medical time. The service would be given in more pleasant surroundings if the NHS had more to spend on new hospitals. The more usual New Right case against public services is that they could never function effectively whatever the amount of resources they might have – but this is not made strongly about the NHS.

The charge against the NHS is that it has failed to deliver an appropriate level of service. The remedy is to unleash the market; that will bring about a large expansion of hospital-based services for the acutely ill. There can be many arguments for and against; but that is a separate story. The main defect of the NHS in the eyes of the New Right is that it has not provided acute services on the American pattern and on the American scale. The debate, then, has to be about the effectiveness of such services. Ironically the key issue in this debate is not about the market versus the state at all – it is merely about the effectiveness of medical care.

Against this failure of sufficiency has to be set two successes. There is no dissent at any point in the range of opinion that the NHS provides a good service for people who are seriously ill and for emergencies, and has made a sustained attempt to improve services for the elderly, the mentally ill and the mentally handicapped. Especially in the case of the elderly the NHS is in advance of many health services.

It is also common ground that the NHS record measured against mortality and morbidity is at least as good as that of other developed countries.[35] In some parts of the country, however, there is a serious problem of waiting for treatment, but there are other ways of dealing with that than by the rapid adoption of an insurance-based scheme.

The New Right's case against the NHS has a shift of emphasis from the demand side to the supply side. In the 1960s Buchanan was virtually alone in making the case mainly on the supply side. Other critics tended to emphasise how a free service with a positive demand elasticity would be swamped by excess demand. Later emphasis on the costs in time and discomfort involved in queuing have reduced the stress put on this excess demand effect.

Until now we have mainly been discussing arguments about the NHS based chiefly on empirical evidence. But there is another part of the New Right's case which relates to a much more general model of economic behaviour. The New Right holds that a market system would lead to more diversity and flexibility. Seldon again has put the case most fully:

> The NHS has done the health of the people a 'dis-service' because it has prevented the development of more spontaneous, organic, local voluntary and *sensitive* medical services that would have grown up as incomes rose and medical science and technology advanced. If it were not for the *politically*-controlled NHS we should have seen new forms of medical organisation and financing that better reflected *consumer* preferences, requirements and circumstances. [36]

The New Right's views here are open to challenge, partly because they have falsely specified the alternative. The alternatives are not between the NHS and an ideal decentralised market system. It is between the NHS and an insurance type system which would have many elements of standardisation and centralisation. It would have to have some basic level of compulsory premium. Standards would have to be monitored for those who were receiving a subsidised service. There would be problems of cost containment to deal with. The alternative system would have to face the same problems of cost containment and of choice among service priorities as the NHS does.

It can be argued that the NHS has done more to protect and encourage variety than the alternative system would have done. The New Right's system would give more power to the medical profession and to consumers who chose to exercise their purchasing power on the NHS. The likely result would be an increase in hospital-based acute care. The NHS has a better balance between community and hospital care than the system of almost any other developed country. It is doubtful whether an insurance-based system, with its strong medical and consumer compulsion, would adequately provide unglamorous services such as the family doctor service or district nursing. The individual decisions of the most powerful producers and the most powerful consumers may not produce a pattern of health care which is either efficient or equitable. The case for the NHS, it is suggested, should rest on four main arguments. The first is the need for a countervailing power to the medical profession. The New Right admits the need for such a power but finds it in the consumer's money. The old case of the consumer's difficulty in getting information weakens this argument. If the consumer's money is not the effective counterforce, who is to check the medical monopoly? The second main argument for the NHS is the need to give some weighting to the preferences of those groups of consumers – the old, the mentally ill and the disabled – who would have few votes in the market system. Public intervention has resulted in services for these groups which are both more efficient and more equitable. Third, the NHS establishes a budget contraint which makes for more realistic choice of priorities.

Finally there is the single most important argument for the NHS. This is the argument from equality, that people will get care according to need rather than according to income or social position. There are still many inequalities within the NHS: but they are less than those which would be present under an insurance-based system. The NHS may not score well against some ideal standard but it is better than the realistic alternative. In fact these other systems have had to add policies which in effect bring them much closer to the NHS in order to hold inequality within tolerable limits. The introduction and survival of Medicare and Medicaid in the United States is only the most striking example of such changes. Any system based on payment must face major difficulties when illness greatly reduces ability to pay insurance premia. Health care can be seen as a consumer good but it is also a line of defence against threats to life and serious illness. In serious illness the NHS will bring about a closer approach to equality of treatment than will be possible under the most likely alternative.

The more usual defence of the NHS in the past has been its superior social ethic. Titmuss has argued that the NHS and its associated services such as blood donation represent the spirit of altruism, as against the self-interest of the market.[37] American society is usually taken as an example of self interest at work as illustrated by practice in commercial blood donation. Ironically some of the areas of greatest difficulty for Americans have been in institutions such as prisons and long-stay hospitals which are well outside the market. But an even greater difficulty is in confining the comparison of social ethic to health services. Are we really comparing British and American society rather than the two health services? The case for the NHS can be made in rather more specific terms.

References

1. D.S. Lees, *Health Through Choice*, London; IEA, 1961, reprinted in R. Harris (ed.), *Freedom or Free for All*, London; IEA, 1965; A. Seldon, *Wither the Welfare State*, London; IEA, 1981. M. Friedman and R. Friedman, *Free to Choose*, London; Secker and Warburg, 1980, pp.112–15.
2. A good statement of these arguments is to be found in H.E. Klarman, *The Economics of Health*, New York, Columbia University Press, 1965, pp.1–10.
3. C.M. Lindsay, 'Medical Care and the Economics of Sharing', *Economica*, Vol.XXXVI, 1969, pp.351–62; A.J. Culyer, *The Political Economy of Social Policy*, London; Martin Robertson, 1980, is a more recent statement of this case.
4. *Health Through Choice*, p.32.
5. *Wither the Welfare State*, pp.20–24.
6. A. Seldon, *Charge*, London; Temple Smith, 1977, p.86.
7. *Free to Choose*, p.115.

8. *Charge*, p.89.
9. M. Friedman and S. Kuznets, *Income from Independent Professional Practice*, New York; NBER, 1945.
10. The classic discussion is in A.L. Cochrane, *Effectiveness and Efficiency Random Reflections on Health Services*, Nuffield Provincial Hospital Trust, 1972.
11. Hugh Elwell: 'Better Medicine by Better Insurance', in A. Seldon (ed.), *The Litmus Papers*, Centre for Policy Studies, 1980, p.110.
12. C.M. Lindsay, *National Health Issues, The British Experience*, Roche Laboratories, 1980.
13. *Wither the Welfare State*, p.38.
14. DHSS, *Priorities for the Health and Personal Social Services in England*, London; HMSO, 1976.
15. A. Seldon, 'The Next 30 Years . . .?' in Lindsay, *National Health Issues, The British Experience*, p.107.
16. OECD, *Public Expenditure on Health*, Paris; OECD, 1977, p.23.
17. *National Health Issues, The British Experience*, Chapter 4.
18. *Free to Choose*, p.114.
19. Max Gammon, *Health and Security*, London; St Michael's Organisation, 1976, p.30.
20. *National Health Issues, The British Experience*, p.75.
21. *National Health Issues, The British Experience*, p.77.
22. *National Health Issues, The British Experience*, p.56.
23. *Wither the Welfare State*, p.38.
24. *Wither the Welfare State*, p.38.
25. B. Abel-Smith and K. Gales, *British Doctors at Home and Abroad*, Occasional Papers in Social Administration No.8, Welwyn Garden City; Codicote Press, 1964.
26. *Free to Choose*, p.114.
27. DHSS communication to author.
28. *National Health Issues, The British Experience*, pp.64–5.
29. *Free to Choose*, p.114.
30. *National Health Issues, The British Experience*, Chapter 3.
31. *Wither the Welfare State*, p.20.
32. M. Friedman, *Capitalism and Freedom*, Chicago; University of Chicago Press, 1962, p.155.

    There is, however, no doubt that the tendency towards group practice has been greatly retarded by the AMA's opposition. It is interesting . . . that the medical association is against only one type of group practice, namely prepaid group practice.

33. J.M. Buchanan, *The Inconsistencies of the National Health Service*, London; IEA, 1965.
34. *The Inconsistencies of the National Health Service*, p.9.
35. This is accepted by Lindsay in *National Health Issues, The British Experience*, Chapter 2 and by the *Report* of the Royal Commission on the National Health Service, London; HMSO, 1979, Cmnd 7615, Chapter 3.
36. A. Seldon, 'NHS – Success? Still on Trial? Failure?', in *The Litmus Papers*, p.5.
37. R.M. Titmuss, *The Gift Relationship*, London; Allen and Unwin, 1970.

12 Education and Housing

In these different worlds, the New Right has had some similar effects. The detailed issues are very different: but the common effect has been towards a polarisation of opinion. The New Right's main impact has been through proposals to unleash the market. The quality of the supporting argument has often been high but it is the simple policy proposals for vouchers and for ending rent control which have made the major impact.

In education the New Right has had to register failure after a long effort of persuasion. After twenty years of advocacy voucher schemes have been confined to one temporary experiment in a small school district in the outskirts of San José. In housing rent control retains its attractions. In spite of such disappointments the New Right's advocacy continues and dominates debate. The casualty in both cases has been chances for reform in ways which did not mean a simple adoption of market principles. For example in education there is much cause for disquiet in the record of the state education services. But the voucher scheme of the kind advocated by the New Right runs up against the one strongest point in the case for public education.

This is its role in assuring at least a minimal amount of equality of opportunity and equality of respect. The chances of rich and poor children are unequal under the state system but they would be even more unequal under Friedman's variant of the voucher scheme. There are different and better ways towards more choice and more variety in education. There is a strong case for change in the balance between voluntary and state initiative in education, but the chances of such change are much reduced by pre-occupation with a stereotyped confrontation between market and state.

Education

In social security and health services we argued that the New Right's evidence of government failure was weak. Its main failings would be in its adjustment to preferences, in high cost and in unfair financing. Government would fail if its services were out of line with consumers' preferences, interpreted broadly to include potential consumers in need as well as consumers with effective demand. Government would fail if it provided services at significantly higher cost than the market. Government would certainly fail if the net effect of taxation and expenditure was perverse.

In education, the case for government failure rests first on the issue of consumer preference. The system, it is argued, has little to offer working-class children beyond minimum literacy. Their progress is much below that to be expected from their IQs. State education seems to be a service of greatest interest to the middle classes and their children. Working-class children leave school as soon as they can, often playing truant well before the official school-leaving age. In some secondary schools in London and Liverpool, truancy rates run at 20 per cent. The problem is not just one of resources. Expenditure differences within the normal range do not seem to have much effect on outcome. Midwinter has compared Sandwell, an industrial area in the West Midlands, with Stockport which has a much larger proportion of middle-class residents:[1]

	Sandwell	*Stockport*
Teacher/pupil ratio	22.6	22.2
Annual expenditure per pupil (£)	275	248
All further and higher education awards as % of school population	6.5	25.7

There is some contrary evidence, however, that very high spending can make a difference. ILEA spends twice as much as the average on secondary education and children in working-class areas of London seem to do rather better than expected, but the gulf between middle-class and working-class performance is still wide.[2] There is wide agreement that the system fails to meet the preferences or to engage the interest of working-class consumers.

The issue of cost has not arisen here: the other suggested area of government failure is in the balance between expenditure and taxation. Friedman has argued that it is perverse to finance higher education from general taxation.[3] Why should tax-payers finance the acquisition of earning power by people who are likely to be much better off than themselves? This argument has grown in importance as the balance of spending has swung in the past twenty years away from elementary education towards higher education.

Government has some traditional aims which are peculiar to education, and we can measure success or failure by these as well. Typically, the external effects of education are used to justify government intervention. West has shown conclusively that such external effects as the reduction in crime and the contribution of education to a better political order are nebulous.[4] Government intervention has often been justified as a way of creating social solidarity. However, Friedman has argued that schools reflect the nature of the residential community.[5] Children in inner-city ghettos are condemned to schools as bad as their homes, while children in better-off families go to school in the suburbs. We shall argue that the record of the public system is rather more mixed than that stereotype would suggest. Even so, public education has had a disappointingly weak effect in reducing class barriers.

Government spending on education has also been justified according to its effects on economic growth. At macroeconomic level, the crude relationship between educational spending and growth rates in Britain casts some doubt on that. Over the last fifteen years there have been large increases in educational spending in a time of faltering growth rates. The argument has also been made through evidence on rates of return to individuals from particular kinds of education. Such calculations relate the benefits of education, mainly those of higher earnings, to the costs including direct costs and earnings forgone by students.[6] On average the rate of return is positive, although it differs between stages of education; that in the early stages of education being much higher than that in the later ones. There are also differences between the rate of return to the individual and rates of return to society.

Individual rates of return are higher. The size of government subsidies enter into the costs to society but not into the costs of the education of an individual. The economic growth argument for investing in school education is more impressive than that for investing in higher education. But new evidence on the variation of earnings in relation to education has cast further doubt on the whole argument. The rates of return reflect average results, but there is a big overlap in earnings between people with education and those without it. Many people without education earn more than people with it. Much of the gain in earnings for the educated simply reflects the higher ability of some of them – they would earn more whether or not they were educated. Conversely, people with ability earn more without education. Even if all the variations in education were removed – for example, if we were all educated for the same length of time – the variations in earnings would be almost the same.[7]

Of the special arguments for government intervention in education only that for social solidarity retains any real strength. Friedman has argued that different classes and ethnic groups live in separate neighbourhoods and therefore the schools cannot be used to provide a social mix. But, though some cities are divided into ghettos and suburbs, many neighbourhoods and smaller towns are more mixed. Children in a high proportion of state schools come from a wider range of backgrounds than do children in most private schools. Private schools with a wider mix are the exceptions. The arguments using external effects and economic growth may have had their days, but the argument for social solidarity still has some strength. Even so the evidence of government failure is much stronger in education than in social security and in health services.

The debate on education has been notable for the quality of analysis. West has contributed a powerful critique of the conventional view on education in the nineteenth century.[8] The symposium on West's work published by the IEA is one of the best in its repertoire.[9] For the United States, there is Jencks's report on his particular scheme for education vouchers described below.[10] In Britain, Maynard has produced a lucid summary.[11] The New Right has also advocated particular proposals for reform over a quarter of a century, although interest in voucher schemes now goes well beyond the Right. In the United States, some of the main support has come from the Left. In Britain, Klein and Watt have suggested experiments to enhance consumer choice by the use of vouchers.[12]

This wide interest has arisen and survived because the idea for vouchers covers two essentially different schemes with entirely different implications. The exhaustive list of schemes is even longer. Maynard's catalogue covers eight different types:[13] but there would appear to be two main variants. One is the Friedman type of voucher. The parent would get a voucher either for the full cost or a proportion of the cost of an average place in a state school. The IEA's Friedman-type voucher has usually had a value at the average cost of a place. Parents would then be free to top up with any amount they chose. The voucher could be spent at any school, public or private, and there would be no restrictions on how the school selected pupils from any waiting list.[14]

Under Jencks's scheme, the voucher covers the full average cost of education. It can be spent at state or private schools, but the schools must undertake not to charge tuition fees. Parents with low incomes receive a compensatory addition to the basic voucher.[15] This allows schools with many children from poor homes to buy additional resources. The voucher must be the only payment made by the parent. The schools must also accept certain conditions about selection. If the demand for places exceeds the supply, at least half the available places have to be allocated at random (for example, out of a hat). Schools have to provide full information about themselves.

The New Right has become known for its advocacy of vouchers, mainly of the Friedman type. The two voucher schemes are, in fact, very different. They differ in their effects on the range of family spending on education. The Friedman scheme would have the immediate beneficial effect of giving extra help to parents who previously had sent their children to private schools. They would be relieved of double taxation and be better off by the value of the voucher. Actual expenditures on education would probably show considerable variation. Jencks's scheme would also give an immediate benefit to those parents who had bought private education before; but the effect on actual expenditure would be to equalise it between all parents. Jencks's scheme is hardly an incentive to parents to spend more on their children's education in the same way as Friedman's scheme. Finally, the schemes differ greatly in their effects on the supply side. Friedman's leaves it uncontrolled while Jencks's proposes elaborate bureaucratic controls.

Voucher schemes have been constantly advocated by Friedman since 1955. Friedman's paper published in 1955 reappears in *Capitalism and Freedom*.[16] Some of the proposals made there have prospered. But this one has had a poor record. Its movement off the blueprint has been slow. In the market of opinion it has found few takers. It is vouchers of Jencks's type which have come closer to acceptance.

The most sustained attempt to launch the voucher was in the United States from 1971 to 1976, and it was sponsored, ironically enough, by an agency of the federal government. There were eight feasibility studies but only one experiment. These have been described in an appendix to a report by Kent County Council in Britain which has also undertaken a feasibility study.[17] The only experiment was undertaken in Alum Rock, one of the smallest and poorest school districts in the United States. An energetic schools superintendent saw the scheme as a way of getting some federal funding for his impoverished district. It did not suffer from any of the usual problems of residential segregation. San José happens to be one of the most integrated cities in the United States. It also has few private schools. The project was fairly successful in stimulating the schools into producing a wider range of options. Parental desire to switch schools was not strong and the voucher scheme has now been replaced by an open enrolment scheme, in which parents choose schools.

The other seven feasibility studies did not move to experiments. In Seattle, it became clear that the issues of bussing and a desegregation imposed unilaterally by the school board had polarised opinion and vouchers were seen as another element in these issues. There was also a great deal of controversy about the inclusion of private schools in the scheme. In Gary, Indiana, opposition by teachers seems to have been the main inhibition. In San Francisco, the issue was also clouded by the conflict over desegregation: 'the community at large showed little interest'.[18] In New Hampshire, there were continual changes in the model proposed to meet the kind of anxieties which the Jencks's scheme tries to meet.[19] These changes did not quell the anxieties and ultimately town meetings voted against the project. In East Hartford, the scheme came closest to success but was in part undermined by the 'failure to develop a sizeable parent constituency in favour'.[20] New

Rochelle and Rochester never got near the starting line. The voucher scheme lacked home-grown appeal. It was escorted locally by a Praetorian guard of consultants from the Centre for the Study of Public Policy at Harvard; the local image of the scheme was poor. On one assessment 'local citizens did not see vouchers as a possible answer to pressing local problems (except perhaps in Alum Rock) but rather as a remedy for abstract problems that bothered intellectuals'.[21]

The one feasibility study in Britain, for a scheme close to the Friedman type, was carried out in the Ashford division of Kent Education Authority.[22] The voucher was to cover the full cost of education in a state school but parents would be free to add to it in private schools. The survey of parents' views showed that there would be a net transfer to private schools. Their response suggested that 9 per cent of parents with children in maintained schools would choose to move them to independent schools. The demand for private education would have varied by social class. Seventeen per cent in social class I would transfer, compared with 5 per cent in social class IV.[23] Private schools would have been willing to participate but only if they retained the freedom to organise their own admissions. On the supply side, there was great hostility from the teachers and possible difficulties with classroom space in the more attractive schools. The voucher scheme would have meant much higher spending on school transport.

Parents in Ashford were certainly very dissatisfied with the amount of information which they were given by schools in the state system.[24] They were also quite dissatisfied with the scope for transfer between schools. However, the feasibility study concluded that there were other ways of achieving improvements than a voucher scheme. 'Freedom of choice, the full information about schools necessary for such choice, a right of transfer between schools and subsidised transport where necessary to the chosen school – these are the critical elements. The decisive factor in making them possible, with or without vouchers, would be the availability of surplus capacity in the schools.'[25] The voucher scheme would increase the total short-term cost of education: parents with children in private schools would be able to get vouchers and there would also be more spending on transport. The voucher scheme would have to be justified as a marginal increase in public expenditure and quite a large one.

Voucher schemes have not shown a robust Hayekian will to evolve. They have not been a socially selected institution which has grown. The New Right might argue that the political power of teachers has interfered with spontaneous choice of parents. But, this hardly explains the parents' apathy to such schemes. Nor can it explain why for centuries the state school has become the dominant type in so many countries. The typical argument about voucher schemes has not been the conflict between the irresistible force of parental preference and the immoveable object of the teachers' vested interest. The forces against the scheme have certainly been there, but the forces for the scheme have been weak and have become weaker with further knowledge.

The real issue is about the Friedman voucher. The Jencks voucher does not give parents any greater freedom to spend their own money. Nor is it likely to produce increased competition between state and private schools. Few private schools would be willing to meet the conditions and controls on fees and admissions policies. The Jencks scheme is hardly likely to go beyond the state system. Once a state system has some places to spare there are other ways of reaching the objectives of wider choice and easier transfer than the Jencks voucher scheme. Open enrolment with parental choice and much fuller supply of information are simpler ways of reaching the same objectives. It is also possible to offer a range of courses or mini-schools within the school and to arrange for schools to expand or contract with demand. Not all education authorities in Britain have adopted Kent County Council's past practice of giving teachers contracts to particular schools and making transfer very difficult.

The question is why the Friedman scheme has made so little progress that the Kent report has been the only feasibility study, with no experiment at all. One reason is the opposition from the teachers. The New Right has here shown one more example of its non-recognition of the power of professions. But there have been other objections to the Friedman scheme which have deprived it of the positive support which would be needed to override the vested interests of teachers. One is that it is likely to make the problem of residential and class segregation in the schools a good deal worse, a problem the New Right claims to hold dear to its heart. We can examine the effects of the Friedman scheme in two types of neighbourhood. One is the Friedman case of a neighbourhood already polarised where the pattern in the schools reflects that of residential segregation. The two communities are likely to live some way apart. Here a voucher scheme is likely to make little difference. With travel costs and the freedom of schools to select their own pupils, there are likely to be few transfers of children to schools in the better-off neighbourhood. The more likely effect would be to encourage the development of private schools in the poor neighbourhood. Instead of a two-way split there is likely to be a three-way one between suburban schools, ghetto private schools and ghetto public schools.

The second type of neighbourhood is one with a more mixed pattern of residence. Here the effect of a Friedman-type voucher would be to increase the demand for private education. There is no reason why the private school should take children who are likely to present them with difficulties. They will choose pupils from a queue, starting with the more eligible. The New Right has often denied that the effect of voucher schemes would be to leave the state schools with all the children who were most difficult to educate. However, this follows from the market pressures which schools are under. The particular form of the voucher scheme would not reduce the problem of residential segregation – it is likely to make it worse. In the type of neighbourhood that Friedman is thinking of class division is likely to widen without doing much about residential segregation. Elsewhere, the voucher scheme is likely to lead to a reduction in the range of children going to state schools.

The New Right claims that voucher schemes will contribute to greater equality – that they will stimulate the interest of working-class parents who will be willing to pay more for their children's education. This implies that, on average, working-class parents will contribute a higher proportion of their income to their children's education than middle-class parents. If they did not, the gap between middle-class and working-class expenditures would widen. Thus the condition for a voucher scheme to produce a greater equality of expenditures is that working-class parents should be willing to pay a larger proportion of a lower income on education. Now it can be argued that they would be willing to do this. Maynard and others suggest that there is a case for experiment to see exactly what would happen.[26] But there would still be an absolute difference between middle-class and working-class expenditures. The biggest purse would still count.

It has been argued that working-class parents would be willing to top up their vouchers. It is difficult to believe that they would do this, given the other claims on their resources. Because their income is lower, the opportunity cost of extra spending on education is greater. It is even more difficult to believe that working-class parents would make these sacrifices when the likely position on the supply side is brought into the reckoning. The Friedman scheme is likely to result in the better teachers moving away from working-class schools. There would be price competition for better teachers. Schools with more purchasing power from topped up vouchers would be able to bid for teachers more successfully. These schools would become more efficient than the others. Many teachers would prefer to work with more teachable children. Thus the results of schools with high proportions of working-class children are likely to be worse. The supply-side effects would provide a further deterrent to working-class parents towards matching the larger purses of better-off parents. The New Right might argue that in the long run supply elasticities might draw more resources into education. But even in the long run, better teachers would tend to go where pay and teaching conditions were better.

The New Right has tended to stress the importance of the parents' interest and motivation. These have vital effects on a child's performance. But children do not belong to their parents. They have interests which are independent of them. For all their weaknesses, state schools provide a setting in which teachers, parents and the children themselves can arrive at decisions after discussion. The Friedman voucher scheme makes the child more dependent on the parents' willingness to purchase education, and the teacher more dependent on that purchasing power. For the child this dependence may have particular problems in secondary education. Young people are becoming more independent at an earlier age. Any system that makes choices and opportunities for 15-year-olds more dependent on their parents' purchasing power must have many drawbacks to it. Enthusiasts for vouchers, such as Friedman and the IEA, have not explained how the separate interests of the child are to be represented. State education has provided a setting within which there can be a third-party contribution to decisions. It represents one way, developed over many years, of balancing the interests of parents and children.

State schools have also represented, however falteringly, some ideas of equal opportunity. They have drawn a lot of support and survival power from the, admittedly vague, idea that the community should have some interest in the well-being of all its children. There is a core of educational opportunity which should have public backing to the extent of public provision. The New Right seems to reject the idea of positive freedom or public interest in fulfilment of potential. They may also argue that there are other ways to achieve minimum standards than by public provision. Nevertheless, whatever might have been, the debate about public education was resolved in one particular way by the 1870 Education Act. This and succeeding Acts have come to have positive associations for many people. Supporters of voucher schemes have not managed to show how they would retain these ideas.

The New Right also underestimates the strength of the argument for social cohesion by state education. It accepts that, in the past, social cohesion justified public provision in the United States. With many different groups of immigrants, the public school system helped to develop a common culture and a common language. It is felt by the New Right that such considerations do not apply so strongly in the United States, and even less in Great Britain, today. It may be that the Left has put too much stress on the role of education in reducing class and ethnic divisions, but the New Right falls into the error of dismissing it completely. There are dangers and losses involved in a divided society, and the issue of social cohesion is not merely of antiquarian interest, nor is the record of the state schools in promoting social cohesion as bad as the New Right suggests. Certainly there are the

Friedman-type neighbourhoods, but generally the range of children is greater in most state schools than in most private schools. These early contacts between children from a range of backgrounds have value and they would be reduced under a Friedman-type voucher scheme. Voucher schemes are also likely to lead to a big increase in sectarian education. For the New Right this does not matter; but, again, quite other judgements are possible.

The failure of the Friedman voucher scheme illustrates some of the general weaknesses in the New Right's position. It has been defeated in part by professional power of the kind which it has constantly ignored. The teachers' opposition has been one very important reason for this failure. But their opposition has had such power partly because of the lack of a strong demand by parents or community for the scheme. The New Right's case for vouchers has not been able to explain how the desire (including that of the New Right) or equal opportunity for all children would be preserved under the system. It has also failed to dispel fears that segregation might be even greater under the voucher scheme. Nor has it been able to explain how the independent interests of children would be maintained. On all these points, government success has been far from complete. Differences in patterns of residence reduce the mix in schools. Neither teachers nor parents will always do what is best for the child. But there is a lack of credibility about the Friedman voucher scheme on these issues. Private schools will not do better; they will almost certainly do worse. As well as its neglect of private coercion by professions, the New Right has been affected by its lack of respect for the idea of positive freedom which, however imperfectly, the state schools represent.

Finally voucher schemes have had an opportunity cost. The cost has been other kinds of reform in education which might have had more attention without this pre-occupation. There are ways in which parents' choice could be increased and in which schools could have provided a bigger choice in types of course. It is possible to imagine a larger private and voluntary sector concerned with children of all levels of ability, not just with the favoured few. It is possible to imagine more schools started by private initiative which showed the spirit of Montessori. There are many unhealthy features about the near-state monopoly in education, but they are not going to be made any better by a Friedman-type of voucher scheme. We need to find ways to encourage diversity and real choice for children of all levels of ability but the main debate has been in stereotypes. There are alternatives to state monopoly other than the market: but the search for alternatives has to show some greater sensitivity to the interests of all children not just those of elites. The pre-school playgroup movement in Britain has shown what can be done through voluntary effort supported by small amounts of public grant. There is no reason why different combinations of voluntary and public initiative should not be encouraged at other stages of education.

The main failure of the New Right has been over vouchers. On student loans, it has won the day in much of the United States. But the reasons why a student-loans system has not been adopted in Britain are of interest. There are some compelling arguments in favour of loan schemes. But the difficulty with loans is that, unless repayments are related to income, they discriminate against women and against people in low-paid vocational jobs. The repayment of the loan may be pitched to ability to pay, in which case it becomes a progressive, graduated tax, an addition to income tax. Alternatively, it has to be repaid by everyone, which would be unfair to women who have lower earnings and are less likely to work full-time while they are having children. There are ways round this, such as giving grace periods of payments, but that begins to make the scheme complicated and bureaucratic. The scheme would also discriminate against those with less capital, often students from working-class backgrounds. The risk involved in taking a loan would be greater for them than for those with some family assets. The redistributive effect of higher education is certainly perverse, but the advocates of loan schemes have never been able to allay the fear that they might simply create a different kind of muddle.

Housing

In housing the New Right has also become more and more identified with a simple market solution. The ending of rent control has been its main proposal. The debate has again been polarised. The need for reform is certainly there and market principles are relevant to a degree, but there are substantial differences between the housing market and other markets. One is the issue of security of tenure. Any reform has to take account of the fact of extreme sensitivity about dispossession. The housing market has also been deeply affected by government policies on taxation and by the strategies of non-profit institutions such as building societies. There is also the slowness of the supply response. Adjustments in the short term are made through price and demand. There are many inhibitions about rationing by price in the housing market.[27]

It would be possible in principle to carry through reforms that would improve the social and economic functioning of the housing market even in the face of all these special difficulties and sensitivities. There is a case for eliminating indiscriminate demand subsidies and for relating prices to costs. There is a case for concentrating assistance on households with low incomes. There is a case for setting rents at a level which will allow a reasonable return and create conditions for investment. But such changes have to be carried through in ways that show some sensitivity to the personal and social issues involved. The New Right's emphasis on a very simple market solution has made it more difficult to carry out reform in ways that did take into account these special characteristics.

Hayek's early analysis of rent control in fact showed much more sensitivity than the later crude prescriptions of Friedman and others.[28] Hayek showed great insight by concentrating on the long-term interactions between demand and supply which would arise from a policy of rent control. It would lead to excess demand for housing both because of the effect on new demand and, as it reduced supply, by encouraging people to hang on to their tenancies. This excess demand would not be met by private investment but would draw in more public investment. But the excess demand would be a poor guide to the true underlying pattern of demand. The location of these new projects would be arbitrary. We might well end up with a combination of long queues and empty houses in unpopular locations. Hayek also showed considerable perception about the difficulties of moving away from rent control. It would be necessary to retain control for existing tenancies; otherwise there would be excess demand, especially for smaller flats.

Hayek was writing about a very strong form of rent control in Vienna where most of the housing stock is in large blocks of flats which are not amenable to individual ownership. In Britain the conditions were there for increased owner-occupation even without rent control. Rent control in Britain has certainly had powerful and damaging effects. But it has not been the only force making for decline in private rented accommodation. Both the nature of the housing stock with its preponderance of small houses and tax incentives have helped to create conditions for a big increase in owner-occupation. Any reform that simply involved the abolition of rent control without changing other incentives would probably be ineffective.

The most important effect of rent control has been in encouraging landlords to hang on and to wait for vacant possession so that they could then get their full capital gain. The level of rents has been too low for adequate maintenance and there has been a steady decline in the condition of the stock. Rent control has helped to keep price well below cost. The durability of housing means that the effects of such policies only become clear after quite a long time – but that time came some years ago. Rent control also implies an arbitrary pattern of subsidies. Some landlords get rich but many do not. There is no reason why the landlord should subsidise the tenant and any subsidy would be much better done through direct payments by government. Rent control is not defensible as an exercise in income redistribution. Its most pernicious effect however is to encourage small landlords to hang on to property long after they are willing or able to manage it properly. The tenant gets a subsidy – but he also gets a declining standard of housing.[29]

The New Right has had a great deal to say and fairly enough about these effects of rent control. But it has had much less to say about the causes of its persistence. It is not only the pressure from the vested interests of tenants which has helped to preserve rent control. It is the strong degree of emotion about eviction. Here again the idea that there is a core of rights which should not be for sale in markets has proved powerful. The opponents of rent control have never been able to overcome the disquiet about families losing their homes so that landlords can make more money.

The New Right believes that private renting run by profit-making firms and landlords can be revived. The whole tale may point however to a rather different moral. It is certainly the case that prices should cover costs including a reasonable return, but it seems very unlikely that this can be achieved by the usual kind of profit-making concerns in the peculiar conditions of the housing market. Only voluntary agencies which can take into account both the economic and social considerations are likely to achieve a reasonable return. The whole history of housing policy suggests that private initiative in the usual sense is likely to run into great difficulties and that economic sense can only be achieved by a different approach. A system based on private landlords is essentially archaic and cannot be revived under present conditions. The real argument should be about how various kinds of agency, some public and some voluntary, can achieve a sensible level of rents while at the same time meeting social obligations. Certainly there are political obstacles in the way of such results, but the chances of reviving the private landlord are even less as far as permanent accommodation is concerned. It is possible to have a combination of economic rents with income-related assistance and guarantees on security of tenure which would reconcile the 'economic' with the 'social'. But this kind of approach is very different from the crude market solution advocated by the New Right.

There is certainly much wrong with public housing as it exists at present in Britain. It aims to relate housing to need and not to money demand. In practice the needy have often found themselves on unpleasant estates which were both poorly maintained and socially stigmatised. The full aim of equality of treatment has not been realised in practice.[30] The reverse dogma of the Left – that public enterprise should do it all – has held the field with rather poor results in practice. Once again the debate has been polarised between different kinds of utopianism. The growing public sector monopoly in rented accommodation has had pernicious results and there is everything to be said for a greater variety of supply. But there are going to have to be other routes towards freedom of choice than through the revival of the private landlord. If the New Right had spent more time on defining what those routes might be, its contribution to real consumer choice might have been a greater one.

The New Right has had one other main concern in housing and its contribution here has been a more effective one. This is its critique of the follies of urban planners and of the business of comprehensive redevelopment. It can claim to have made the first systematic exposition of the follies of these redevelopment policies. In the United States Anderson and Jane Jacobs were the main contributors.[31] Opposition to the Federal (or Municipal) Bulldozer has now become part of the conventional wisdom, and we are all in favour of organic change in cities. But the New Right certainly made a major contribution in the best Hayekian tradition to discrediting the idea of the replanning of cities by large bureaucracies. In Britain the message took rather longer to sink in, but again IEA authors such as McKie made a distinctive contribution.[32] McKie's surveys of central Peterborough showed that owners and tenants had plenty of will to carry on and ideas about how to do it. In Rochdale surveys of older terrace housing in the mid-1960s showed that there was much more life in it than had been thought by the planners.[33] All this contributed to the swing in ideas in favour of more gradual renewal of towns. Here the New Right's analysis and suggested lines of policy have had a very different spirit from the utopianism which marked their discussion of rent control.

References

1. E. Midwinter, *Education Choice Thoughts*, London; Advisory Centre for Education, 1980, p.8.
2. 'Getting Caned', *The Economist*, 12 December 1981, p.34.
3. M. Friedman and R. Friedman, *Free to Choose*, London; Secker and Warburg, 1980, pp.181–3.
4. E.G. West, *Education and the State*, 2nd edn., London; IEA, 1970, Chapter 3.
5. *Free to Choose*, pp.157–8.
6. Mark Blaug, *An Introduction to the Economics of Education*, London; Penguin, 1970, Chapter 6.
7. R. Layard *et al.*, *The Causes of Poverty*, Royal Commission on the Distribution of Income and Wealth, Background Paper No.5, London; HMSO, 1978, p.41.
8. E.G. West, *Education and the State*, London; IEA, 1965 (2nd edn., 1970).
9. *Education, a Framework for Choice*, 2nd ed., London; IEA, 1970.
10. C. Jencks, *Education Vouchers*, A Report on the Financing of Elementary Education by Grants to Parents, Cambridge Center for the Study of Public Policy, 1970.
11. Alan Maynard, *Experiment with Choice in Education*, London; IEA, 1975.
12. D. Watt and R. Klein, 'Commentary: Towards a New Centre Party', *Political Quarterly*, April–June 1981.
13. *Experiment with Choice in Education*, pp.27–33.
14. *Experiment with Choice in Education*, pp.31–2.
15. *Experiment with Choice in Education*, pp.31–2.

16. *Capitalism and Freedom*, Chapter VI.
17. Kent County Council, *Education Vouchers in Kent:* Appendix 4, The American Experience, Kent County Council, 1978, pp.88–92.
18. *Education Vouchers in Kent*, p.91.
19. *Education Vouchers in Kent*, p.92.
20. *Education Vouchers in Kent*, p.92.
21. *Education Vouchers in Kent*, p.89.
22. *Education Vouchers in Kent.*
23. *Education Vouchers in Kent*, p.13.
24. *Education Vouchers in Kent*, p.13.
25. *Education Vouchers in Kent*, p.39.
26. *Experiment with Choice in Education*, pp.46–8.
27. There is an excellent discussion in F.G. Pennance, *Housing Market: Analysis and Policy*, London; IEA, 1969. This comes to the different conclusion, however, that the special characteristics don't actually matter very much.
28. Reprinted in F.A. Hayek *et al.*, *Verdict on Rent Control*, London; IEA, 1972. The best Friedman exposition is M. Friedman and G. Stigler, 'Roofs or Ceilings? The Current Housing Problem', in Hayek *et al.*, *Verdict on Rent Control.*
29. The effects may not be so great if the level of rents is above the long-run equilibrium level. But this hardly seems likely either for controlled or for fair rents in Britain. R. Robinson, *Housing Economics and Public Policy*, London; Macmillan, 1979, Chapter 6, is the best discussion.
30. Ironically council housing is quite redistributive in cash terms, but a complete evaluation has to take into account other aspects. For redistribution see J. Le Grand, *The Strategy of Equality*, London; Allen and Unwin, 1982 Chapter 5.
31. M. Anderson, *The Federal Bulldozer*, Cambridge, Mass; MIT Press, 1967; Jane Jacobs, *The Death and Life of Great American Cities*, London; Jonathan Cape, 1962.
32. Robert McKie, *Housing and the Whitehall Bulldozer*, London; IEA, 1971.
33. Ministry of Housing and Local Government, *The Deeplish Study*, London; HMSO, 1966.

13 Macroeconomics

The social policies of the New Right are still mainly intentions and, in the case of vouchers, would seem to have a diminishing chance of adoption. The position is very different in macroeconomics. Some policies have had an actual trial. Ironically, a movement which stresses the importance of markets and microeconomics is ending up without any distinctive successes at the market but with a new dominance in macroeconomics. In this chapter we shall ask whether the experiment in macroeconomics reveals more general lessons about the philosophy of the New Right.

The victory of the New Right in macroeconomics has been the more complete because of the nature of the suggested main alternative. This maintains that government fiscal policy can bring about large increases in real output indirectly through raising levels of expenditure. In some variants of this alternative, effects on the balance of payments are dealt with by import controls.

With or without this policy for side-effects, the extreme Keynesian view would be that government policy can and must increase expenditure enough to bring about full employment. That is sometimes seen as a return to past Keynesian policies of demand management which have been abandoned because of political prejudice. More unkindly, this view could be described as 'punk Keynesianism'.

The alternative suggested here is rather different. I make this case as one of 364 economists who signed the statement in March 1981 condemning monetarist policies.[1] I do not argue that government can influence real output enough to bring about an early return to full employment. But there is no reason to go to the other extreme and to argue that government fiscal and monetary policy can have *no* effect on real output. In particular, it is argued that governments can and should take responsibility for moderating recessions. Government policies for expenditure, interest rates and exchange rates can make adjustments in the real economy either easier or more difficult. Government policy should also recognise the heavy costs of long-term unemployment without any compensating benefits to the people involved. Government should both aim at least to arrest the rise in unemployment and reduce the costs to the individual of long-term unemployment.

The macroeconomics of the New Right are usually summed up in the one word: monetarism. This is misleading because there are three different versions of monetarism. The version which has had some practical effect is a peculiar British version of Friedmanite monetarism.

The term 'monetarism' is also unhelpful because one does not have to be a supporter of the New Right to accept the importance of limiting the growth of the money supply. Adherence to monetary and financial disciplines is not a policy only advocated by the New Right. It is misleading, too, to include Hayek among the monetarists. Hayek has a very different view of macroeconomics.

Our main discussion here is of British monetarism, and it will suggest some general lessons to be learned about the New Right. One is its faith in mechanistic approaches which is perhaps Friedman's most influential contribution. The fiasco by which money supply targets were made the end-all for British economic policy has some wider lessons. But, perhaps most important, there is a vacuum of social ideas at the heart of monetarism. In one sense it is close to its main rival, Keynesianism, in its belief in the potential of long-term growth. In the short term, there are difficulties: but in the long term if only we reduce the role of government we will come into a new time of abundance. It is a policy of simple rules for moving towards an unclear destination.

The three main versions of monetarism are Monetarism I (Friedman's version), Monetarism II (or 'rational expectations' monetarism) and British monetarism. In addition, there is Hayek's rather different approach.

Monetarism I

Friedman's version would include the following propositions:

1. Inflation is brought about mainly by increases in the money supply. The crude 'quantity theory' is still the beginning of understanding.
2. Increases in the money supply are brought about by political pressures. It is not enough now as it might have been twenty years ago to concentrate on the contingent monetary causes of inflation. We also need to know about the political pressures which cause governments to accommodate inflation.
3. There is a long-run equilibrium in the economy set by underlying forces of productivity and thrift. These forces set the natural rate of unemployment in the labour market and the rate of growth of GDP.
4. Government policy can alter real output only temporarily. In the long run, increases in expenditures will lead to accelerating inflation with little increase in real output.
5. There will be painful side-effects on output and employment during the monetary detoxification which takes the economy away from accelerating inflation and back on its long-run equilibrium. The cure should be carried out gradually and with an advance announcement. 'The most important device for mitigating the side-effects is to slow

inflation *gradually but steadily* by a policy announced in advance and adhered to so it becomes credible.'[2]

6. The pains of adjustment are severe, partly because there is so little flexibility in wages and prices in a modern economy.

7. Apart from inflationist policies, there are other forces which could push an economy away from a long-run equilibrium. Mistaken monetary policies could lead to money itself being a major source of economic disturbance. People adapt their expectations gradually and this can compound the effects of the original change. There are political pressures towards inflation, but they can be offset by the political will of a strong government.

These propositions form the basis for an economic policy of gradualism. Other monetarists put even more stress on the dangers of rapid disinflation and would introduce policies to reduce its effect on real income and employment.

Monetarism II

In this version we are very close to long-run equilibrium – so close that a short, sharp, monetary contraction will bring us there. Participants in labour and product markets make careful plans for the future based on rational expectations of relevant variables, including government policy. Government policy cannot alter the real economy because people will simply change their behaviour in order to offset its effects. Firms and workers have made their plans and will keep to them, however much fog and confusion is set up by government manipulation.

British Monetarism

This has taken over the core policy of Monetarism I, that a sustained reduction in the money supply is the essential step towards reducing inflation. But the British version has given less attention than most gradualists would consider wise to policies for the side-effects on output and employment. It has also shown a greater concern with targets for the PSBL. The medium-term financial strategy is derived from Friedmanite monetarism, but with certain differences of emphasis.

British monetarism has also brought in certain arguments of a general kind to support its detailed policy prescriptions:

1. Britain has been involved in a 'rake's progress' of rising unemployment and falling growth rates. This decline has its origins a long time back, in the period of Keynesian economics. The rise in unemployment since 1979 is mainly a hangover from these past evil ways.

2. Britain suffers from a severe problem of overmanning. Falling

employment may have positive effects if it is associated with rising productivity.

3. The costs of inflation are very great; greater than the costs of unemployment. Wood has summed this up well: 'Models where the costs of inflation are trivial are models which omit an important feature of the world. It is worth reducing inflation to low single figures – and preferably to zero. There are costs of doing so – but the costs of not doing so are greater.'[3]

Hayekism

Hayek accepts that there is a clear monetary cure for inflation but in current circumstances this knowledge is trivial. He has a rather different analysis of the side-effects. Inflation creates distortions in the structure of employment: it creates a range of jobs which collapse as the inflation recedes. But the main special feature is Hayek's analysis of the political and social difficulties in the way of a monetary cure. There is no doubt that the cure will work – and speedily. But there are strong vested interests in trade unionism and politics at work against its adoption. Hayek has come to believe that basic political and social changes will be needed: the reduction in union power and even possibly the end of the central bank monopoly in money creation – the de-nationalisation of money. It is unlikely that any government under current political conditions will stick to the cure. The economics of inflation are simple, but the politics much more difficult. He has also some disagreements about the mechanistic approach of the monetarists to the quantity theory.

The Record of British Monetarism

It is clear that Britain since 1979 has had a rather worse recession than any other country except for Belgium. The case against British monetarism is that it made the recession worse than it should have been. It added to the rate of inflation and it failed to take reasonable steps to moderate the fall in real output. Some rise in unemployment was inevitable, but it need not have been so severe. The usual problems about the timing of government policy do not arise because it was very clear by the third quarter of 1980 that the economy was in a serious recession and action taken then could have reduced the fall in output.

British monetarism puts a great deal of weight on control of the money supply as the means of controlling inflation. It pays little attention to the pressures which form expectations other than those in the monetary sphere. Changes in utility prices and in taxes may increase pressure on real incomes and strengthen expectations. Control of the money supply is certainly necessary to controlling inflation, but there are other helpful means of changing an inflationary climate. Government decisions to increase indirect taxes and to raise nationalised industry prices sharply in 1979 added about 5 per cent to inflation. The changes came about at a time when the rate of inflation was accelerating anyway because of the rise in oil prices and pressure in pay bargaining. This meant that the economy had to go through a much more drastic deflation of demand to achieve a given reduction in inflation than would otherwise have been the case. In an economy where government has important indirect and direct influence on prices, it was irresponsible for the Government to increase the burden of adjustment falling on the private sector at a time when that burden was increasing for other reasons.

The case for these changes might have been stronger if nationalised industries had been running deficits as large as they were in 1974. They were not: the aim of economic pricing could have been put off for a year. It would have been reasonable to give priority to the aim of reducing inflationary pressure.

One further effect of these changes was to increase the pressure on firms. They were faced by falling orders and rising costs. The government's policies added further to their costs. Their position was made even worse by the falls in expenditure and the rise in the exchange rate between mid-1979 and mid-1980. The Government did little to help firms overcome these difficulties. Other main criticisms of British monetarism are that government should attempt to stabilise real output in recessions, and that it should attempt to reduce the effects of an appreciating exchange rate on the real economy. A government should have targets for the real economy as well as for the money supply.

Government has to influence real output indirectly through influencing expenditure. Brittan has shown how the relationship between money expenditure and real output has changed for the worse.[4] More of any given increase in expenditure has gone into raising prices and into imports: less has gone into raising domestic output. There is no doubt that it is now much more difficult to influence real output through general changes in money expenditure. However this does not mean that government should have no aims for expenditure and thus, indirectly, for real output. It is possible to be selective in the ways that expenditure is raised. Different kinds of expenditure have very different effects on real domestic output. Policy changes designed to stimulate investment in the building industry, for example, would have much more effect on real output than a reduction in income tax. It may well be no longer realistic to expect that government could influence real output enough to bring about full employment, but it should have targets both for expenditure and for real output and it can have some influence on real output through selective changes in expenditure.

It becomes the more important to have such targets if the aim of policy is to raise the profit share. British monetarism accepts that it would be highly desirable to raise the share of profits. For example, the Chancellor said in his Budget speech in 1981: 'Between 1977 and 1980 the real after-tax income of individuals rose by about a sixth. But the real disposable income of industrial and commercial companies fell by a quarter.'[5] In an economy where most of the adjustment comes through output rather than through prices, the reduction in output is bound to lead to further pressure on profitability. Reductions in expenditure make it even more difficult to increase profitability. The aims of monetarism in distribution are undercut by its effects in reducing output and profitability.

British monetarism also lacks any worked-out view of the relationships which run from changes in money markets via the exchange rate to changes in real activity. Again the Hayekian monetarists have had a much clearer approach to this. Hayek has always maintained – quoting the authority of Ricardo on earlier exchange crises – that decisions on exchange rates were of great importance to the real economy. He opposed the return to the gold standard in 1925. His view would seem to be that there can be such a thing as an overvalued exchange rate. The British monetarists' position on this is much less clear. They do not appear to accept that attempts at monetary restriction by pushing up interest rates could have effects first on the exchange rate and through the exchange rate on real activity. The rigorous pursuit of domestic monetary targets could have perverse effects both on the internal monetary balance and on real activity. High interest rates could lead to inflows of currency which could offset the effects of the restrictions in the domestic money supply. These inflows would lead to increases in the exchange rate which would reduce export competitiveness. It could be argued that wage flexibility could be promoted in order to offset the rise in the exchange rate – but this was notoriously difficult, even in the 1920s. All these difficulties would be greater in a market such as the foreign exchange market affected by swings in confidence and mood which could produce movements in and out of currencies greater than could be explained by real factors. This argument cuts both ways in the sense that it also makes difficult a policy for fine tuning the exchange rate. But it suggests that policy has to be concerned with more than the internal monetary balance. It has to be concerned with the interactions between the internal and external monetary balance and with the possible effects of the exchange rate on real activity.

Monetarism has run into its most obvious problems in its attempts to turn the simple plan into a reality through policy for controlling the money supply. The British monetarists are handicapped by a crude version of the quantity theory and by the sheer difficulty of controlling the variety of money-creating institutions and money substitutes. Nor has the policy provided a reliable way of influencing real output. Its level of achievement in controlling the money supply in an open economy through indirect monetary means alone has pleased neither friend nor enemy.

It may help to illustrate what an alternative approach to 'British' monetarism might have meant in 1979–81. It would have involved some reflation concentrated on investment and stock-building in the private sector at the end of 1980. The state of the economy by then was clear and there was little possibility that fiscal policy would have a perverse effect in accentuating a boom that had already started. It was also clear that there were serious falls in output – especially in manufacturing – and increases in unemployment, and that both were likely to continue.

The Government had by then produced two Budgets. It certainly inherited a rising rate of inflation which would cause difficulties. It made the generally admitted mistake in the 1979 Budget of adding to inflationary pressure by increaseing indirect taxation. In its 1980 Budget it unveiled the medium-term financial strategy. However, it could well be argued that though the fall in output and the rise in unemployment began in the first quarter of 1980, the extent of the recession was not clear at the time of the Budget. By the end of 1980 the degree of the fall in output and the prospect for more were all too clear, as some of us wrote at the time, most strongly the Bank of England in its *Quarterly Bulletin* for December 1980.[6] There was no doubt that the Government was not going to meet the financial targets in the medium-term financial strategy. This was partly because of once-and-for-all changes to do with ending exchange controls and the abolition of the corset, but it was also partly from the effects of the recession itself in raising the PSBR through higher unemployment payments, higher industrial subsidies and lower tax revenues.

The Government's reaction was to increase taxation and to cut its spending in the Budget of 1981 in order to move towards the targets in the medium-term strategy. The alternative approach would have been to give a stimulus to private and public sector investment and to stock-building. It would also have been possible to introduce special employment measures, particularly of the marginal employment subsidy type, to reduce the cost of training and recruitment. Such a package would have been a much better use of an increase in the PSBR than the higher unemployment payments which materialised. These suggestions were made at the time and were fairly obvious. It was argued that 'The severe recession over the past year reflects especially intense pressure on the company sector. It would be possible to relieve some of this without a general consumption-led reflation and without relaxing the general restraint on public spending.'[7] The Chancellor argued that there had been no shortage of money demand over the previous years. This may well have been true as a long-term proposition – but it was certainly not true at the end of 1980.

The alternative policy can be summed up as follows:

1. There should be targets for expenditure and real output as well as monetary targets. In fact because the achievement of monetary targets is to an important extent dependent on targets for expenditure and real outputs, even within a monetarist framework, it makes little sense to have one without the other.[8] These targets are perhaps more important in Britain than elsewhere because of the well-known fragility of British manufacturing.

2. The main aim of government policy should be to prevent falls in output, and if possible, to contribute to a modest expansion, by selective stimulus to investment. The realistic target for Britain is to stop unemployment from rising yet further. Government has a particular responsibility to offset recession, to intervene when it is clear that output is falling and unemployment rising. This is an approach which concentrates on trying to alleviate the worst possible case rather than to bring about a hypothetical best. The aim also suggests the choice of detailed instruments. The emphasis would be on expenditure changes that would have a reasonably precise effect on unemployment and output within the private sector, rather than on general measures of reflation. Such measures as marginal employment subsidies and reductions in employers' social security contributions would figure rather than changes in income taxation.

3. The aim should be to keep inflation down to under 10 per cent. Below that the unemployment costs would have to be weighted seriously. Perhaps most importantly of all, the highest priority should be to prevent unexpected increases in the rate of inflation.

4. Incomes policies can play a role in helping to guide expectations down. It is often argued that incomes policies have failed: but the alternatives may well have shown to be an even greater failure.

In the past, incomes policy was misused as a substitute for other policies. In particular, the 1972–4 incomes policy was used to reduce the inflationary stress which was bound to be produced by a rapid expansion of demand. A better precedent was the 1975–7 experience where the evidence suggests that incomes policy helped to temper expectations and to reduce inflation. The case has been well made that an incomes policy cannot be a substitute for tolerably sane fiscal and monetary policies, but that it could be complementary to such policies. In an economy in which there are coercive pressures to comparison and in which those with the most power may be well protected from the market, the degree of demand deflation required to reduce prices may well be great. Any policy that could reduce these short-term costs should surely be tried. Monetarists would argue that incomes policies have been completely ineffective – even harmful – in discouraging the adoption of sensible monetary policies. But this is an argument against the type of policies brought in by Heath in Britain and Nixon in the USA. Even Brittan and Lilley show a tiny hint of agnosticism about the effects of the 1975–7 policy in Britain.[9] There can be differences of view but it is a reasonable proposition that an incomes policy can have a role – in association with sensible monetary and fiscal policies – in bringing down a rising rate of inflation. The aim should be to moderate the struggles over distribution at those times when they are likely to do most damage to the real economy. These are the times when any strong drive to maintain real income in wage-bargaining is likely to lead to higher unemployment and to further falls in real income.

This alternative policy does not mean a return to the Keynesianism which was typical of the post-war full employment period. It is a policy of trying to prevent falls in output with their multiplying effects on employment and real income, as well as their implications for social conflict. It is a policy which concentrates on the worst possible case. It is a policy of giving some help in a selective way to recovery. It also attempts to prevent side-effects of disciplined monetary policies through the exchange rate on real output. It is above all a policy for preventing the shocks of rapid increases in the rate of inflation and falls in output to which Britain has been particularly vulnerable. Within the context of greater stability in output levels and inflation rates, there will be a greater chance of getting to grips with the well-known problems of industrial competitiveness. It is a plea for a strategy for the real economy, but one with very modest aims.

British monetarism can also be criticised for its very casual view of the costs of long-term unemployment. These costs are not evenly distributed: they are borne overwhelmingly by the young and the old. For the young they may well interfere with their ability to acquire skills and to make a success of their future. For older workers unemployment is often the step towards leaving the labour force entirely. The effects on individuals are not easily measurable but are probably more pernicious than is generally realised. More recognisable are the severe effects of long-term unemployment on the stability of communities – Northern Ireland is the most obvious example.

In Britain long-term unemployment is a relatively much more important part of the unemployment burden than it is in the United States. Britain, too, has had a more severe regional problem – most notably in Northern Ireland, Clydeside and Merseyside – than have most other Western countries. The costs of unemployment are borne by a minority and are not accompanied by any long-term benefits to the individuals bearing them. Short-term costs may well be accompanied by further long-term costs of personal decline. Once this high level of long-term unemployment is established, it is very difficult to reduce it, for reasons which have to do with both the supply side and the demand side of the affected labour markets. Thus, although there may be benefits to society or to some other group in that society from reducing inflation, there are unlikely to be any benefits to the groups who are experiencing rising unemployment.

A rise in unemployment means heavy costs for relatively small groups of individuals while the benefits of low inflation and of growth are more diffused and do not accrue very strongly to the same individuals. The costs are heavy, pointless, and irreversible for the people carrying them. The costs are of a kind which also do not lead to strong political protest. They affect groups of people who were particularly weak already. Unemployment leads to reductions in both income and self-esteem which further reduce the ability and the desire to take part in society.

There are ways in which the position of at least some of the long-term unemployed could be improved. One would be to treat them reasonably generously within the social security and benefit system. There are some improvements that could be made without great damage to labour market incentives. One would be to make some of the long-term unemployed eligible for the long-term rate of supplementary benefit. Far from doing this the Government reduced the real value of the short-term rate. The long-term unemployed are now relatively worse off in the social security system.

Another policy of benefit to the long-term unemployed would be to pay employers a premium for six months to take them on. A small experiment was made with this kind of marginal employment subsidy in three local labour markets in 1978–9. But this was not conclusive and a further experiment on a larger scale with more publicity is needed. Such a policy would not change the total number of people in the dole queue, but it would ensure that the long-term unemployed are nearer to the front of it.

These policies could help a few and reduce some of the costs of unemployment, but the fate of the long-term unemployed depends mainly on what happens in the economy generally. There can be little hope of an early return to full employment, but the approach to running the economy set out above offers a better hope of avoiding further damage and of making a gradual recovery. British monetarism has produced the certainty of very heavy costs in the present with the romantic hope of gains at some time in the future. In macroeconomics the New Right's approach seems to lack realism and to have little patience with some of the ways in which immediate social costs might have been reduced.

References

1. 'Economists Lay Mass Censure at Howe's Door', *The Guardian*, 30 March 1981.
2. M. Friedman and R. Friedman, *Free to Choose*, London; Secker and Warburg, 1980, p.277.
3. G. Wood, 'Can 364 Economists All Be Wrong?', *Journal of Economic Affairs*, Vol.I, 1981.
4. Samuel Brittan, *How to End the 'Monetarist' Controversy*, London; IEA, 1981, p.24. I am very much indebted to the discussion in this pamphlet.
5. Sir G. Howe, Budget Speech, *The Times*, 11 March 1981.
6. N. Bosanquet, *The Guardian*, 8 January 1981; Bank of England *Quarterly Bulletin*, December 1980, p.403.
7. N. Bosanquet, *The Guardian*, 8 January 1981. The letter was called 'A Tragedy in the Making'.
8. Brittan suggests that a target should be set only for expenditure. But it would be a useful discipline for government to have to translate the expenditure target into real output.
9. Samuel Brittan and Peter Lilley, *The Delusion of Incomes Policy*, London; Temple Smith, 1977, p.176.

14 An Alternative View

The social philosophy of the New Right has not yet been fully adopted, although Western societies are moving in that direction. The central proposition is that a major reduction in the role of government is both a necessary and a sufficient condition for progress. The Hayek case for this, even in the latest version, is a highly sophisticated and subtle one. But more commonly the proposition is supported by appeal to simpler ideas about markets, consumers and freedom. Adam Smith's view of the role of government is still the crucial one.

My first proposition is that the case for government in principle should be looked at separately from the performance of government in practice. It might be that the performance of government would be so bad as to undermine the case in principle. But unless the case in principle has been made, there can be no fair assessment of government failure anyway.

The New Right maintains that the correct decision in principle is for the functions of government to be limited to maintaining law and order, external defence and providing a very limited range of public goods. It would go beyond these only in a few very strong cases in which the market generates social costs, though even there other ways might be more appropriate than government action for dealing with the problem. The only correction to income distribution required is to provide a minimum income consistent with preventing destitution.

Economists have attempted to suggest why government might go beyond this range of functions. The usual defence is that there are elements in some private preferences which cannot be met through the market or charitable giving. The existence of altruism has been used as an argument for state intervention to provide health services or to redistribute income. The main source of state action is to be found in certain feelings of concern about others. In a sense this implies a sunny view of human nature in which the better off have strong impulses to help the less fortunate.

We turn now to the case for government in principle. Usually assessment of the role of government is confined to particular programmes such as education or social security: but it is argued here that before we can make sensible statements about particular programmes, we should examine the role of government in a more general sense. Are there reasons for expecting government to have an active and increasing role in society?

The justification in principle rests on the following main arguments:

1. In society there are strong tendencies towards the use of coercive power by private individuals, groups and organisations. The natural state of society is not one in which, in the absence of government, freedom flourishes, even in the negative sense. It is one in which private interests will seek to organise to win advantages for themselves both through political and through commercial means.

Government's function in rule-making has been interpreted far too narrowly by economists. Government is not just a referee setting the rules of a sporting contest. Government is involved in a society in which the strong are often preying on the weak. Private coercion could be exercised by economic interests, by people with certain opinions or religious beliefs, by certain social or class groups, or by ethnic groups. An appeal to a third party, or government, is one of the few recourses open to the weak against various forms of coercive power.

2. Motives count for far more in determining action than do consequences. Motives are provided by the immediate relationships and experience of the individuals – consequences outside this circle or far in the future will carry little weight. There is a case for a third party to make sure that consequences are more fully taken into account, particularly when they are far in the future. This need to increase the weight of consequences is the greater in a society with advanced technology in which the capacity for remote danger is much greater.

3. There is a difference in power, information and resources between the household and the large organisation, so great that it casts doubt on the contention of the New Right that contracts between such parties are free. Friedman has argued in *Capitalism and Freedom* that

> Despite the important role of enterprises and of money in our actual economy, and despite the numerous and complex problems they raise, the central characteristic of the market technique of achieving coordination is fully displayed in the simple exchange economy that contains neither enterprises nor money. As in that simple model so in the complex enterprise and money exchange economy, co-operation is strictly individual and voluntary *provided*: (a) that enterprises are private so that the ultimate contracting parties are individuals and (b) that individuals are effectively free to enter or not to enter into any particular exchange, so that every transaction is strictly voluntary.[1]

Thus, General Motors and the household of a car worker are held to be freely contracting parties. The contention here is that the imbalance of resources between the household and the enterprise continually threatens this freedom. The capability of the enterprise to take decisions which in its view are quite minor but which have major consequences for individuals is also significant. There has been an increase in the scale of organisation in private industry and in the public sector, and this makes the individual household more vulnerable. The individual has a constant struggle for survival against the large organisation. One of his few resources is the vote. In search of protection against the large organisation the household turns to a third party – government.

4. The New Right claims that there is no agenda for distribution other than the provision of a minimum income. We have seen, however, in Chapter 8 that the pattern of income over the life cycle does not fit well to the pattern of family responsibilities. There are also issues about distribution affecting the economically active and dependants about which economists have said little. There is, in principle, a wider case for government action to alter the distribution of income.

5. The idea of a social minimum is relevant in a society which is committed to ethical notions of common humanity and to equality of opportunity. We can measure the living standards of children, the retired, and other dependants against this very rough standard. The New Right maintains that the development of the economy will mean that fewer people fall below this minimum. The natural course of distribution will be benign, and will make it possible for government to discharge its minimal responsibility very easily. It has been argued that the course of distribution in the past fifteen years has shown a distinct movement towards greater inequality. The development of the labour market presents some further issues which in principle require government action: without it the living standards of many households in the poorest third of the population would have fallen in absolute terms over the past fifteen years. The likely pressures in the future are also threatening to absolute standards. The issue is not just one of equality: it is one of pressure on the absolute standards of dependants and of those who are less well placed in the labour market.

6. The idea of negative freedom requires a complement of responsibility. The minimum condition for freedom and responsibility cannot be reduced to the absence of government. Security is required in family and social life for responsibility to develop. Even the functioning of the market depends on beliefs and experiences outside the market. In practice a minimum core of security, income and resources for participation in society is a pre-condition for freedom and responsibility. In principle if government could do anything to ensure that people have this then it should.

All these are arguments why, in principle, a society composed of households and organisations might generate a considerable volume of work for a third-party 'government'. The pressure for government might be offset if private interests were to win complete control of the machinery of the state, but that would require the abolition of freedom of speech, a free press and the right to vote. In a society with these features but with many large and powerful organisations there will naturally be very strong pressure on government to intervene in order to protect households. The usual state of such a society will be one of constant struggle between households using the weapons of civil rights and the organisations with their potential for secretly planned and far-reaching action. Proposals for unleashing the market and for drastic reduction in the role of government simply shift the balance between the households and the organisations in favour of the latter. They confer greater freedom of action on various types of corporate enterprise in relation to the households.

The case for government in principle arises from the need for a counterweight to private coercion, and because long-term consequences will be often neglected. On issues of distribution the agenda is longer than that suggested by the New Right. Finally, there is a constant struggle for survival by households. All these make the case in principle. Starting from it we can now set a definition of government failure which allows us to assess the record in practice.

The main general task of government in a society with freedom of private organisation is to act to offset the bias in favour of the strong and away from the weak. In such a society the net effect of market and power forces will be to put pressure on the living standards of those at the end of the social ladder. There will also be continuing pressure on these poorer households from commercial or bureaucratic organisations or from those sponsored by better-off households in order to improve their own position. Government can use a variety of means to carry out this general task: it can redistribute income; it can confer civil rights on households; and it can redistribute resources other than income.

It would be possible that government would not undertake this task at all. Why is it that government does not act in a single-minded way to reinforce the strength, power and resources of better-off households and the large organisations? Why is it that government undertakes any policies at all which have the intention of redistributing income and resources? Many political decisions simply reflect the interests of the better-off households, but there is some intention in a number of government programmes to do the opposite. We can take issue about the effects, but the intention is there. The strength of intention has varied a great deal but it has never completely disappeared.

The sources of this intention can be sought partly in self-interest and partly in ethical considerations. Anxiety about dependence and about the costs of child-rearing and old age are not confined to the less well off households. There is the possibility of demotion for those households among the better off which face a heavy or an unexpected burden of dependence or sickness. Only government can do an effective job in ensuring certain types of income security and in raising income during the period of life in which family commitments are heavy. A sufficient number of better off households have interests parallel to those of the less well off to bring into being some policies which have a redistributive intention. Many better off households have some sense of inferiority and of threat from large organisations and this helps to bring into being policies which strengthen the rights of households. Ethical ideas about common humanity and about equality of opportunity do something to reinforce this intention.

The central task of government is to assist less well off households in achieving a certain minimum of security, rights and protection against private coercion. Advocates of the New Right would have various approaches to such a definition of aim. They would not be of one mind on the principle. Hayek would argue that such an aim was illegitimate – meaningless at the collective level. Friedman might accept that it was in some sense a good idea for less well off households to have such a minimum. There is nothing wrong with the aim, but he would maintain that the market would do a more effective job in bringing it about than government. Indeed government would be outstandingly ineffective in bringing it about.

We have argued the case in principle that government should play a particular role: we have suggested some reasons why it might actually do so. We turn now to the question of practice, and to particular programmes. There are different assessments which might be made of the government record. The first is the romantic assessment which underlies many proposals for large, quick increases in public spending. Such proposals imply that the record of public spending is extremely good. It has achieved its objectives with creditable levels of cost and standards of efficiency, and we need a lot more of it quickly. There is no strong preference for one programme rather than another. They are all good and we need more spending on all of them. At the other extreme is the New Right which maintains that public spending has failed to reach most of its objectives, that its costs are discreditably high, and that we need much less of it. The indictment would be both of particular programmes and of general public spending.

I would argue that government performance is seriously defective but not beyond redemption. Reforms are feasible in public choice to reduce fiscal illusion. On the supply side, reforms are needed to increase the influence of consumers; but such reforms should be attempted. The defects of practice are not so irreparable that the strong case in principle has to be abandoned. Even in its current state, the public sector does better in assisting households to achieve a social minimum than would the most likely alternatives.

This assessment begins from a distinction between *government* and *public expenditure*. There are certain functions that government should in principle perform. These suggest some rather obvious types of programme: social security, health services and education. Certain patterns of financing and procurement turn these government functions into public spending. But public spending can also grow from other reasons and other sources. In Britain, the effect of low growth has been to increase public spending on industrial subsidies. Many of these new kinds of public spending have little to do with the traditional welfare functions of government.

We can sum up the main propositions underlying this middle assessment as follows:

1. Government has valid functions beyond those set out by Adam Smith and Milton Friedman.
2. Government performance of these functions should not be judged against idealised versions of either the market or some pure state of redistribution. Government performance in social security, health services, and education should be assessed against the most likely alternatives. Thus the National Health Service should be assessed against an insurance-based system rather than against an ideal model.
3. The translation of these functions into public spending raises increasingly serious questions over the past few years. Problems of cost, efficiency and inequality have become far more serious on a day-to-day basis.[2] Effective management has been at a discount and the major decisions have become part of a political business cycle.

In essence, the current operation of the public sector has been undermining the case in principle for government. Instead of argument about the ends, we have become more involved in argument about the means. The public spending share of GNP has certainly shown significant growth in Britain over the last twenty years.[3] This growth has been a result of policy decisions in two periods: 1962–4 and 1972–4. These were years when governments were at particular points in the political business cycle. Not all the motives for the increases in public spending were of a crude vote-buying kind. No doubt there was a real ethical concern for the effects of high unemployment and low growth. But the main impulse came from politics. Between these two periods, public spending has shown a much slower increase but, until recently, a steady rise in its real cost. There is no doubt that public sector outputs now involve a higher opportunity cost in terms of lost private sector outputs now than in the early 1960s. We have to forgo more private consumption for a given amount of public sector output. Most of the increase in the relative price effect came between 1960 and 1975.

The rise in public spending has led to attempts at halting it through growing centralisation which have, in turn, further reduced its local flexibility. We can sum up the main defects of the current situation as follows:

1. Decisions about particular services and outputs are not taken on their merits but as the by-product of a crude political battle over a generality called 'public spending'.[4]

2. Fiscal illusion – by which voters and their representatives are taking decisions about the expenditure side without having to face the consequences in taxation – has become more important. One important source of fiscal illusion is in the use of deficit financing at the national level. Another is in the high proportion of local government spending that is financed by grants from the central government. Although there has been some slight reversal of both trends in the last few years, since the early 1960s there has been a major increase both in the PSBR and in the proportion of local government spending financed from central government grants.

3. Public services are now on a larger scale and are more bureaucratic.

4. Public services are now more inflexible. The services have enormous difficulties in adjusting their activities to meet new needs: difficulties which partly reflect the self-interest of professions and unions. The traumatic experiences of the health and other social services in trying to provide for mentally handicapped people is one sign of this.

5. The crisis in public spending has not had an even impact on all functions of government. Some services are more efficient than others. The crisis has widened the spread of efficiency in the public sector. The degree of government failure – in relation to the role in principle – varies very much. The social security system is very successful: the NHS less so but still has greater merit than the most likely alternative.

Reforming Government

There is an odd similarity between the reactions of Left and Right to the crisis in public spending. Both show a swing towards simple, almost utopian, solutions. In the Left's view public spending has come to take on a magical aura. More public spending is seen as the cure for almost all ills. The Right's view of the market shows a similar tendency to Utopia.

The political Left and the political Right have an oddly similar view of the political process. A majority vote elects a government with a mandate for sweeping change. The majority acting through government has both a steady intention and the ability to carry it through. The democratic process is about distilling a powerful general will, and once this is known it can be translated into actions quite quickly. Bureaucracies can have only a temporary power to bring about delay and can be turned by bringing in new men at the top.

Both also unite to condemn the traditional middle of the mixed economy, and it is in this they find their strongest argument and their greatest appeal to uncommitted opinion. The mixed economy, in the meaning used after 1945, depended on certain economic and social prerequisites. One often cited is a rapid rate of growth: but more important is the compatibility between the economy's rate of growth and the society's code of practice on distribution.[5] Within this code, it was possible to reconcile various demands of private consumption, a high rate of investment and modest improvements in public spending.

The mixed economy is usually traced in macroeconomic numbers of growth and inflation from its rise after 1945 to its decline after the mid-1960s. But it involved far more than certain levels of economic performance. It embodied a certain approach to distribution, with a lack of will to exploit sectional bargaining power. It involved understandings about the role of government which were such that at times it was actually possible to suggest that government was doing too much. The philosophy of voluntarism was accepted by all the parties to industrial relations in Britain. Politics was dominated by a stable, elderly corporatism.

There can be no return to this world of the 1950s and any alternative to the dogmas of Left and Right has to be on a very different basis to that of the mixed economy of those days. Any alternative cannot start by taking political equilibrium for granted in the face of evidence on its break-down. There is no underlying consensus on distribution. Patterns of public spending show greater influence of producer groups and sectional interests. The range of issues coming into the political process is extending at a time when the political system is showing a growing inability to resolve problems. The records of British and American democracy since 1960 have been far from impressive.

The argument about reform of collective choice has sometimes been seen as an unimportant part of a wider argument about social conflict. The changed role of the state simply reflects a changed level of social conflict in society. The political difficulties simply reflect the collapse of a consensus about distribution and of the unspoken understandings which are more important than constitutional forms. The suggestions here assume that it is possible to have such a reform of public spending in a narrow sense. We look first at desirable directions for such reform and then at possible incentives to bring it about.

The New Right has done a service in drawing attention to the very real weaknesses of public spending. Yet it always seems to assume that reform means a major reduction in the role of government. Typically it shows little interest in the reforms of government; instead it prefers to impose a solution through increased centralisation. As Hayek has argued, the conservative is less concerned with reducing the powers of central government than with wielding them himself.[6]

We need a basic reform of the fiscal and political system in order to provide more informed choice on the demand side and to reduce the power of vested interests on the supply side. But this may not, given the strength of the case in principle for government, produce less public spending. It may well produce a rather different pattern and much alteration in the way the public sector operates – but not necessarily less. The outcome might go any way. We are interested here in improving the way in which the decision is taken.

The New Right has usually sought reform through constitutional safeguards. These have included new voting rules requiring two-thirds majorities, constitutional amendments requiring balanced budgets; limitation on taxations, and, even in the case of Hayek, limitations on the suffrage. These suggestions imply that the behaviour of voters and their representatives can be altered by changes in the rules. The suggestions made here give more weight to the underlying conflict of opinion. If the intention is there, the rules will not be necessary: if it is not, they will be of little use. The New Right also seems to stress particular single changes, within the possible constitutional amendments. A great deal of stress is put on one particular change in altering behaviour. Here the emphasis is more on defining a range of principles and then seeing what changes might help to get them adopted in the main practical decisions. There is no one magic constitutional change at the centre which will infallibly improve the operation of government in detailed areas of policy.

Changes are needed to ensure that government concentrates on its core functions of offsetting the bias towards greater inequality in the market, and of giving support to households in their struggle with large organisations. The need for such concentration will be greater in the next few years because without government action there is likely to be a substantial increase in poverty. The role of government in redistribution implies a considerable increase in financial commitment. The central issue of moral concern is this increase in poverty and inequality, and this involves a much starker choice of priorities than is usually admitted.

The danger is that the resources needed to deal with the real functions of government will be pre-empted by a gradual increase in inefficient, producer-dominated kinds of public spending. This is more likely than another major all-round increase through a new spasm of vote-buying. The current level of taxation is such that politicians of all parties have to recognise it as a major constraint, and financial markets set limits to government's ability to fund increases in the deficit.

Government has become more and more diversified in its functions, and this is weakening its ability to carry out its core functions. Broadening of the functions of government has usually been a subject of complaint only by the Right. But it should be recognised far more widely as a major problem. Such broadening of functions reflects insistent political pressures. There has been a drift towards government assuming an omni-competent role, which started well before the recent recessions, but has inevitably been strengthened by them. Centrally, the power of producer groups and bureaucracies and the extent of fiscal illusion all tend to reduce the inhibitions to adding new functions to government. There is also a greater split between the spending gains by particular groups and the financial consequences. The gains from particular programmes to particular small groups are often quite large, while the consequences in higher taxes are diffused. If there is to be effective response to the problem of poverty there have to be frontiers to state action even though they are rather different from those set out by the New Right.

These extensions of government's role also make it more difficult for government to carry out its essential function of strengthening the rights of households in their struggle for survival against organisations. The changes tend to turn government into yet another producer organisation whose activities may be just as arbitrary and damaging to households as any large capitalist organisation. The question of individual rights should be much more central to the role of government, yet increasingly the pattern of government activity is blurring this role and creating difficulties about playing the role at all.

Government has also got the job of providing certain services. For all their weaknesses, some basic public services are better than the most likely alternatives in providing a minimum of rights and opportunities. A health service with a fair degree of competition between autonomous units can provide a more effective service than the most likely alternative of an insurance-based system. Public education, for all its faults, is better than Friedman's voucher scheme. But in these basic services there are problems of inflexibility, inequality and lack of response to consumer preferences.

One way of improving collective choice would be to strengthen local government and to give it greater responsibility both for its spending and for raising revenue. The evidence is strong that all the problems of choice and efficiency are far greater in large areas with infrequent elections and complicated systems of taxation. The aim would be small units which would raise most of their own revenue. In practice, in Britain this would mean concentrating most functions on the present districts and metropolitan districts. It would raise some problems of scale – the units, ranging from 100,000 to 500,000, are quite small. For those few services that would need larger areas, such as secondary and further education, it would be better to set up consortia of authorities to run the services than to have a higher tier of county councils. The arguments for economies of scale in government have been vastly overstated. There would also be problems of inequality in revenues between local government units. The most likely sources of revenue would be a combination of local income tax with the rate or property tax.

There has traditionally been great suspicion of giving more responsibility to local government. This is partly because of the view that the same standard should be available to everyone wherever they live. But at best, a central setting of standards can apply only to inputs and there may, in practice, be rather little association between the amount of inputs and outputs. The quality of output could be rather more affected if the service is locally-based and consumer-led. The proposals made here imply that the gains from decentralisation outweigh those from centralisation. The decisions of local government should be made, however, within a framework of rights set centrally. The other main ground for opposition to local government has been what was once called the 'Mississippi problem' where one local government unilaterally takes away rights. It is the role of central government to set standards in rights. A more effective programme of income redistribution by central government would also reduce the inhibitions to increasing the role of local government.

Another function of central government is to establish a framework that would ensure more competition on the supply side for local government units. They would have to acquire goods and services through competitive tendering, and more areas of activity would be subject to tendering procedures which now affect building by local government. Central government can also stimulate competition through setting up autonomous agencies which would compete with local government in certain functions and which should be largely self-financing. For example, housing associations funded by the Housing Corporation provide a growing alternative to the local government monopoly in rented housing. The small size of these new units would in any case limit their monopoly power against the consumer.

These changes would create the possibility of a more effective collective choice and a more efficient supply. They would add to the responsibility of the elected representative, a responsibility which has become blurred by the size of government and by the complexity of the way it is financed. There might or might not be a different pattern of activity and a higher level than that envisaged by the New Right; but decisions would not be produced by a combination of voter apathy, representative inadvertence and producer domination.

One aim of the changes would be that more public spending would be subject to local control. Public spending should be more related to detailed choices of ordinary people than to an abstract process of central economic management. This approach also implies that real reform in public spending has got to start at the local level. The imposition of rules about balanced national budgets, even if desirable, is not in itself likely to control public spending effectively. These changes could help to produce more cost-effective and responsive services within the core functions of government.

We come now to the most difficult question: how to set some limits to the enlargement of central government action. Government has some functions in economic management. These were defined in Chapter 13. Government has certain core functions in offsetting inequality. But how do we ensure that it really concentrates on these? The continuing extension of government functions has made it very difficult to finance and manage the core functions adequately. It is suggested that the following steps could contribute:

1. A plan to reduce government spending and staffing outside activities relating to the core functions. There is a very wide range of other functions in which there should be a larger market element. Where a complete introduction of competition would be difficult, public institutions such as universities should raise more of their revenue through services sold directly to the public.

2. The ending or weakening of public sector monopolies in nationalised industries. These monopolies have contributed very largely to heavy spending on industrial subsidies and have diverted public spending away from the core functions. The efficiency of nationalised industries varies with the degree of competition to which they are subject.[7]

This programme is very different from that of the New Right. It is envisaged that overall public spending might be much the same as now, but its composition would be different. There might be relatively more spent on the core functions, especially on social security. There would be rather less on many other things. The programme also differs from that of the New Right in its view of the role of the market. For reasons discussed in detail in the chapters on health and education, only a small role is seen for profit-making enterprises in health services and education, though even in these services there is scope for a bigger role for voluntary alternatives to state services. The increased role for the market is in reducing monopoly power in the nationalised industries. Finally, the programme differs most crucially in its approach to local government. The New Right has paid lip-service to local government but has, in practice, limited its role. But whatever the immediate exasperation with the current activities of local government, it alone offers real hope of improved collective choice by elected representatives. From its sheer size, national government will always be dominated by civil servants.

These proposals would help to create a new framework and a new climate for collective choice. The pattern of decisions might go in the direction which the New Right seeks towards a general limitation of all the functions of government: that is for the future. The task of the present is to bring about a reform of the serious defects in collective choice in public spending: its growing ineffectiveness, its remoteness from consumers and voters, and the excessive influence of producers. There is only a very short time to preserve the legitimate core of government by a fundamental reform of collective choice in public spending. Unless such a reform is carried out, the New Right's case, which is against both government and public spending, will carry the day.

Finally these changes would concentrate the activity of national government on two other important functions. One is in redistribution through the social security system. This would remain an important responsibility of central government. The first priorities here should be to improve conditions for the long-term unemployed and for families through better child benefit. The other main function is in acting as a countervailing force to private coercion and to oppressive actions by bureaucracies.[8] The Ombudsman system should be extended to cover all large organisations whether in the private or the public sector. A much greater amount of parliamentary time needs to be given to issues of civil liberties. There are of course difficulties in that some of the worst problems of oppression and lack of accountability have occurred directly in the public sector. First there must be a decision in principle covering methods of giving households greater rights in their dealings with all types of organisation. Then, particular resistance will become easier to wear down. Government must create countervailing forces both to private coercion and to its own potential for oppression. The potential for oppression is there for enterprises and bureaucracies of all kinds whether they are large firms, unions or ministries. The most important division is between the individual and the organisation rather than between 'private' and 'public'.

The essence of the changes suggested is to shift emphasis away from government's role as a producer organisation. The main task of government is to set limits to inequality and to give individuals and households more rights and protection against large organisations.

We come finally to the question of incentive. What changes in the political system could help to bring these aims about? The key here will be the struggle for opinion. There are some signs of a weakening hold of utopian thinking and the strengthening of a more empiricist approach to politics. Such changes in opinion could be greatly assisted by changes in administrative and political practice. There is a strong case for opening up government through a Freedom of Information Act and for giving the individual the protection of a Bill of Rights. But there is no one magic cure by constitutional change or anything else. Rights have to be established in one detailed area of policy after another. 'The observance of justice', in Hume's words, must again be made 'the immediate interest of some particular persons.'[9]

References

1. M. Friedman, *Capitalism and Freedom*, Chicago; University of Chicago Press, 1962, p.14.
2. Julian Le Grand's recent work (J. Le Grand, *The Strategy of Equality*, London; Allen and Unwin, 1982), has produced much interesting new evidence showing that better off households demand and get more from public services than do poorer ones. But his results do not amount to an evaluation of the services for two reasons. First they do not compare outcomes under the most likely alternatives. Secondly the results do not cover outputs in terms of satisfaction. In fact if they did the rank order of success might be very different. Thus by Le Grand criteria public housing scored well as in the past the general subsidy was highly redistributive. The NHS scores badly. But in terms of satisfaction by poorer consumers the results are probably the other way round. Public housing gives little satisfaction and the NHS rather more.
3. J. Tomlinson, 'The Economics of Politics and Public Expenditure: a Critique', *Economy and Society*, November 1981, pp.381–402.
4. The best discussion of the whole process in Britain is in S. Brittan, 'The Economic Contradictions of Democracy', *British Journal of Political Science*, April, 1975, pp.129–59. See also S. Brittan, *Capitalism and the Permissive Society*, London; Macmillan, 1973, and S. Brittan, *The Economic Consequences of Democracy*, London; Temple Smith.
5. Dan Usher discusses the importance of this system of equity in his interesting book: *The Economic Prerequisite to Democracy*, Oxford; Blackwell, 1981.
6. F.A. Hayek, *The Constitution of Liberty*, London; Routledge and Kegan Paul, 1960, pp.397–411.
7. The evidence is very clearly set out in R. Pryke, *The Nationalised Industries, Policies and Performance since 1968*, Oxford; Martin Robertson, 1981.
8. R. Delbridge and M. Smith (eds.), *Consuming Secrets*, London; Burnett Books, 1982, is a good account of just how far there is to go.
9. David Hume, 'Of the Origin of Government', in H.D. Aiken (ed.), *Hume's Moral and Political Philosophy*, New York; Hafner, 1972, p.100.

Index

MIX
Papier aus verantwortungsvollen Quellen
Paper from responsible sources
FSC® C105338

If you have any concerns about our products,
you can contact us on
ProductSafety@springernature.com

In case Publisher is established outside the EU,
the EU authorized representative is:
Springer Nature Customer Service Center GmbH
Europaplatz 3, 69115 Heidelberg, Germany

Printed by Libri Plureos GmbH
in Hamburg, Germany